MODERN HUMANITIES RESEARCH ASSOCIATION
NEW TRANSLATIONS
VOLUME 15

RAMÓN MARÍA DEL VALLE INCLÁN
SAVAGE COMEDIES

MODERN HUMANITIES RESEARCH ASSOCIATION
NEW TRANSLATIONS

The guiding principle of this series is to publish new translations into English of important works that have been hitherto imperfectly translated or that are entirely untranslated. The work to be translated or re-translated should be aesthetically or intellectually important. The proposal should cover such issues as copyright and, where relevant, an account of the faults of the previous translation/s; it should be accompanied by independent statements from two experts in the field attesting to the significance of the original work (in cases where this is not obvious) and to the desirability of a new or renewed translation.

Translations should be accompanied by a fairly substantial introduction and other, briefer, apparatus: a note on the translation; a select bibliography; a chronology of the author's life and works; and notes to the text.

Titles will be selected by members of the Editorial Board and edited by leading academics.

General Editor
Dr Ann Lewis

Editorial Board
Dr Ann Lewis (French)
Professor Ritchie Robertson (Germanic)
Dr Mark Davie (Italian)
Dr Stephen Parkinson (Portuguese)
Professor David Gillespie (Slavonic)
Professor Duncan Wheeler (Spanish)
Professor Jonathan Thacker (Spanish)

www.translations.mhra.org.uk

Ramón María del Valle Inclán
Savage Comedies

Translated and edited by
Christopher Colbath and Luis M. González

Modern Humanities Research Association
New Translations 15
2022

Published by

The Modern Humanities Research Association
Salisbury House
Station Road
Cambridge CB1 2LA
United Kingdom

© The Modern Humanities Research Association 2022

Christopher Colbath and Luis M. González have asserted their right under the Copyright, Designs and Patents Act 1988 to be identified as the author of this work. Parts of this work may be reproduced as permitted under legal provisions for fair dealing (or fair use) for the purposes of research, private study, criticism, or review, or when a relevant collective licensing agreement is in place. All other reproduction requires the written permission of the copyright holder who may be contacted at rights@mhra.org.uk.

First published 2022

ISBN 978-1-78188-969-5

CONTENTS

	Introduction	1
	Valle-Inclán: Life and Work	2
	The *Savage Comedies*	5
	Modernism, Decadence and Nostalgia: The *Savage Comedies* as Modern Tragedies	8
	The *Savage Comedies* on the Stage	13
	Our Translation	16
	Works Cited	17
1	*Golden Boy*	19
2	*The Blazoned Eagle*	102
3	*Wolves Rampant*	207

INTRODUCTION

Among Ramón del Valle-Inclán's (1866–1936) diverse and prolific writings, the *Savage Comedies* occupy a special place. Key dramatic works from the early twentieth century, the trilogy of *The Blazoned Eagle* [*Águila de blasón*] (1907), *Wolves Rampant* [*Romance de lobos*] (1908) and *Golden Boy* [*Cara de plata*] (1922), which comprise the *Savage Comedies*, represent a break from contemporary commercial theatre,[1] with which Valle-Inclán clashed throughout his life.[2] The author of *Divine Words* [*Divinas palabras*] (1919) was not alone in his desire to breathe new life into the theatre. A series of writers had emerged on the European stage since the end of the nineteenth century who independently undertook a project through which Western drama would be renewed. The theatrical works of George Bernard Shaw, Anton Chekhov, T. S. Eliot, Luigi Pirandello, W. B. Yeats and Bertolt Brecht are just a few examples of efforts to free the theatre from the constraints imposed by the realist aesthetics of the nineteenth century. As Bert Cardullo writes: 'The new movements were fed by the other arts as much as they were provoked by conventional drama itself. Poets, painters, filmmakers, musical composers, circus performers, architects, choreographers, photographers, cartoonists, sculptors — any but professional or commercial dramatists — were models and sources for the radical shift in the aesthetics of theater and drama'.[3]

In this introduction we view the *Savage Comedies* against the modernist

---

[1] At the beginning of the twentieth century the Spanish stage was dominated by the 'comedy of manners' of Jacinto Benavente, the poetic-nostalgic drama of Eduardo Marquina, and the comic theatre of the Álvarez Quintero brothers and Pedro Muñoz Seca, among others.
[2] In an interview granted to a contemporary theatre critic, Valle-Inclán responded to the question, 'Why don't you write for the theatre?': 'For the stage? No. I haven't written, do not write, nor do I intend to write for the stage. I am very fond of dialogue, as my novels show. And, of course, I like the theatre, and have done theatre, always trying to overcome the difficulties inherent in the genre. I've done theatre, taking Shakespeare as my mentor. But I haven't written, nor will I write, for Spanish actors... Spanish actors haven't as yet learned to speak. They babble. And as long as there isn't one who knows how to speak, it seems to me ridiculous to write for them. It would be stooping to the level of illiterates' (*ABC*, 23 June 1927; quoted in Robert Lima, *The Dramatic World of Valle-Inclán* (Woodbridge: Támesis, 2003), p. 44).
[3] Bert Cardullo and Robert Knopf, *Theater of the Avant-Garde, 1890–1950: A Critical Anthology* (New Haven: Yale University Press, 2001), p. 2.

backdrop and examine Valle-Inclán in the social, political and cultural context of his time. We then address some of the issues prevalent in the trilogy. We consider the nostalgic — but not uncritical — gaze Valle-Inclán fixes on the old world of the *mayorazgos* and *vinculeros* (two of the various titles given to Don Juan Manuel in the plays) — a world which, in the second half of the nineteenth century, was in full decline.[4] Finally, before surveying the production history of the *Savage Comedies* in Spain and internationally, we locate the plays in a literary tradition that encompasses Attic tragedy, Shakespeare, Calderón de la Barca and the myth of Don Juan, which Valle updates in the figure of the protagonist of the trilogy: Don Juan Manuel Montenegro.

Valle-Inclán: Life and Work

This great, goat-bearded Ramon
Summed up in that smile of his
Like an old god, arrogant and elusive
Like a cold statue coming to life.
  Rubén Darío, 'Sonnet for Don Ramón del Valle Inclán'[5]

My face wears a hundred fictional masks which succeed each other under the base dictates of an insignificant fate. Perhaps my true expression has yet to reveal itself; perhaps it cannot emerge from under the numerous veils accumulated day after day and interwoven by my many hours. I myself do not know who I am; perhaps I am condemned to suffer that ignorance forever. I ask myself frequently which among all the sins is mine and so interrogate the masks of vice: Arrogance, Lust, Vanity, and Envy have left their imprints on my carnal face as well as on my spiritual demeanor; yet I know that all but one will disappear in due course, that one to remain fixed on my features when death arrives.[6]

Ramón del Valle-Inclán was born on 26 October 1866 in Vilanova de Arousa in the province of Pontevedra, in the north-west of the Iberian Peninsula, to a family of the Galician aristocracy. These aristocratic origins instilled in the

---

[4] The title of *mayorazgo* is a remnant from the medieval period. It was given legal definition in 1505 during the reign of Isabel and Ferdinand. Etymologically the term *vinculero* refers to the idea of hereditary lands being 'linked' yet indivisible. Land was generally to be passed on to the eldest son in a primogeniture system, the main goal of which was to preserve the aristocratic houses and prevent their atomization. In the mid-nineteenth century, the liberal government began to dissolve this archaic institution, but the terms of its dismantling were vague and without a clear timeline. This convoluted process culminated in the late nineteenth century during the time in which Valle's trilogy is set.
[5] Rubén Darío, *El canto errante*, ed. with an introduction and notes by Ricardo Llopesa (Valencia: Editorial Instituto de Estudios Modernistas, 2006), p. 171. All translations from the Spanish are ours unless otherwise noted.
[6] Ramón del Valle-Inclán, *The Lamp of Marvels: Aesthetic Meditations*, trans. by Robert Lima (New York: Inner Traditions, Lindisfarne Press, 1986), pp. 119–20.

author of the *Savage Comedies* a strong elitist and anti-bourgeois character that he would evince throughout his life. In 1888 Valle-Inclán began studying law at the University of Santiago de Compostela. He interrupted his studies to settle in Madrid in 1890, where he collaborated on the periodicals *El Globo* and *Heraldo de Madrid* until he moved to Cuba and then Mexico in 1892. His first publications were two collections of romantic short stories with female protagonists: *Femeninas* (1895) and *Epitalamio* (1897). Between 1902 and 1907, the year he married the young actress Josefina Blanco, Valle-Inclán published the *Sonatas: Memorias del Marqués de Bradomín* (1902–1905), a series of four novels that recount the amorous life of a decadent Don Juan, 'ugly, Catholic and sentimental', as well as a collection of short stories, *Jardín umbrío* (1903), and the short novel *Flor de santidad* (1904).

In 1906, Valle-Inclán published his first play, *El Marqués de Bradomín: Coloquios Románticos*. The second of March 1907 marked the premiere of *The Blazoned Eagle*, the first of the *Savage Comedies*, in Barcelona. *Wolves Rampant* would be published in 1908. His affinity with the right-wing Carlist movement inspired Valle-Inclán to compose the trilogy of novels *La guerra carlista*, comprising *Los cruzados de la causa* (1908), *Guerifaltes de antaño* (1908) and *El resplandor de la hoguera* (1909). June 1911 saw the premiere of *Voces de gesta*, an epic tragedy through which Valle-Inclán again defended the Carlists.[7] The excellent biography recently published by Manuel Alberca describes Valle-Inclán's enthusiastic collaboration with supporters of the Carlist cause.[8] However, other scholars tend to minimize Valle's ideological commitment by highlighting the purely aesthetic nature of his fidelity to the ultraconservative Carlist movement, as if the ideas advocated by the Marquis of Bradomín in *Coloquios románticos* were Valle's own.[9] In this play, the Marquis of Bradomín articulates this position in various contexts: 'Mr. Abbot, I am Carlist for aesthetic reasons. Carlism has for me the beauty of the great cathedrals. [Like them,] Carlism should in my view be seen as a national monument' and 'The Carlists are divided into two great sides: me on one and everyone else on the other'.[10] This critical tendency reflects readers' difficulty reconciling

---

[7] The long-lived, and still active, Carlist movement in Spain has stood in opposition to the encroaching tides of modernity (democracy, bourgeois values...), initiating three civil wars over the course of the nineteenth century. The last of these took place between 1872 and 1876, during which these plays and some of Valle's novels are set. In the twentieth century, the Carlists were important players in the last Spanish civil war, supporting Franco's fascist coalition.
[8] Manuel Alberca, *La espada y la palabra. Vida de Valle-Inclán* (Barcelona: Tusquets Editores, 2015).
[9] Joaquín Hernández Serna, 'Historia y literatura: el carlismo estético de Valle-Inclán', in *Historia y humanismo. Homenaje al Prof. Pedro Rojas Ferrer* (Murcia: Universidad de Murcia, Servicio de publicaciones, 2000), p. 674.
[10] Ramón del Valle-Inclán, *Obras Completas, IV, Teatro* (Madrid: Fundación José Antonio de Castro, 2017), p. 75.

a writer of the aesthetic avant-garde with a political reactionary whose Carlism consistently opposed enlightened modernity. In fact, this apparent contradiction was characteristic of many artists of the time. Valle is hardly the sole example of a modernist writer to be strongly drawn to sociopolitical movements of markedly conservative, even fascist character. Alongside him can be placed a long list of names including T. S. Eliot, Ezra Pound, Gabriele D'Annunzio, Luigi Pirandello, Mircea Eliade, Wyndham Lewis, F. T. Marinetti, Gottfried Benn, Georges Sorel and Louis-Ferdinand Céline, among others.

Valle-Inclán remained productive in various genres. Besides the dramatic works, the publication in 1916 of *La lámpara maravillosa*, an essay explicating his aesthetic and philosophical ideas, deserves mention. Commissioned by the newspapers *Prensa Latina* and *El Imparcial*, in April 1916 he visited the front lines in France where the Battle of Verdun was taking place. The result of this experience was a series of articles published under the title *La media noche: Visión estelar de un momento de guerra* between 1916 and 1917. In these pieces Valle used Tolstoy's writings on war as a model. Like the author of *War and Peace*, he sought to combine various individual subjective viewpoints with a panoramic view of military action from above — an 'aerial' view. And although this technique applies to the prose works, it informs the dramatic pieces as well, especially their cinematic qualities, which we discuss below.

Following the 1919 book of poems *La pipa de Kif* and the play *Divinas palabras*, which would be reworked for the stage in 1933, the 1920s were marked by theatrical writings (although Valle-Inclán never abandoned his work as a novelist). In 1920 he published the plays *Farsa y licencia de la reina castiza*, *La enamorada del rey* and *Luces de bohemia*. That year he would collaborate with Cipriano Rivas Cherif in the Teatro de la Escuela Nueva project, and in 1922 *Golden Boy* appeared, the last of the *Savage Comedies*.

On 13 September 1923 General Miguel Primo de Rivera led a coup d'état and, with the assistance of King Alfonso XIII, ushered in a dictatorship that would last until the proclamation of the Second Republic in April 1931. Valle-Inclán's fierce opposition to the authoritarian regime earned him a brief stay in prison.

In 1927 Valle-Inclán published *Retablo de la avaricia, la lujuria y la muerte*, a volume made up of several short dramas: *La rosa de papel*, *La cabeza del Bautista*, *Ligazón*, *El embrujado* and *Sacrilegio*. Three years later came another collection of plays, *Martes de carnaval*, which contained *Las galas del difunto*, *La hija del capitán* and *Los cuernos de don Friolera*. In prose, Valle-Inclán published *Tirano Banderas* in 1926 and *La corte de los milagros* in 1927, the first novel of the series *El ruedo ibérico*, which was followed in 1932 by *¡Viva mi dueño!*

During the years of the Second Republic, Valle-Inclán complemented his artistic work with various institutional positions, including Conservador

General del Patrimonio Artístico Nacional [General Curator of the National Art Collection], and later on in 1933 he was appointed director of the Academia Española de Bellas Artes de Roma. In the latter capacity he would remain in Rome until 1934. During this time, he was a fervent supporter of Mussolini and his fascist regime. However, the true nature of his political affiliation is complex and difficult to define. In 1933 he participated with other intellectuals in the creation of the Asociación de Amigos de la Unión Soviética. Throughout his life Valle-Inclán sympathized with the Carlist movement, anarchism, communism and finally with fascism. He died on 5 January 1936 in Santiago de Compostela.

The *Savage Comedies*

One of the most striking features of the plays in this volume, immediately clear from the author's designation of the trilogy, is the peculiar brand of irony which permeates both dialogue and stage directions. As we hope to demonstrate, the *Savage* (lit. 'barbaric') *Comedies* are essentially tragedies. Although the irony operates in a unique fashion, and although the plays are formally innovative, Valle's work here is in line with other modernist projects which broke from the past while at the same time referring to and situating themselves within a very specific literary tradition.[11]

There are two literary characters Valle-Inclán fuses into the protagonist of this trilogy, Don Juan Manuel Montenegro: Shakespeare's King Lear and the Don Juan of the Spanish tradition, specifically *Don Juan Tenorio* by José Zorrilla (1844), in which Don Juan is pardoned in the final moments. From the former Valle-Inclán takes filial conflict and desolation, which plague the patriarch in his autumn years. From the latter, he draws on the dynamics of sin, repentance, death and redemption.

Montenegro is the final representative of a certain type of declining rural nobility in Spain. Nineteenth-century progress and industrialization diminished the importance of the agricultural social structure that rested on the institution of the *mayorazgos*. In this way, the trilogy is linked to a current of nineteenth-century literature that documented these transformations. The work of Emilia Pardo Bazán, *Los pazos de Ulloa* (1886) and its continuation *La madre naturaleza* (1887), *Os Maias* (1888) by the Portuguese Eca de Queiroz, and *El abuelo* (1897) by Benito Pérez Galdós depict the death throes of a society

[11] Olga Taxidou writes: 'Modernism in general exhibits a profound and complex relationship with the workings of tradition, particularly the classical European tradition against which it appears to be rebelling. The canonical European models of theatre from the Greeks to the Renaissance to German Romanticism are constantly evoked throughout the period as signifiers of the Enlightenment and its economies of representation' (*Modernism and Performance: Jarry to Brecht* (New York: Palgrave Macmillan, 2007), p. xvi).

that in the time in which Valle's plays are set, the second half of the nineteenth century, was yielding to capitalism and a new bourgeois order. Russian writers from Turgenev to Bunin would document comparable changes, as would Faulkner later in the American South.

The protagonist of the trilogy is 'one of those despotic, lusty, short-tempered yet magnanimous noblemen preserved in old portraits in the ghostly townships, the villas that evoke with their feudal names the clanking of rusty armour'.[12] Don Juan Manuel lives on his Lantañón estate, separated from his wife, Doña María, 'a wan, mournful woman wearing a Franciscan habit' (*BE*, II. 6), together with their six sons, for whom he harbours no affection — with the important exception of the youngest, Don Miguel, nicknamed Golden Boy, who, like his Suebian forebears,[13] 'has golden hair, happy green eyes and an aquiline nose' (*GB*, I. 2).

Golden Boy (literally, and in other translations, 'Silver Face') lends his name to the trilogy's chronologically first play, which revolves around two intertwining conflicts, one public and one private. After years of allowing local peasants and merchants to enter the lands of Lantañón on the way to the Viana del Prior fair, to which they travel to sell their goods and livestock, Don Juan Manuel (old Montenegro) decides to ban them from passing, prompting angry protests by both the villagers and the Abbot of Saint Clement of Lantañón, to whom Golden Boy, in a tense encounter, denies passage at his father's behest.[14] In retaliation, the man of the cloth forces his niece Isabel, nicknamed Sabelita (with 'her honey blonde hair pulled back in two braids, her skin buffed and fair, her nubile figure draped in a Nazarene habit', *GB*, I. 2), the god-daughter of Montenegro and his ward at his estate of Lantañón, to leave the latter's house and return to him at the rectory.

At the end of the play, Montenegro saves Sabelita from the mad vagrant Filthy Fuso's advances and takes her back to his home, where she will become his mistress, provoking the wrath of both his distant relation the Abbot and his son Golden Boy, who is in love with her. It is the youngest of the Montenegros who menacingly raises an axe against his father. It does not fall but rather foreshadows the final murder of Don Juan Manuel at the hand of another of his children. *Golden Boy* concludes with Don Juan Manuel triumphant in the struggles both against the Abbot and his son, but acknowledging that he has gone too far, as he exclaims: 'Perhaps I really am the Devil incarnate!' (*GB*, III. Final Scene).

---

[12] *The Blazoned Eagle*, Act I, Scene 2. References to the plays in the present edition are hereafter given in parenthesis in abbreviated form, followed by act and scene numbers.

[13] The Germanic Suebian tribes migrated from central Europe and founded a kingdom in the Roman province of Gallaecia in the first half of the fifth century.

[14] Viana del Prior is a fictional location created by Valle-Inclán, situated in southern Galicia in the provinces of Orense and Pontevedra.

The Blazoned Eagle, the first work of the trilogy to be written but second in terms of plot development, begins some years later in the house of Don Juan Manuel, where he lives openly with Sabelita. The plot of this play centres on the lack of retribution for an attempted burglary of Montenegro's house and assault on his person.[15] Don Juan Manuel suspects that one of his sons, aided by a gang of thieves, has tried to rob him. The patriarch shares his sorrow with Don Galán, a kind of inverse of the nobleman ('hideous and old, deceitful, fearful, and a teller of ribald tales. In the master's house he also plays the role of fool', *BE*, II. 2).

The second act portrays another villainous deed on the part of Don Juan Manuel's progeny. This time it is Don Pedrito, who rapes Liberata la Blanca, the wife of the miller Pedro Rey. Liberata will later become the mistress of Don Juan Manuel once the repentant Isabel quits the house of the Montenegros in the face of Doña María's reproaches. His long-suffering and estranged spouse, aware of the attempted robbery, has come to convince him to distribute the inheritance among his children precisely to forestall these sorts of crimes.

Isabel, the plays' sinner-saint Magdalene figure, wanders through the lands of Lantañón and happens upon a pregnant woman and her family, whom she assists in a ritualistic remedy. At the same time, Golden Boy confides to his mother his intention to join the Carlist expedition led by the famous Marquis of Bradomín. Before riding off to war, Golden Boy, along with his concupiscent cleric brother Don Farruquiño and the prostitute Moaning Pichona, will dominate one of the trilogy's most grotesque scenes, in which sex and death intermingle in an uncomfortably literal fashion. The play closes with a new farewell between Doña María and the old knight, who is now left with Don Galán and Liberata as his sole companions. Doña María forgives Sabelita and takes her under her wing, and Golden Boy has found a purpose with the Carlists.

Wolves Rampant begins with Don Juan Manuel running into the Procession of the Damned,[16] which serves as a premonition of the play's, and the trilogy's, tragic conclusion. Reinstalled in his ancestral home, and alone save for the

---

[15] Plots built around lack of action are of course one of the major currents in modernist drama (see Beckett, Pirandello, etc.). But whereas such plots typically rise to the level of content and theme, the Shakespearean grandiloquence and portentous gestures in Valle's trilogy obscure the fact that very little actually happens. This is especially true of *Golden Boy*, the tragic action of which consists simply of old Montenegro taking on a new mistress. Other than that, the plot consists of little more than a series of idle threats.

[16] The Procession of the Damned, or *Santa Compaña* (literally 'Holy Company'), is a tradition that dates back to the medieval period. It was especially strong in the rural northwest of the Iberian Peninsula. The Procession was typically led by someone bearing a cross or some other holy object. Other participants holding candles would follow, often chanting or reciting scripture. For a general idea of what it may have looked like, the reader might refer to Ingmar Bergman's 1957 film *The Seventh Seal*.

company of his fool and a few loyal servants, Don Juan Manuel receives news from a sailor that Doña María now lies on her deathbed at her home in Flavia-Longa. Despite the adverse weather conditions, Montenegro forces the ship's crew to embark on the journey, not knowing that Doña María has just died and that their sons, with the exception of Golden Boy, are ransacking the house. The vessel which Montenegro forces to set sail then capsizes, and as the sole survivor he is washed up on the coast. At precisely this moment the old nobleman shows the first signs of contrition. He encounters a group of beggars who will accompany him on his personal *Via Crucis*. Meanwhile, his sons take over the estate of Doña María. A violent encounter occurs between Don Juan Manuel and his son Don Pedrito. The final scenes of *Wolves Rampant* focus on the repentance of Don Juan Manuel and his ritualized death at the hands of another of his sons, Don Mauro.

Modernism, Decadence and Nostalgia: The *Savage Comedies* as Modern Tragedies

Realizing that his eldest son, Don Pedrito, has tried to rob him, Don Juan Manuel commiserates with his ancient housekeeper: 'In my veins runs the last drops of truly noble blood; in yours, the last of the true and loyal servants' (*BE*, II. 3). This sense of an ending — a central motif in modernist literature, according to Frank Kermode — is found in the nobleman protagonist as well as his servants.[17] Representing the common people, an Old Woman exclaims: 'Nobility is a thing of the past! Oh, if you had known Grandfather Don Ramón María! He was the foremost knight of these lands, the likes of whom we'll never see again!' (*BE*, II. 5). And, some time before, Doña Rosita, referring to Don Juan Manuel's children, states: '[Old Micaela] has witnessed the birth of all Don Juan Manuel's sons — all good-for-nothings who, it must be said, have brought disgrace to his line. From their father they've inherited only despotism, nothing of his nobility. Don Juan Manuel has a kingly nature' (*BE*, II. 5).

The works of Edmund Burke, Johann Gottfried Herder, Thomas Carlyle, Hippolyte Taine and Ernest Renan, to mention just a few examples, emphasize the decay and degradation that accompany the emancipatory ideology of enlightened modernity. In the twentieth century, the German historian and philosopher Oswald Spengler significantly influenced modernist authors with the publication of *The Decline of the West* in 1918. In Spain, where

---

[17] In *The Sense of an Ending*, Frank Kermode argues that modernist authors were witnesses to the end of an epoch. Thus, 'apocalyptic time' was a central motif in modernist art (*The Sense of an Ending: Studies in the Theory of Fiction* [1967] (New York: Oxford University Press, 2000), p. 98).

the Enlightenment never fully took hold, this sense of decadence would be exacerbated after a humiliating defeat in the war against the United States in 1898 and the subsequent independence of Puerto Rico, Cuba and the Philippines. Losing even the vestiges of a vast colonial empire both horrified and inspired many writers and intellectuals. Ramiro de Maeztu, Antonio and Manuel Machado, José María Pemán, Miguel de Unamuno, Pío Baroja, Azorín, and Ramón del Valle-Inclán, among others, would echo a widespread sense of decline and of the end of an era. These authors responded to the sociopolitical crisis in various ways. In 1921, one year before the publication of *Golden Boy*, the Spanish philosopher José Ortega y Gasset analysed the decline of Spain in *España invertebrada*. In this book, Ortega argues that 'the decadent era in society is characterized by the minority leadership's — the aristocracy's — losing its qualities of excellence — precisely those which conferred on it its privileged position'.[18]

This is Valle's main argument in the *Savage Comedies* and hence his interest in highlighting the moral turpitude of the Montenegros. With the exception of Don Miguel/Golden Boy, Don Juan Manuel's sons have abandoned the obligations of the ruling minority and neither want nor know how to lead the people; nor do they have the opportunity. Towards the end of the first novel of the Carlist War trilogy, Valle-Inclán, through the voice of the Marquis of Bradomín, provides a detailed analysis of the causes of the Spanish decline:

> That is lineage! As Liberalism could never understand, destructive as it is of all the traditions of Spain. The entailed estates preserved the history of the past and should have been the history of the future. Those ancient, generous country gentlemen who owned them were the fruit of a military selection. The only Spaniards who could love the history of their line, preserve the cult of their ancestors and the pride of four syllables to a surname.[19]

The decline of the Montenegros' house, caused, in part, by their inability to adapt to the new ways, pushes them into a struggle for economic survival in which robbery and violence will play a fundamental role. It is a violence that is exerted from top to bottom. Don Juan Manuel is despotic and violent with the servants and with his mistresses Isabel and Liberata. All of his children have inherited this authoritarian and violent manner. Miguel, the 'golden boy', will threaten his father with an axe. Don Pedrito brutally rapes Liberata. And ultimately Don Mauro murders his father.

Given this bleak outlook, which foregrounds economic collapse and moral degeneration, it is not surprising to hear voices predicting the end of the world.

[18] José Ortega y Gasset, *España invertebrada. Bosquejo de algunos pensamientos históricos* (Madrid: Espasa Calpe, 2002), p. 92. All translations of critical works are ours, unless otherwise indicated.
[19] Ramón del Valle-Inclán, *The Carlist War*, trans. by Michael Perceval (London: CreateSpace Independent Publishing Platform, 2017), p. 43.

Filthy Fuso repeatedly screams in a prophetic tone that 'The world is doomed! Doomed!'; that 'The world is hopelessly misguided. In a blink of an eye it will burst into a thousand pieces' (*GB*, II. 1). In *The Blazoned Eagle*, 'the servants begin speaking about how in the mountains a cow gave birth to a two-headed calf' (*BE*, III. 1).

For many characters in the trilogy, this apocalyptic vision exists alongside a feeling of nostalgia for a world that was better but is now irretrievably lost. The action of the *Savage Comedies* is located in quasi-mythical space where time seems to have been suspended. It is a time that contains all times, but where a medievalizing vision prevails, as in much Romantic literature. The landscape is dominated by 'the ruins of a castle' where 'horses graze on the sacred grass of the ancient Celtic burial mounds' (*GB*, I. 1). Viana del Prior, where Valle-Inclán located several of his works, 'once the hub of the manorial holdings, as evidenced by the awesome stonework, resounds with the rough reverberance of its courtyards and atriums. Preserving its stories in sonorous stone, it sings songs of feudal freebooting and rebellious guilds rising up against crown and mitre. Ancient manses, ancient dynasties, ancient documents, the coats-of-arms over the archways all declaim gothic tales featuring the heraldic symbols of Galicia' (*GB*, II. 1). The region's post-Roman, Celtic heritage is evoked: 'receding over the Celtic hillocks in the crystal-dewed morning and weaving lines of epic verse formed from mercantile chatter and the barking of dogs' (*GB*, I. 1) — this verse derives both from the medieval and the Homeric epics. This is mythic time, lost in the mists of history, before the process of democratization ushered in by modernity.

The servants share this preference for a better and simpler past. Ginger-Micaela states that Montenegro's manor 'used to be happy, like the fires of San Juan. The servants gathered daily 'round the stove — twelve of us, just like the Apostles. At harvest time or when picking the grapes there were more than fifty. Telling stories, folk laughing, young ones singing and playing without a care!' (*BE*, III. 4). Here the attitude is not only uncritical but idealizing. The servants, representing all of the masses, in the terms of José Ortega y Gasset, are happier in that hierarchical and organic old world.

Valle-Inclán is aware of the irreversibility of a historical process that is guided by the advances of enlightened modernity and, in that sense, part of his work is presented as the swansong of a lost era. The interesting thing here is that the author of *Bohemian Lights* depicts and frames that past in a critical way. In *The Future of Nostalgia*, Svetlana Boym defines modern nostalgia as 'a mourning for the impossibility of mythical return, for the loss of an enchanted world with clear borders and values'.[20] Boym distinguishes two types of nostalgia: restorative and reflexive. Valle-Inclán's nostalgia is restorative in

[20] Svletana Boym, *The Future of Nostalgia* (New York: Basic Books, 2001), p. 8.

that it 'proposes to rebuild the lost home and patch up the memory gaps... [Restorative] nostalgics do not think of themselves as nostalgic; they believe that their project is about truth. This kind of nostalgia characterizes national and nationalist revivals all over the world, which engage in the antimodern myth/making of history by means of a return to national symbols and myths...' (p. 41). However, a reflexive nostalgia also permeates Valle-Inclán's work. This type of nostalgia centres on individual experience, on 'the irrevocability of the past and human finitude' (p. 49). Of interest here is not the project of faithfully recovering the past but rather providing a critical reflection on history and the passage of time. This type of nostalgia is 'ironic, inconclusive and fragmentary' (p. 50) and 'lingers on ruins, the patina of time and history, in the dreams of another place and another time' (p. 41).

In *Bohemian Lights*, the poet protagonist Max Estrella states that 'the tragic sense of Spanish life can only be expressed through an aesthetic of systematic deformation' and to that end, Valle-Inclán creates the *esperpento*,[21] which, although not a tragedy, retains the essence of the genre.[22] Since the beginning of his literary career Valle-Inclán had tried in various ways, including in the *Savage Comedies*, to create a modern tragedy that denounced the ruin and decay of the modern world and exposed the enormous political and social crisis that these changes had wrought in Galicia and other societies.[23] The *Savage Comedies* should be read in the context of the modernist revival of tragic theatre promoted by authors such as D'Annunzio, Pirandello and Anouilh, among others, with whose work we can link Valle-Inclán's. This resurgence coincided with a strong rejection of progressive modernity and its rationalist program, as we see in the philosophy of Friedrich Nietzsche.[24]

Scholars agree that tragic art is a symptom of periods of historical transition in which different incompatible social models coexist and give rise to extraordinary social unrest and anxiety.[25] The *Savage Comedies* depict a

---

[21] *Esperpento* is a term coined by Valle-Inclán. It is an artistic mode that makes use of deformation, ugliness and the grotesque in order to depict the modern world. In many ways it can be considered the Spanish variant of Expressionism, although for Valle-Inclán it also draws on the Spanish artistic tradition — for example, the paintings of El Greco and Goya.
[22] Dru Dougherty, 'Valle-Inclán y La Tragedia Moderna', *Anales De La Literatura Española Contemporánea*, 33, 3 (2008), 469–500 (p. 469).
[23] In an interview published in *Heraldo de Madrid* on 15 March 1918 Valle-Inclán states: 'Now I will restart my literary career writing tragedies, which I call "Savage Comedies"' (Dru Dougherty, *Un Valle Inclán Olvidado: Entrevistas y Conferencias* (Madrid: Fundamentos, 1983), p. 97).
[24] In *The Birth of Tragedy* Nietzsche argues that Attic tragedy reached its apogee in Athens during the fifth century BCE in the works of Aeschylus and came to an end with Euripides. The latter, according to Nietzsche, all but eliminates the original Dionysian element, replacing it with Socratic scientific rationalism. Therefore, in the modern context, a renascence of tragedy was only possible after a rejection of modern science.
[25] Vernant and Vidal-Naquet were pioneers in pointing out that Greek tragedy was born

profound social crisis in which all of the characters are immersed. The liberal government's suppression of the ancient institution of the *mayorazgos* was depriving society of its organic structure; in this view, the change was purely negative. Don Juan Manuel will try unsuccessfully to stop this process, arguing that, for him at least, 'nothing has changed' (*BE*, III. 2). Nevertheless, in *Wolves Rampant*, we will witness his tragic fall as the leader of the beggar band (which functions much like the chorus in classical tragedies) in a revolutionary uprising which has as its first goal razing to the ground this new-old world. His quasi-anarchist speech constitutes an ideological high point of the trilogy.

Old Montenegro's revolutionary plans are decisively quashed in the climactic patricide; however, in a sense they soon come to fruition in various ways all across Europe (both the German and Russian examples share parts of their ethos with Don Juan Manuel). The desire for a radically new beginning was in the air. Don Juan Manuel's violent death transforms him into the scapegoat of a society in crisis.[26]

The *Savage Comedies* revolve around the thematic axes of decadence, nostalgia, redemption and death. The structure of the plays is paradigmatic of certain modes of avant-garde modernism but also very much in the centuries-old tragic tradition. Despite the formal innovations, the plays are deeply conservative from an ideological point of view.

---

in a society which was undergoing a period of historical transition (Jean P. Vernant and Pierre Vidal-Naquet, *Myth and Tragedy in Ancient Greece* (New York: Zone Books, 1990)). Raymond Williams states that tragedy 'attracts the fundamental beliefs and tensions of a period' (*Modern Tragedy* (Stanford: Stanford University Press, 1966), p. 45). In a similar tenor, Terry Eagleton believes that tragedy 'deals in the cut-and-thrust of historical conjunctures' (*Sweet Violence: The Idea of the Tragic* (Oxford: Blackwell, 2003), p. xiii). Likewise, Sarah Annes Brown notes that tragedy 'seems to have been most potent at moments of cultural or political upheaval, reflecting and anticipating change' ('Introduction: Tragedy in Transition', in *Tragedy in Transition*, ed. by Sarah Annes Brown and Catherine Silverstone (Malden, Oxford, Carlton: Blackwell Publishing, 2007), pp. 1–15 (p. 1)).

[26] Naomi Conn Liebler, following the works that established the connection between ritual sacrifice and tragedy in the field of cultural anthropology, concludes that the tragic protagonist 'serves as *pharmakos*, the sacrificial victim required by all purgative rituals, whose efficacy as sacrifice signifies above all the symbolic embodiment of whatever threatens the community in crisis. The tragic hero is the community's surrogate. She could not be its surrogate if she did not resemble it in critical ways. And because she stands for what must be methodically eliminated, she must be destroyed' ('Introduction: Wonder Woman, or the Female Tragic Hero', in *The Female Tragic Hero in English Renaissance Drama*, ed. by Naomi Conn Liebler (New York: Palgrave, 2002), pp. 12–13). In a similar tenor, Eagleton adds that 'Rebuffing the claims of the symbolic order... [s]uch figures... incarnate the inner contradictions of the social order, and so symbolize its failure in their own' (*Sweet Violence*, p. 280).

The *Savage Comedies* on the Stage

One of the tasks of a book introduction is to cultivate enthusiasm. We hope that the light we have shed on the contradictions and peculiarities of Valle-Inclán's writing leads to inspiration and creative interpretation. But that hope is tinged with a note of failure. While twenty-first century renderings of the *Savage Comedies* are beginning to draw on the potential of their textual source, there has yet to appear anything like an adequate version for the stage.[27] Cinematic adaptations exist but tend to be marred by excessive naturalism.[28]

This note of failure followed the plays from the beginning. Valle-Inclán was deeply dissatisfied with Spanish productions of his plays and was not hopeful of a Spanish interpretation which would match his vision. He expressed this displeasure on multiple occasions: 'I can think of nothing more excruciating than witnessing the translation of my plays to the stage. Everything tried has been quite different from what I had in mind. Does it have something to do with the way I compose my stage directions? I feel as though my directions provide a better interpretation than any actual adaptation'.[29] This sentiment must have been one of the motivations for creating his own company in late 1926, 'El cántaro roto'.[30] However, as Manuel Azaña recalls, the new project failed at

---

[27] Only one of the trilogy's three plays was staged during Valle-Inclán's lifetime. On 2 March 1907 *Águila de blasón* premiered in Barcelona at the Teatre Eldorado. To celebrate the centenary of Valle-Inclán's birth, La Compañia Nacional de Teatro staged all three plays: *Águila de Blasón* (Adolfo Marsillach, 1966), *Cara de plata* (José María Loperena, 1967), *Romance de lobos* (José Luis Alonso and Agustín Alezzo, 1970). In Argentina, a full version of the *Savage Comedies* premiered in 1970, directed by Agustín Alezzo. In 1974 the Frankfurt Stadt Schauspielhaus staged *Barbarischen Komödie* (Augusto Fernándes). The Avignon Festival, 9 July 1991, presented *Les Comédies Barbares* (Jorge Lavelli). The same production was staged at the Teatro de la Colina de París and the Festival de Tardor in Barcelona. *Comedias Bárbaras* were presented by Centro Dramático Nacional in 1991 (José Carlos Plaza). In 1993 at Teatro Espace Libre de Montreal, Jean Asselin presented a complete version of the trilogy. In 1995 the Gate Theatre premiered *Barbarous Comedies*, directed by David Johnston. The Edinburgh Festival witnessed a premier of *The Barbaric Comedies* by the Abbey Theatre on 14 August 2000, directed by Calixto Bieito. Other productions include: Bigas Luna, *Comedias Bárbaras* (2003); Etelvino Vázquez, *Cara de Plata*, 2003; Ramón Simó, *Cara de Plata*, 2005; Angel Facio, *Romance de lobos*, 2005; Centro Dramátic Nacional, *Montenegro* (Ernesto Caballero, 2013). In April 2017 second-year Edge Hill University drama students presented *A Season of Plays by Ramón del Valle-Inclán*, including *Ballad of Wolves*.
[28] Luis Miguel Fernández ('Romance de lobos en el cine: ¿un proyecto frustrado?', *Anales de la literatura española contemporánea*, 26, 3 (2001), 99–110) points to an unfinished 1919 project to adapt *Wolves Rampant* for the screen, which demonstrates that the *Savage Comedies* have been viewed in cinematic terms from a very early date. Other actual films based on Valle-Inclan's works include: *Sonatas* (Juan Antonio Bardem, 1959), *Flor de Santidad* (Adolfo Marsillach, 1972), *Beatriz* (Gonzalo Suárez, 1976), *Luces de Bohemia* (Miguel Ángel Díez, 1985), *Divinas Palabras* (José Luis García Sánchez, 1987), *Tirano Banderas* (José Luis García Sánchez, 1993) and *Esperpentos* (José Luis García Sánchez, 2009).
[29] Valle-Inclán, *Obras Completas, IV, Teatro*, xxv.
[30] Lima, *The Dramatic World of Valle-Inclán*, p. 37.

the beginning of the following year: 'Valle, who directed the affair alone and despotically, dragging in all his friends and disinterested parties, ended up at odds with them'.[31]

Looking elsewhere for environments more consonant with his dramatic vision, the Spanish aristocrat and (proto-)fascist in his later years pinned his hopes on Soviet Russia, of all places. As Lima notes, Valle-Inclán 'was specially enthused by correspondence with Russia in 1931, which promised to open a new public not only in his novels but also to his plays'.[32] Unfortunately, the Soviet Russian path led to another dead end. In the 1930s, Stalinism crushed the avant-garde experiments in theatre and cinema that reverberated so powerfully in the decade following the revolution. Still, twenty-first-century readers have something to gain by speculating on the form that collaboration between the Spanish modernist and his Russian counterparts might have taken.

We suggest reading the *Savage Comedies* in line with what Sergei Eisenstein called 'the principle of montage'. In various writings, the Soviet director went to considerable lengths to prove that montage, which in most writings on cinema refers simply to editing but which Eisenstein understood more broadly as the intentional sequencing and presentation of images in a work of art, pre-dates cinema and in fact underpins human cognition. The artist may possess the organizing consciousness that makes montage possible, but the reader/viewer, in assembling and assimilating the material, contributes actively to overall meaning. In his analysis of passages from a diverse range of authors such as Milton, Shelley and Mayakovsky, Eisenstein provides us with the framework for a kind of mental storyboarding approach that can be profitably applied to the 'stage' directions of the *Savage Comedies*.

Consider the opening lines of the trilogy (if we consider, as Valle-Inclán did, the chronologically first play *Golden Boy* as the proper opener):

> A brisk sunrise. Communal pastures undulate in the hills of Lantaño. Above the rocks, the ruins of a castle, and nestled in the soft verdure — the Arcas de Bradomín. A group of herdsmen are camping out there, taking shelter among the noble stones... Their horses graze on the sacred grass of the ancient Celtic burial mounds. From slightly higher ground, the sound of bovine indignation begins to crescendo as a cattle driver takes a calf away from its mother and off to market. (*GB*, 1.1)

The full stops function as cinematic cuts. It is a visual depiction that is not merely descriptive but sequential, diachronically fluid. As Eisenstein acknowledged, the eye can travel — especially if a successful artistic design guides it — over a single picture in a way that actualizes the montage principle. But in this passage and generally in his scene-setting, Valle-Inclán marshals a

---

[31] Cited in Lima, *The Dramatic World of Valle-Inclán*, p. 38.
[32] Lima, *The Dramatic World of Valle-Inclán*, pp. 44–45.

wealth of sensory material, more of it than a single picture or stage design could possibly reproduce.

Valle-Inclán's readers need to possess this kind of cinematic imagination, and part of their imaginative work entails looking past the dull interpretations of the *Comedies* that have been attempted thus far on screen. As much as he complained of Spanish actors' inability to *speak* his dialogue, what the plays required was someone to *see* them properly. The artistic experiments in Russia in the years following the revolution of course entailed a rejection of much of the past, but there was also a breathing of life into old traditions as well. Sergei Eisenstein cites approvingly the symbolist author Andrei Bely and his studies of Gogol's prose and comedies.[33] In the mid- to late nineteenth century, the period of Realism, Gogol was viewed as a satirist who faithfully documented squalor and social injustice in imperial Russia. His comic masterwork *The Inspector General* was subjected to one lifeless naturalistic production after another. Bely championed the great theatre director Vsevolod Meyerhold, Eisenstein's teacher, who gave the play its first properly expressionist staging.

Valle-Inclán called his plays *esperpentos*. Their maximalist, expressionist design is immediately evident. The disappointing cinematic adaptations of his work that have appeared so far should not deter our inner cinematographers from picturing them in their true colours… We imagine *Rancho Notorious* as directed by David Lynch, *Red River* as directed by… Sergei Eisenstein.

Thus, when it comes to our interpretations of the plays, the notes of failure and disfavour are worth exploring rather than explaining away. We suggest that Valle-Inclán's frustrations with contemporary Spanish dramaturgy impelled him to refine a style of writing for the stage which paradoxically rendered the staging of his plays impossible.[34] This is not a question of their content — that is, we do not suggest that the plays speak to the impossibility of tragedy as an artistic mode. Rather, it is primarily a formal question.

Not needing to take into consideration theatre directors or actors, Valle-Inclán was free of the requirement to compose practical stage directions.[35] It is

---

[33] See Sergei Eisenstein, *Selected Works, vol. 2: Towards a Theory of Montage*, ed. by Michael Glenny and Richard Taylor, trans. by Glenny (London: British Film Institute, 1991), pp. 354–55, and *vol. 4: Beyond the Stars: The Memoirs of Sergei Eisenstein*, ed. by Richard Taylor, trans. by William Powell (London: British Film Institute and Calcutta: Seagull Books, 1994), pp. 638–46.

[34] 'I believe my plays to be perfectly stageable… I feel that my *Esperpentos* could be done to perfection by our actors since the plays possess something akin to popular farce, between the tragic and the grotesque' (quoted in Lima, *The Dramatic World of Valle-Inclán*, p. 44).

[35] It should be noted that the author downplayed the significance of his descriptive stage directions and did not intend for them to impinge on the plays' content: 'I write in a scenic form, in dialogue, almost exclusively. But I'm not concerned whether or not the works are staged later on. I write in this form because it pleases me greatly, because it seems to me the best literary style, the most serene, the most impassive in conveying the plot. I

these passages where his originality comes to the fore. In fact, taken together, they can scarcely be considered stage directions at all. Reeling off one exquisite sensory detail after another, the voice seems to belong at once to a novelist, a poet and a painter. Furthermore, and in line with our interpretation, the remarkably visual quality of the descriptions suggests the art of cinema.

Our Translation

The tragic grandeur of Don Juan Manuel Montenegro notwithstanding, the main character of Valle-Inclán's work is arguably Galicia and its culture. Hence it is no surprise to find the author's Spanish to be heavily seasoned with Galician terms and phrases. As translators, we encountered several instances that set us on a tortuous quest for answers. Valle-Inclán's terminology and topography required some detective work.

We have tried to produce a translation unmarked by any one regional or dialectal peculiarity. For specific purposes (and not without reason, given the Celtic dimension of Galician culture that Valle-Inclán emphasizes again and again), Maria Delgado's version of *Cara de plata* (Silver Face) is rendered in Irish-English. While this approach generally works well, our goal has been to produce a text that reflects the linguistic diversity of the original. We aim to be faithful first and foremost to the uncanny and beautiful atmospheres conjured in the text.

It is at the level of discourse, and not language as such, that Valle-Inclán's style is truly fascinating. Crude colloquialisms accompany formal, almost courtly, phraseology; and blunt, naturalistic dialogue is often bookended by ornate, archaic diction that is baroque sometimes to the point of solecism. In this sense, these works are as much post-modernist as modernist. At times, the abruptness of these stylistic transitions is less acute in our translation; at other times it is exaggerated. For example, we could not refrain from having the Baby Jesus speak in a kind of notional Elizabethan English, because isn't this how a pious nineteenth-century noblewoman would want her Baby Jesus to express himself? Beyond such fluctuations, there are surely other occasions where our American-English origins show through. However, our intent is to retain Valle-Inclán's polyphonic literary style.

In our choice of titles, we have eschewed literalism in a couple of important ways. The most obvious case is *Golden Boy*. Previous translations have gone with 'Silver Face', which rolls off the tongue nicely but misleadingly suggests

---

love impassivity in art. I want my characters to present themselves and to be themselves without the commentary, the explication, of the author. Everything should be the plot itself' (interview by Montero Alonso, *La Novela Semanal* 6 (1926); cited in Lima, *The Dramatic World of Valle-Inclán*, p. 36).

something portentous while losing its primary meaning as an affectionate nickname. Readers who insist on some kind of metallurgical symbolism at work in the text may be dismayed, but we believe the Golden Boy moniker to be a better fit for Don Miguelito.

The Blazoned Eagle is the most straightforward of the three titles. In this case we chose 'blazoned' over the more common 'emblazoned' to emphasize the heraldic theme. Just as Valle-Inclán's commitment to ultra-conservative political ideologies is complex and multi-dimensional, he depicts the Montenegro coat-of-arms paradoxically both as an emblem of something essential and as a dead symbol, the moribund endurance of pure form. With *Wolves Rampant* (Romance de lobos), we carry forward this theme where Valle-Inclán does not. And the primary meaning of the word 'rampant' contains an apt irony: the Montenegros, all of them, are up to all manner of unpleasantness, but they are actively destroying themselves (and others) rather than flourishing or spreading unchecked. A literal rendering would convey Valle's fusion and manipulation of generic conventions, but given the meanings attached to the term 'romance' by Northrop Frye and other critics, we feel that its use here would lead to interpretive dead ends rather than possibilities. For example, Valle-Inclán clearly draws on Shakespearean tragedy, especially *King Lear*, but there are few or no connections to those plays of Shakespeare which in some critical traditions have been termed 'Romances', such as *The Tempest*.

Our attempts here to contextualize and interpret the *Savage Comedies* are not intended to circumscribe their meaning. In the history of literature, they remain strange and unique creations. In the end, we hope that our versions of these plays inspire readers to 'produce' them in their minds with maximal freedom and with pleasure.

Works Cited

ALBERCA, MANUEL, *La espada y la palabra. Vida de Valle-Inclán* (Barcelona: Tusquets Editores, 2015)

BOYM, SVLETANA, *The Future of Nostalgia* (New York: Basic Books, 2001)

BROWN, SARAH ANNES, 'Introduction: Tragedy in Transition', in *Tragedy in Transition*, ed. by Sarah Annes Brown and Catherine Silverstone (Malden, Oxford, Carlton: Blackwell Publishing, 2007), pp. 1–15

CARDULLO, BERT, and ROBERT KNOPF, *Theater of the Avant-Garde, 1890–1950: A Critical Anthology* (New Haven: Yale University Press, 2001)

CONN LIEBLER, NAOMI, 'Introduction: Wonder Woman, or the Female Tragic Hero', in *The Female Tragic Hero in English Renaissance Drama*, ed. by Naomi Conn Liebler (New York: Palgrave, 2002), pp. 1–31

CHILDS, PETER, *Modernism* (London: Routledge, 2000)

DARÍO, RUBÉN, *El canto errante*, ed. with an introduction and notes by Ricardo Llopesa (Valencia: Editorial Instituto de Estudios Modernistas, 2006)

DOUGHERTY, DRU, *Un Valle Inclán Olvidado: Entrevistas y Conferencias* (Madrid: Fundamentos, 1983)
—— 'Valle-Inclán y La Tragedia Moderna', *Anales De La Literatura Española Contemporánea*, 33, 3 (2008), 469–500
EAGLETON, TERRY, *Sweet Violence: The Idea of the Tragic* (Oxford: Blackwell, 2003)
EISENSTEIN, SERGEI, *Selected Works, vol. 2: Towards a Theory of Montage*, ed. by Michael Glenny and Richard Taylor, trans. by Michael Glenny (London: British Film Institute, 1991)
—— *Selected Works, vol. 4: Beyond the Stars: The Memoirs of Sergei Eisenstein*, ed. by Richard Taylor, trans. by William Powell (London: British Film Institute and Calcutta: Seagull Books, 1994)
FERNÁNDEZ, LUIS MIGUEL, 'Romance de lobos en el cine: ¿un proyecto frustrado?', *Anales de la literatura española contemporánea*, 26, 3 (2001), 99–110
HERNÁNDEZ SERNA, JOAQUÍN, 'Historia y literatura: el carlismo estético de Valle-Inclán', in *Historia y humanismo. Homenaje al Prof. Pedro Rojas Ferrer* (Murcia: Universidad de Murcia, Servicio de publicaciones, 2000)
KERMODE, FRANK, *The Sense of an Ending: Studies in the Theory of Fiction* [1967] (New York: Oxford University Press, 2000)
LIMA, ROBERT, *The Dramatic World of Valle-Inclán* (Woodbridge: Támesis, 2003)
ORTEGA Y GASSET, JOSÉ, *España invertebrada. Bosquejo de algunos pensamientos históricos* (Madrid: Espasa Calpe, 2002)
PAZ GAGO, JOSÉ MARÍA, *La revolución espectacular. El teatro de Valle-Inclán en la escena mundial* (Barcelona: Edhasa/Castalia, 2011)
TAXIDOU, OLGA, *Modernism and Performance: Jarry to Brecht* (New York: Palgrave Macmillan, 2007)
VALLE-INCLÁN, RAMÓN DEL, and SANTOS ZAS, MARGARITA, *Obras Completas* (Madrid: Fundación José Antonio de Castro, 2018)
—— *The Carlist War*, trans. by Michael Perceval (London: CreateSpace Independent Publishing Platform, 2017)
—— *The Lamp of Marvels: Aesthetic Meditations*, trans. by Robert Lima (New York: Inner Traditions, Lindisfarne Press, 1986)
WILLIAMS, RAYMOND, *Modern Tragedy* (Stanford: Stanford University Press, 1966)

Golden Boy

Dramatis Personae

DON JUAN MANUEL MONTENEGRO aka the Lord of the Manor, the Vinculero and the Mayorazgo

His sons: DON MIGUELITO, known as GOLDEN BOY, DON PEDRITO, DON ROSENDO, DON MAURO, DON GONZALITO, and DON FARRUQUIÑO

ISABEL, called SABELITA, god-daughter to DON JUAN MANUEL and niece to the ABBOT

THE ABBOT of Lantañón and his sister DOÑA JEROMITA

THE SEXTON, THE SEXTON'S WIFE, the sexton's LAZY DAUGHTER and THE CHORUS OF LITTLE ONES

FILTHY FUSO, a madman

DON GALÁN, the Mayorazgo's Fool

The group of five herdsmen: PEDRO ABUÍN, RAMIRO DE BEALO, MANUEL TOVÍO, MANUEL FONSECA and SEBASTIÁN DE XOGAS

THE ELDER OF CURES[1] and A SHEPHERD

'Moaning' PICHONA, LUDOVINA the tavern keeper and a TAVERN MAID from another establishment

THE MARAGATERIAN,[2] THE PENITENT, THE BLIND MAN OF GONDAR, THE INDIANO,[3] THE DEACON OF LESÓN

AN OLD BUSYBODY

VOICE FROM THE CHIMNEY

OTHER OLD WOMEN, CRIES and INSULTS, SHOUTS, THE HAGS, CHANTED PRAYERS, CURSES and EXCLAMATIONS, THE LIGHTS OF THE HOLY VIATICUM

---

[1] Pronounced KOOR-es.
[2] La Maragatería is a region located in the province of Leon, south of Galicia.
[3] An 'Indiano' is a Spaniard who has made his fortune in the Americas and returned to Spain.

Act One

Scene One

A brisk sunrise. Communal pastures undulate in the hills of Lantaño. Above the rocks, the ruins of a castle, and nestled in the soft verdure — the Arcas de Bradomín.[4] A group of herdsmen are camping out there, taking shelter among the noble stones: MANUEL TOVÍO, MANUEL FONSECA, PEDRO ABUÍN, RAMIRO DE BEALO *and* SEBASTIÁN DE XOGAS. *Their horses graze on the sacred grass of the ancient Celtic burial mounds. From slightly higher ground, the sound of bovine indignation begins to crescendo as a cattle driver takes a calf away from its mother and off to market.*

PEDRO ABUÍN
   Lantaño cattle, they've always been granted free passage through Lantañón.
RAMIRO DE BEALO
   Not anymore. The local mayors lost the case in court. There's no point in protesting.
PEDRO ABUÍN
   For the time being, perhaps.
RAMIRO DE BEALO
   You don't just file a lawsuit with the lords in the high towers.
PEDRO ABUÍN
   An arrogant lot! The legal privileges they enjoy could disappear if all of us joined together. They put themselves on par with the King!
SEBASTIÁN DE XOGAS
   Plenty of kings in the past found themselves at the wrong end of a rope.
RAMIRO DE BEALO
   In other lands.
MANUEL FONSECA
   The Montenegros — what a black-hearted clan!
PEDRO ABUÍN
   We'll see how this bunch of renegades fares without bread, without a roof over their heads. Nobler houses have fallen!
MANUEL TOVÍO
   But for now, passage through Lantañón is denied. These days everything works against us!

---

[4] The Marqués of Bradomín is the nephew of Don Juan Manuel and the protagonist of Valle's 1906 play *El Marqués de Bradomín: Coloquios Románticos*, and of the *Sonatas*, a series of four modernist novels published between 1902 and 1905 in which the character appears as a Don Juan figure, but a 'feo, católico y sentimental' [ugly, Catholic and sentimental] version.

Isolated groups of itinerant herdsmen and merchants — from Cures and Trans-Cures, from Taveirós and Nigrán — proceed along the winding mountain roads. They shout and goad their ornery herd, receding over the Celtic hillocks in the crystal-dewed morning and weaving lines of epic verse formed from mercantile chatter and the barking of dogs.

PEDRO ABUÍN
  Stop, friends!
VOICES IN THE DISTANCE
  What do you want?
PEDRO ABUÍN
  It appears they've revived an ancient law in Lantañón which denies transit to and from the Viana market. What do you think of that?
THE ELDER OF CURES
  Well, if it's the law…
PEDRO ABUÍN
  It's not a law. Neither the law nor its enforcement is of the exclusive provenance of the Vinculero Don Juan Manuel.
THE ELDER OF CURES
  I wouldn't bank on that.
SEBASTIÁN DE XOGAS
  I wouldn't bet the whole bank, perhaps, but it's worth considering. Past legal agreements granted us the right to cross the lands of Lantañón. Our elders secured that right for us!
RAMIRO DE BEALO
  There's no fighting it. The Vinculero won the lawsuit against the mayors.
PEDRO ABUÍN
  Hardly a just decision! I say we all pass through together and see what these pieces of paper are worth.
THE ELDER OF CURES
  When a judge returns with his verdict, good or bad, right or wrong — the case is closed. There's simply no going against it. It's always been that way!
PEDRO ABUÍN
  Verdict or no verdict, Montenegro can't keep us all down! Such is my verdict!
THE ELDER OF CURES
  Arrogance doesn't win lawsuits.
SEBASTIAN DE XOGAS
  What choice do we have here? Take the cattle by ferry?
THE ELDER OF CURES
  We'll ride up to the gates of the estate and ask the Vinculero's permission.

PEDRO ABUÍN
  He's too proud to yield!
THE ELDER OF CURES
  We should all go together — strength in numbers!
PEDRO ABUÍN
  And if he is unmoved by our appeals?
THE ELDER OF CURES
  Then we wait for his mood to improve. What you propose is open rebellion against the court's decision, right? I suggest negotiation and avoiding bloodshed. Time will tell who is right!
RAMIRO DE BEALO
  We lose nothing by going there!
MANUEL TOVÍO
  He will hurl abuse at us, though, if we catch him at the wrong moment.
PEDRO ABUÍN
  I am quite happy to trade insults with him!
THE ELDER OF CURES
  That talk will get you nowhere!

A SHEPHERD *standing off to the side on a crag participates in the council by marking circles with his crook on the thousand-year-old lichen which blankets the stones.*

THE SHEPHERD
  This idea of yours — others have tried it. And what did it get them? Slander! When I appealed to him, how was my politeness repaid? With insults! He stroked his beard as he heard me out, then suggested that my 'better half' come to make the case instead.
MANUEL FONSECA
  To make the case in his bedroom, that is!
THE SHEPHERD
  Someone should close his case — for good!
RAMIRO DE BEALO
  He enjoys unlimited privileges.
THE SHEPHERD
  You could bring him one of your prize cows.
PEDRO ABUÍN
  Ramiro's probably tried that already.
RAMIRO DE BEALO
  You can go to Hell!
PEDRO ABUÍN
  What is our decision, comrades? I vote we take the cattle through Arcas. But

we must all be of one mind. If what they say is true, that there was a time when the lords' towers burned to the ground, then perhaps that time is upon us again.

THE SHEPHERD

Let's stop wasting time and go, while the grey-maned wolf is alone in his cave.

PEDRO ABUÍN

What do you think, good merchants? Shouldn't we go together to assert our right to pass?

THE ELDER OF CURES

As the elder here, I maintain that we stand to gain more from diplomacy than from acts of rebellion.

PEDRO ABUÍN

Those of this opinion can go ahead and speak first.

THE ELDER OF CURES

Amen! Without peace between the upper and lower classes, the world would writhe in chaos.

VOICES OF THE COW-HANDS

Move along, Marela! Move along, Bermella!

MANUEL FONSECA

Let's see what Quinto de Cures can accomplish.

RAMIRO DE BEALO

He's got nothing to lose.

THE SHEPHERD

He'll get what others got before him.

PEDRO ABUÍN

He'll get insults and abuse!

SEBASTIAN DE XOGAS

Listen please! We have plenty of time for an uprising. In my view, we can postpone any quarrel until after the Corpus fair in Viana.[5] For now we need to sell our cattle at the fair. We can worry about protesting against the Vinculero's decision later.

PEDRO ABUÍN

Montenegro, we'll be back!

SEBASTIAN DE XOGAS

You'll get what's coming to you, Montenegro!

THE SHEPHERD

Our only salvation is to set fire to his fields!

---

[5] Corpus Christi is a Catholic holiday for the celebration of the Eucharist. It falls sixty days after Easter. Local fairs marking the holiday are organized by merchants and farmers, as in the present example.

The cavalcade of herdsmen departs, and THE SHEPHERD, *high on the rock and silhouetted against the sky, waves them off with a shout. In the crystalline daybreak a distant flock of doves circles the Tower of Lantañón.*

Scene Two

Dawn breaks over the Lantañón Estate. A stone stairway descends to the arch opening onto the atrium whose courtyard is lined with lemon trees. SABELITA *is high up on the stairway, her honey blonde hair pulled back in two braids, her skin buffed and fair, her nubile figure draped in a Nazarene habit. A corner of the courtyard is taken up by a group of* HAGS *prattling behind their fruit stalls.*

THE HAGS
 Is it true that we are not allowed to pass? The detour around is so long! Mother of Christ! Mother of Christ! We've already had such a long road! Sweet Mother! We've journeyed so far! Farther than San Quinto de Cures!

THE HAGS *in the marketplace make way for an approaching rider. He is a handsome young nobleman, surrounded by greyhounds and other hunting dogs. The peddling* HAGS *rush to protect their goods, screaming out threatening insults. Some secure the baskets balancing on their heads, others prevent the collapse of their stalls.* DON MIGUEL MONTENEGRO, *the gallant young son of* DON JUAN MANUEL, *leaps from the saddle and ties his horse to a large iron ring fixed to the wall. His fine looks and manners have earned him the nickname* GOLDEN BOY.

THE HAGS
 Don Miguelito, please let us pass! Be merciful, dear Golden Boy! We're coming from the world's end! Listen to your heart!
PICHONA
 Such a sweet face should have a kind heart to match, Don Miguelito.
GOLDEN BOY
 All right, the hell with you, just go!
PICHONA
 Long live Sir Golden Boy!
GOLDEN BOY
 When are you going to give it to me, Pichona?
PICHONA
 Oh, you're a smooth talker!
THE HAGS
 God bless you! God bless you!

The group of HAGS *rushes into the inner courtyard through the large arch adorned with the Montenegro coat of arms.* SABELITA's *sweet, lilting voice echoes through the morning sky. The intense violet tones of her habit burn against the old stones of the patio and the lush green lemon trees.*

SABELITA
How is my godmother?
GOLDEN BOY
As usual, locked away, reading her hymnbook and fingering her rosary. And you, when are you coming home?
SABELITA
When my godfather commands it.
GOLDEN BOY
Mother is waiting for you.
SABELITA
Why doesn't she ask me herself? I very much want to go.
GOLDEN BOY
Because of me?
SABELITA
Don't start with that.
GOLDEN BOY
Please help me figure out what's going on with this damned dog. He's limping.
SABELITA
If he was running around in the bushes, it must be a thorn.
GOLDEN BOY
Come here, Carabel!

The dog approaches him with a paw in the air, and the handsome youth flips him over to examine his paws. SABELITA *is close to him, kneeling on the tile floor, smiling and attentive.*

SABELITA
Watch out, he might bite!
GOLDEN BOY
If he does, you can tend to my wounds.
SABELITA
I am no doctor.

GOLDEN BOY *puts his wrist in the dog's jaws, but the dog only whimpers without biting.* SABELITA *stares at him, her eyes ingenuous and open as a little girl's.*

SABELITA
You've lost your mind!
GOLDEN BOY
Bite, Carabel!

SABELITA

The animal has more sense than you do!

GOLDEN BOY

Then let him take out the thorn himself!

GOLDEN BOY *jumps to his feet in a gesture of refined violence. He has golden hair, happy green eyes and an aquiline nose.* SABELITA, *kneeling down next to the dog on the stone floor, tries to remove the thorn stuck in its paw. The Mayorazgo's handsome young son returns to her side.*

SABELITA

You're crazy!

GOLDEN BOY

Why don't you cure me?

SABELITA

There is no medicine for you.

GOLDEN BOY

Your voice can be my medicine.

SABELITA

I don't know any magic spells.

GOLDEN BOY

I need to speak with you tonight, Isabel.

SABELITA

Aren't we talking now?

GOLDEN BOY

It will be a different kind of talk, under the moonlight.

SABELITA

Lunar fantasies for the lunatic!

GOLDEN BOY

You don't love me, Isabel?

SABELITA

Not in the way you have in mind.

GOLDEN BOY

Then you don't love me at all.

SABELITA

I guess I don't.

GOLDEN BOY

We will continue this conversation tonight in your chambers… between the sheets.

SABELITA

You're out of your mind!

GOLDEN BOY

Will you open the door for me?

SABELITA
So, you are a pirate now?
GOLDEN BOY
If I find the door locked, rest assured I will break it down.
SABELITA
Barbarian!
GOLDEN BOY
Don't cry when you see me burst through the door!
SABELITA
You have no integrity!
GOLDEN BOY
What would happen if I really came to your bedroom tonight?
SABELITA
You have clearly put a lot of thought into this scenario! But I am not scared of you, little Golden Boy... If you really love me, show me decency and respect.

With his shotgun on his arm and hound at his side, DON JUAN MANUEL MONTENEGRO *approaches from the orchard and stops at the gate, wild-haired and ready to attack the morning. He is a despotic, womanizing nobleman, renowned for his hospitality and his violent moods: the Suebian lord of the Lantañón estate.*

DON JUAN MANUEL
Golden Boy, say farewell to your lovely companion and come here. I expected you back yesterday. Has the road from Viana grown longer?
GOLDEN BOY
My horse was limping.
DON JUAN MANUEL
I sent men to find you so that we could count the cattle and brand the young steers. Your brothers are already at Viana. The best head must be sent to the fair there. Your elder brothers are in charge of these transactions... they know the herdsmen's wiles and ways. But I'm trusting you with the money. I hope you won't gamble it away like I know those wastrel brothers of yours would.
GOLDEN BOY
No one is free from temptation.
DON JUAN MANUEL
Well, if you are tempted, you had better win. Otherwise don't let me lay eyes on you again.
GOLDEN BOY
That vote of confidence will be my guiding light.

Montenegro's anger is tinged with good humour: for this son he reserves an indulgent, rough affection. The fine young man stands before his father, his mouth set in a serious expression but with a twinkling gleam in his clear green eyes.

DON JUAN MANUEL
Is your mother in good health?
GOLDEN BOY
Yes, sir.
DON JUAN MANUEL
How does she pass the time?
GOLDEN BOY
With the usual pieties.
DON JUAN MANUEL
And yet she has abandoned me!
GOLDEN BOY
She complains you did the same to her in Viana.
DON JUAN MANUEL
Your mother and her imagination! Anyhow, what about this story Pedro Rey came to me with?
GOLDEN BOY
A stray cow fell into the river, and I jumped in to save her.
DON JUAN MANUEL
That version I heard had you riding the cow who then sank beneath your weight and swallowed so much water that she died right under the bridge.
GOLDEN BOY
She's not dead. Almost, but not quite.
DON JUAN MANUEL
Pedro Rey would have me pay for the carcass. I told him to bring me the animal to me, dead or alive. I will strike a deal with him.
GOLDEN BOY
He's after your money. When I dived into the river, the cow was already drowning. Don't pay him for it.
DON JUAN MANUEL
I'm not talking about paying for it. I will make a deal with him: he leaves me the cow and takes you in trade. What do you say?
GOLDEN BOY
Filial devotion is my foremost quality.
DON JUAN MANUEL
Enough, let us speak seriously. I would have you act like the nobleman you are, one whose pure blood obliges him to fulfil the responsibilities that come with it!
GOLDEN BOY
I see to my obligations, father.

DON JUAN MANUEL
   Your brothers have set a bad example and corrupted you. Listen to me. I'm not asking you to be a saint — youth must have its day — but do not be like your degenerate brothers and ignore the responsibilities that come with noble blood.

Heaving a great sigh, his hands on the young man's shoulders, Montenegro finishes his speech. GOLDEN BOY *briskly and indulgently kisses the old man's hand.*

GOLDEN BOY
   Father, when it comes to what I do, good or bad, neither they nor anyone have any influence on me.

DON JUAN MANUEL
   Well, then obey my command and head up the hill.

GOLDEN BOY
   Amen. And what time did my brothers leave?

DON JUAN MANUEL
   They were up with the sun.

As his old sire looks on proudly, the handsome young son unties his horse, who scrapes the ground in the shadow of the rough stone arch. The Vinculero's goddaughter, golden as an ear of wheat as she basks in the sunshine, smiles like a young child.

SABELITA
   Be sensible, Golden Boy!

GOLDEN BOY
   You have driven all sense from me!

DON JUAN MANUEL
   That scoundrel is sweet on you?

SABELITA
   He is all bluster.

DON JUAN MANUEL
   What did he say to you?

SABELITA
   When?

DON JUAN MANUEL
   Just then.

SABELITA
   I don't remember what he said.

DON JUAN MANUEL
   And do you recall your response, perhaps?

SABELITA
   I wasn't listening.

DON JUAN MANUEL
  You are not meant for him.
SABELITA
  I don't pretend to be.
DON JUAN MANUEL
  Your destiny is greater.
SABELITA
  Many sorrows are my destiny.
DON JUAN MANUEL
  And who is the source of these sorrows?
SABELITA
  He who is the source of all.
DON JUAN MANUEL
  When you're young, there is no sorrow. That comes with age… Just don't fall for that scoundrel son of mine!
SABELITA
  I don't listen to him, godfather.
DON JUAN MANUEL
  I wish I were ten years younger!
SABELITA
  I wouldn't want that.
DON JUAN MANUEL
  Well, I would! Then you would look at me instead of sitting there and staring at the ground like a nun!

At the edge of the courtyard, a mad beggar with a contorted face begins to howl. It is FILTHY FUSO, *a hunched and ragged heretic who travels the road between Lugar de Condes and Lugar de Freyres with his cap full of pebbles.*

FILTHY FUSO
  Too-porroo-too! A rebellious bunch gathers together! Too-porroo-too! Here they come! To burn the Tower down! Too-porroo-too!

FILTHY FUSO *sticks out his tongue and contorts his body in fear. His rags expose a throbbing black buttock. Too-porroo-too! Suddenly he turns and starts dancing, plaiting his legs together unnaturally. Too-porroo-too!*

Scene Three

The Lantañón estate, situated between Lugar de Condes and Lugar de Freyres. Pastures, chestnut groves and wheat fields. Lugar de Condes surrounds the church, and Lugar de Freyres is nestled into the mountain. The Lantañón Bridge connects them. Baroque archways bookend the bridge, each bearing coats-of-

arms and emblems. Near the parapets, in the clear morning light comes a herd of cattle, the sun glistening off their horns. His back to the sun and facing the mountain, GOLDEN BOY *rides at a gallop. He is met by the friendly greeting of the* ELDER OF CURES.

THE ELDER OF CURES
Gallant Vinculero, noble lord! Is it true that access is now denied?
GOLDEN BOY
It is true.
THE ELDER OF CURES
And we have to drive our cattle to the river, then cross by ferry, if we want to take them to the great Viana Fair?
GOLDEN BOY
That is what was decided.
THE ELDER OF CURES
When the laws are unduly harsh, judges should be merciful, as the ancients said.
GOLDEN BOY
My father has grown tired of showing mercy.
THE ELDER OF CURES
If we were at least allowed access to the Corpus Christi Fair... It's once a year! The old laws granted us that right!
GOLDEN BOY
My father respected those laws, and you took him to court.
THE ELDER OF CURES
The people of Cures had nothing to do with that. Your noble father should be disabused of that notion. I am the oldest oak in the forest. If we count all my married children and grandchildren, there are over thirty households that I, Quinto Pio, also known as Quinto of Cures, could call home. There it is! A Christian to the core, although nowadays people see no difference between a lifelong Christian and a convert.[6] There it is! We're all good Christian folk here, except for that one English missionary. Anyway, filing that lawsuit was not the work of the people of Cures.
GOLDEN BOY
Yet you bore false witness.
VOICES OF THE CATTLEMEN
You are misinformed! We wouldn't do such a thing! Someone's poisoned your ear!
THE ELDER OF CURES
Your father's blood runs true in you, but you will never succeed in barring

---

[6] In this case, 'converts' refers to those Jews who, in the Middle Ages and especially following the 1492 decree which threatened banishment, converted to Christianity.

our passage! Our customs date back to ancient times, and custom is the law. But the people of Cures are not rebellious by nature, so starting today we will take the river route. There it is! Just know that the horseman riding here now will not be turned away. Even the king bows to other kings.

GOLDEN BOY

Elder of Cures, if pedestrian traffic is denied, then the same rule should apply to those on horseback.

THE ELDER OF CURES

It stands to reason!

GOLDEN BOY

My father's mind is made up!

THE ELDER OF CURES

Amen! The son follows the father and is fettered by his commandments. There it is!

THE ELDER, *his shepherd's crook held high, begins to turn the herd around. The cows are flustered by voices and the prodding of his children and grandchildren, the great brood of Quinto de Cures, and they lock horns in confusion. Trotting toward them in the sun rides* THE ABBOT *of San Clemente de Lantañón.*

GOLDEN BOY

My dear Abbot, turn your horse around!

THE ABBOT

Why? What's wrong?

GOLDEN BOY

The way is barred, good sir.

THE ABBOT

You young Absalom, do not delay me with your pranks. I must make haste to Lugar de Freyres on the Lord's errand.

GOLDEN BOY

If it were only a prank!

THE ABBOT

Are you drunk and looking for trouble?

GOLDEN BOY

Hardly!

THE ABBOT

Stand down and let me pass!

GOLDEN BOY

I cannot!

THE ABBOT

Think, you barbarian! Think carefully before you insult my holy office!

GOLDEN BOY
No insult is intended, but you deserve the same justice as Quinto de Cures. If those on foot are denied access, the same rule should apply to those on horseback!
THE ABBOT
Save your foolish reasoning for another time. A man's soul is at stake. And Death does not tarry!
GOLDEN BOY
He'll have to.
THE ABBOT
Move aside, you vile apostate! I told you I am on my way to administer the last rites. Move aside in the name of the Lord!
GOLDEN BOY
I cannot!
THE ABBOT
Satan has taken possession of you, boy!
GOLDEN BOY
Yes, and with his tail he made the sign of the cross over me.
THE ABBOT
Think about what you are doing!
GOLDEN BOY
I have.
THE ABBOT
You are not speaking to one of your brutish coevals. These games are not to be played with a minister of the Lord.
GOLDEN BOY
My father won the lawsuit, and you must respect the court's decision, my dear Abbot.
THE ABBOT
Ridiculous! That decision does not apply to me.
GOLDEN BOY
It applies to you and to the king himself.
THE ABBOT
Ridiculous! In Lantañón you keep a little pigeon from my coop. Remember that!
GOLDEN BOY
I haven't forgotten!
THE ABBOT
I will come for her!
GOLDEN BOY
I'm sure you will!

THE ABBOT
You can forget about her now!
GOLDEN BOY
I'm already forgetting.
THE ABBOT
We will see whether your father approves of this appalling display of yours.
GOLDEN BOY
The way can be opened to all or to none. Do not expect my father to rescind the order.
THE ABBOT
Sacrilege! You would detain me while a sinner lies desperate for absolution! One who is at death's door! One whom the fires of Hell now await! One for whose sake you would risk excommunication!
GOLDEN BOY
I'll take all that into consideration.
THE ABBOT
You would gamble with your soul so recklessly?
GOLDEN BOY
If there is no alternative!
DISTANT VOICES
This is the King's road! Passage is free to all! To all passage is free! No law can close it off!
GOLDEN BOY
Force your way if you can!

THE ABBOT turns his horse around and digs in his spurs. Up on the rocks the men's agile silhouettes flit about, shouting and waving while scattered herds graze all around. The voices of the shepherds and the howling of their dogs reverberate through the gorge.

Scene Four

Along with an escort of herdsmen and cattle-drivers, THE ABBOT of Lantañón enters the green churchyard, rides up to the rectory gate and dismounts. BLAS DE MÍGUEZ, THE SEXTON, approaches and takes the horse's bridle. Tumultuous voices disrupt the green, pastoral silence. Without a word the inscrutable tonsured arrival strides through the doors of the sacristy. As if on stilts, the black angular figure disappears past the dark recesses and ancient statues of saints. A short while later he returns to the doorway and steals a look at the herdsmen while pretending to take stock of the weather. The merchants continue to argue, gesticulating and waving their staves. Suddenly, on the rectory patio appears the skeletal lady of the house, her wide skirts flying at her side. With her spindle and distaff in hand, she spits on her finger and threads her needle. She is DOÑA JEROMITA, *the Abbot's sister.*

DOÑA JEROMITA
  Sweet Jesus, stop with the noise! This isn't the front door of a tavern! Don't jabber all at once, you rubes! Brother, some peace and quiet please!
THE ABBOT
  Don't look to me to make peace.
DOÑA JEROMITA
  Ave María!
THE ABBOT
  My clerical dignity has been insulted by a mere whelp!
DOÑA JEROMITA
  Sweet Jesus!

THE ABBOT *goes inside again using the sacristy door.* BLAS THE SEXTON *follows him, jangling the keys to the church.* DOÑA JEROMITA, *with the spindle cinched to her belt and her arms outspread, descends the stairway.*

DOÑA JEROMITA
  Don't all talk at the same time, I can't understand. Who was my brother quarreling with?
SEBASTIÁN DE XOGAS
  With one of the Mayorazgo's sons.
DOÑA JEROMITA
  But they are kin to us!
PEDRO ABUÍN
  In Lantañón they care nothing for family. Power and pride are all that matter to them.
DOÑA JEROMITA
  Passage through the arches is still under dispute? When will it finally be resolved?
MANUEL TOVÍO
  The quarrel will pass down to our children.
DOÑA JEROMITA
  How did the Abbot get involved?
MANUEL TOVÍO
  Golden Boy denied him access, even though he was on his way to administer the last rites.
DOÑA JEROMITA
  Sacrilege! And what are you looking for here?
PEDRO ABUÍN
  For someone to lead us.

DOÑA JEROMITA
  My brother?
PEDRO ABUÍN
  Correct. That is my petition!
SEBASTIÁN DE XOGAS
  And ours! It's not only you! You are one of many, don't put yourself first. We all come to petition the Abbot to act as our leader.

The stooped, slender black figure of THE ABBOT *reappears at the door of the sacristy, the missal in his hands. The crowd of herdsmen and cattle drivers falls silent, and the skeletal lady of the house, her distaff cinched to her belt and spindle hanging at her side, clutches the outstretched edge of her skirt in her bony hands.*

THE ABBOT
  What are you waiting for?
SEBASTIÁN DE XOGAS
  We await your decision.
THE ABBOT
  And I wait to see whether old Montenegro will condone his son's foul behaviour.
DOÑA JEROMITA
  My brother, allow the healer to apply leeches. By the Virgin, how did such a vile course of events come about?
THE ABBOT
  Why do you ask if you already know?
DOÑA JEROMITA
  Sweet Jesus! Was it really Golden Boy?
THE ABBOT
  That Lucifer!
DOÑA JEROMITA
  He must have been drunk!
THE ABBOT
  That cursed clan!
DOÑA JEROMITA
  Brother, do not speak ill of them; they are our distant relations. Remember that our niece resides under their roof. She was raised in Lantañón!
THE ABBOT
  I will save her from that iniquitous cave. If the father authorizes his son's use of brute force, I will forever break our friendship.
DOÑA JEROMITA
  I can easily imagine the father acting like that! And although I also think the elder brothers capable of any foul deed, I'm surprised to hear little Golden

Boy mentioned. After all, he is in love.
THE ABBOT
The Archfiend moves him!
DOÑA JEROMITA
He was certainly drunk.
THE ABBOT
Imagine if I had needed to administer a man's last rites!
DOÑA JEROMITA
Sweet Jesus!
THE ABBOT
The poor soul would be condemned to Hell! Irremediably condemned!
PEDRO ABUÍN
Abbot, please, it is only right and natural that you lead your parish at a time like this!
THE ABBOT
I have already told you that I will wait.
SEBASTIÁN DE XOGAS
So, you advise caution.
THE ABBOT
I will wait, wait, wait.
SEBASTIÁN DE XOGAS
That is convenient for us as well, at least until the Viana Fair winds down. After that, we will see.
PEDRO ABUÍN
We've seen enough already. We need to drive these cattle through Lantañón. I say we do that and then deal with the consequences.
SEBASTIÁN DE XOGAS
Pedro Abuín, there is no sense without prudence. What does our Abbot counsel?
THE ABBOT
I have given no counsel. Each one of us is free to protest in the way that he chooses, violently or peacefully.
RAMIRO DE BEALO
If we go to him as supplicants, the Lord Mayorazgo will change his mind. We have to wait until his mood improves.
DOÑA JEROMITA
Go call on him then.
PEDRO ABUÍN
Others tried and failed, receiving only abuse for their efforts.
THE ABBOT
I will go and I won't fail.

SEBASTIÁN DE XOGAS
  He may be full of pride, but he must respect the holy vestments.
THE ABBOT
  I will go without them!
DOÑA JEROMITA
  Enough words!
THE ABBOT
  Jeromita, bring a pitcher of wine so that our friends can refresh themselves. I am going to consult my missal.

Hurriedly crossing himself, THE ABBOT *strolls under the shade of the wall and starts reciting his prayers. The group of herdsmen spreads out along the edge of the churchyard, awaiting the jug of wine — the Rectory's famous vintage.*

Scene Five

Lemon trees line the atrium at the Lantañón estate. DOÑA JEROMITA *approaches, riding side-saddle on a donkey whose gait is puppet-like. Her symmetrically outstretched skirt spreads over the cushioned saddle, and broaches hold her mantle, which trails behind her.* BLAS THE SEXTON *walks alongside, goading the burro with a green hazelnut switch. They pass through the grand feudal archway with its heraldry and groaning chain mechanism. Taking care to cover her bony legs, the gaunt lady dismounts onto a stone bench, and* THE SEXTON, *who out of respect for her delicacy does not dare to touch her, mimes his obsequious assistance.*

DOÑA JEROMITA
  Sweet Jesus!
THE SEXTON
  I'm surprised they haven't set the dogs on us.
DOÑA JEROMITA
  Don't frighten me!
THE SEXTON
  This visit is pointless, Doña Jeromita.
DOÑA JEROMITA
  We will see about that.
THE SEXTON
  We are but two lambs pitting ourselves against a wolf. Two helpless lambs!
DOÑA JEROMITA
  Stop trying to discourage me with your stories!
THE SEXTON
  The good Abbot should be making this petition, not us.

DOÑA JEROMITA
    They are two of a kind, my brother and the Vinculero.
THE SEXTON
    Exactly! Pit one fierce beast against another.
DOÑA JEROMITA
    Arguments between two such men usually end with one dead on the ground and the other condemned to the gallows.
THE SEXTON
    Well…
DOÑA JEROMITA
    I believe old Montenegro will hear me out.
THE SEXTON
    I still think it would have been better not to come at all and to wait for him to have a change of heart.
DOÑA JEROMITA
    Even if that day comes, I cannot allow my niece to remain under this roof one moment longer!
THE SEXTON
    There is no way the Vinculero will willingly turn over his little dove. He loves her like a daughter!
DOÑA JEROMITA
    We have the law on our side.
THE SEXTON
    The Vinculero scoffs at the law.
DOÑA JEROMITA.
    Sweet Jesus!

SABELITA *appears in the shade of the lemon trees, her purple habit standing out dramatically against the green penumbra. The maiden wears the doleful expression of dahlias in a vase. Catching sight of the gaunt woman, she runs over to her.*

SABELITA
    Is anything wrong, aunt?
DOÑA JEROMITA
    You don't know?
SABELITA
    No, nothing!
DOÑA JEROMITA
    I sent you a message.
SABELITA
    I was not told anything.

DOÑA JEROMITA
I've come to take you away from here. Prepare yourself.
SABELITA
What's going on?
DOÑA JEROMITA
Your uncle, on his way to administer the last rites, was turned away by Lucifer himself, the despicable Golden Boy.
SABELITA
Dear Lord!
DOÑA JEROMITA
And so I've come to take you away.
SABELITA
Does my godfather know what Golden Boy did?
DOÑA JEROMITA
Yes, he knows and he approves. Let's go tell him that we are leaving.
SABELITA
And how is my uncle?
DOÑA JEROMITA
His rage consumes him. He requires the leeches.
SABELITA
Dear Lord! And you are taking me away forever?
DOÑA JEROMITA.
Forever! Unless your godfather condemns this Barabbas' foul deed.
SABELITA
Golden Boy!... Madman! All blood and thunder with him!
DOÑA JEROMITA
And destined for Hell!
SABELITA
He is not as bad as he seems.
DOÑA JEROMITA
A reprobate!
SABELITA
Listen to me, aunt. Don't talk to my godfather.
DOÑA JEROMITA
What are you afraid of?
SABELITA
Return to the rectory.
DOÑA JEROMITA
I will return — with you.
SABELITA
Wait, aunt. Don't take me.

DOÑA JEROMITA
: You are already crying? You care less for your own kin than you do for this Judas?

SABELITA
: They raised me!

DOÑA JEROMITA
: You rebel against your own blood! Stay here then!

SABELITA
: I'm not rebelling!

DOÑA JEROMITA
: Sweet Jesus! Dry those tears! I don't want to see them!

SABELITA
: Perhaps… I don't know… Golden Boy… if I speak to him… Because he's not so bad.

DOÑA JEROMITA
: He's a miscreant!

SABELITA
: But how would I talk to him?

DOÑA JEROMITA
: Sweet Jesus! Say something, child! What is going on between the two of you?

SABELITA
: Nothing!

DOÑA JEROMITA
: He is not courting you?

SABELITA
: That's just gossip!

DOÑA JEROMITA
: Do you swear?

SABELITA
: Why should I swear if you won't believe me?

DOÑA JEROMITA
: So, what is all this about intervening for the sake of this apostate? What do you mean to do?

SABELITA
: It was just an idea.

DOÑA JEROMITA
: Just what is your plan?

SABELITA
: Just that he apologize to uncle.

DOÑA JEROMITA
: You really think he would?

SABELITA
 I don't know.
DOÑA JEROMITA
 You have that kind influence over this Satan?
SABELITA
 Heavens! It was only an idea.
DOÑA JEROMITA
 An idea only?
SABELITA
 Only.
DOÑA JEROMITA
 Forget about him, my child! Forget that bad seed now and forever; bury your feelings for him! Come now, let us go.
SABELITA
 Wait, aunt.
DOÑA JEROMITA
 Why are you stalling?
SABELITA
 We can fix everything.
DOÑA JEROMITA
 That is my goal. Where can I find your godfather?
SABELITA
 Aunt, don't talk to him, don't go to him!
DOÑA JEROMITA
 What are you afraid of?
SABELITA
 His temper.
DOÑA JEROMITA
 Don't try to scare me!
SABELITA
 My godfather is a king!
DOÑA JEROMITA
 Then I shall act the queen. I will meet this grey-maned wolf and see if he condones his son's actions to my face.
SABELITA
 Auntie, if you are to take me away, do it now! Take me before he notices!
DOÑA JEROMITA
 Sweet Jesus! You are quick to change your mind! What is it you fear?
SABELITA
 He could stop us!
DOÑA JEROMITA
 The law is on my side! I will put questions to your godfather, and his answers will determine our next step.

SABELITA
  That's him!
DOÑA JEROMITA
  Good.
SABELITA
  Don't interrogate him, aunt!
DOÑA JEROMITA
  With me now.

DON JUAN MANUEL *opens the door of his tower and lingers there in the majestic shadow and stone.* BLAS THE SEXTON, *surrounded by retrievers, bloodhounds and other hunting dogs, squirms and whines at his side, his ear gripped by the nobleman's index finger and thumb. The squire holds him in a gesture of undisguised feudal contempt.*

DON JUAN MANUEL
  It would seem this snivelling sacristan has a message for me.
THE SEXTON
  An errand at the service of our crucified Lord Jesus!
DOÑA JEROMITA
  Blas, you meddler!
THE SEXTON
  Oh, the dogs are tearing at my clothes!
DOÑA JEROMITA
  For having a big mouth.
THE SEXTON
  I was trying to prevent a civil war! The dogs keep tearing at my clothes!
SABELITA
  Let him go, godfather! He is scared!
THE SEXTON
  Oh, my torn clothing!
DON JUAN MANUEL
  Silence, blackguard! They haven't even broken the skin yet.
DOÑA JEROMITA
  Sweet Jesus!
THE SEXTON
  I am more concerned about my clothing than myself!
DON JUAN MANUEL
  Ha! A true philosopher.
THE SEXTON
  I am a poor soul who has nothing.
DON JUAN MANUEL
  Repair to the kitchen and console yourself with a mug of wine.

THE SEXTON
   Oh, my torn clothes!

THE SEXTON *limps down the tiled hall, and in the shadow of the archway old* MONTENEGRO *emits a mirthless feudal laugh.*

DOÑA JEROMITA
   Such an unchecked disposition!
DON JUAN MANUEL
   And how is my friend the cleric?
DOÑA JEROMITA
   Livid. The physicians are bleeding him now, as I'm sure you know.
DON JUAN MANUEL
   Really? He was always the image of gentility at the dinner table.
DOÑA JEROMITA
   Sweet Jesus! His ailments owe to another cause: the insults heaped upon him by a scion of your house!
DON JUAN MANUEL
   The case is familiar to me.
DOÑA JEROMITA.
   And how do you judge it?
DON JUAN MANUEL
   It is not for me to break the rod of justice which the Devil put in my hand!
DOÑA JEROMITA
   Sweet Jesus!
DON JUAN MANUEL
   I cannot set such a bad example in my own house.
DOÑA JEROMITA
   But you set still worse examples.
DON JUAN MANUEL
   Perhaps! But this one I did not set.
DOÑA JEROMITA
   Sweet Jesus! You mean to defend your boy's heresy?
DON JUAN MANUEL
   I am obliged to.
DOÑA JEROMITA
   You are aware of what he did?
DON JUAN MANUEL
   I am. Yes, it is lamentable.
DOÑA JEROMITA
   So, you would defend him at the cost of breaking off our friendship?
DON JUAN MANUEL
   I am not breaking it off! But the rod of justice must remain straight.

DOÑA JEROMITA
Sooner or later it will bend.
DON JUAN MANUEL
Don't count on it. I realize your purpose here. I know why you have come.
DOÑA JEROMITA
And what do you have to say about it?
DON JUAN MANUEL
Nothing.
DOÑA JEROMITA
Go on, say it!
DON JUAN MANUEL
I have nothing to say.
DOÑA JEROMITA
You are not surprised that I've come to claim my lost lamb here?
DON JUAN MANUEL
I'm not at all surprised.
DOÑA JEROMITA
And you won't try to stop me from taking her away?
DON JUAN MANUEL
I will not!
DOÑA JEROMITA
With such discord reigning between our families, I see no choice but to take my niece back to her proper home. Am I not right?
DON JUAN MANUEL
Go to Hell!
DOÑA JEROMITA
Sweet Jesus!
SABELITA
Farewell, stones of Lantañón!
DOÑA JEROMITA
Wipe those tears away this instant!
DON JUAN MANUEL
Don't cry, child. You will return, for time brings changes.
DOÑA JEROMITA
And death.
DON JUAN MANUEL
And death.
DOÑA JEROMITA
And punishment.
DON JUAN MANUEL
Perhaps! Come, god-daughter.

DOÑA JEROMITA
  Kiss your godfather's hand and let's be off.
DON JUAN MANUEL
  Don't cry, my girl! Understand that I cannot bend on this issue.
SABELITA
  You must remain firm, I know. Goodbye forever, godfather!
DON JUAN MANUEL
  Not forever. You will be back.
SABELITA
  Who knows?
DON JUAN MANUEL
  If God doesn't return you, the Devil will!

A drunken, dancing BLAS THE SEXTON *emerges from the tower door still holding a jug of wine. The gaunt woman clutches the hem of her skirt, and the old lord resumes his scornful laughter, slowly running his fingers through the hair of* SABELITA, *who is on her knees and kissing his hand. Her purple habit cries piercingly against the green shade of the lemon trees.*

Act Two

Scene One

Viana del Prior, once the hub of the manorial holdings, as evidenced by the awesome stonework, resounds with the rough reverberance of its courtyards and atriums. Preserving its stories in sonorous stone, it sings songs of feudal freebooting and rebellious guilds rising up against crown and mitre. Ancient manses, ancient dynasties, ancient documents, the coats-of-arms over the archways all declaim gothic tales featuring the heraldic symbols of Galicia. Viana del Prior! Its famous fair takes place following the Corpus Christi festivities and attracts visitors from Portugal and Castile.[7] A green field with oak trees. Buskers, entertainers. Crowds. Cattle. Colourful tent stalls. Portuguese sword belts, saddle blankets from Zamora, brown twill fabric. Petticoats of yellow, green and scarlet. Shades of blue ornament the stockings and the trim on the capes. Tent stalls display hanging vanity mirrors, straight razors. The fair festoons the narrow, sloping stone-paved streets, which resemble old Roman roads, and all manner of hucksters, mountebanks and craftspeople ply their trades. Under huge umbrellas, goods and gambling spread out over long tables, gypsy merchants run shell games on the side and cheat the local peasants. Blind bards, led by their guides, sing ballads.

A PEDDLER
  A fine edition of *Ciprianillo*![8] A book that belongs in every household!
ANOTHER PEDDLER
  Leeches from Limia! Leeches!
A THIRD PEDDLER
  Fabric! Blankets! All the way from Zamora!
THE MARAGATERIAN
  Get the hell out of here, Lucero! Shoo!
PICHONA
  A quarter a piece! Rosaries! Cards! Blades! Clothespins! All for a quarter!

---

[7] Viana del Prior is a fictional location created by Valle-Inclán, situated in southern Galicia in the provinces of Orense and Pontevedra. Cures and Tras-Cures are on the coast, Taveirós lies inland in the province of Pontevedra, and Nigrán is located near the large city of Vigo.
[8] The Book of St Cyprian is a folkloric tome popular in Spain and Portugal, attributed to the third-century Catholic saint Cyprian of Antioch.

In front of the inn, a sallow, sour-faced peasant dressed in a hermit robe chants the details of his once dissipated, now penitent life. Sin, blood — and now the cleansing power of confession.

THE PENITENT
　Take heed of the example of this genuine sinner! One whom signs and omens taught to shun gambling and womanizing!

PICHONA
　Rose-water for the eyes! Tobacco pouches from the Ceuta Prison! Something for everyone on the Wheel of Fortune! My friends, don't you recognize Pichona? All for a quarter! Only two bits!

THE BLIND MAN OF GONDAR
　Mouths tire of singing! Feet tire of dancing! Men tire of sticking it to the same woman! But the eyes never get enough of taking in the world's sights!

The baronial sound of galloping horses and jangling spurs: a group of six gallant young riders enters the town square and dismounts at the tavern door. They are GOLDEN BOY *and his brothers:* DON PEDRO, DON ROSENDO, DON MAURO, DON GONZALITO *and* DON FARRUQUIÑO, *who is the youngest of the six, wearing a tricorn hat and sash, timeless emblems of the seminary of Viana del Prior. With their riding crops they bang on the door and demand the innkeep. The* TAVERN MAID *appears.*

THE TAVERN MAID
　What'll it be?

GOLDEN BOY
　Pour a jug of wine.

THE TAVERN MAID
　Ribeiro or the house wine?

DON PEDRITO
　As long as it's not watered down, it can come from Hell's own cellars!

THE TAVERN MAID
　None of our wine's watered down.

DON MAURO
　A jug of each then, Marela!

THE TAVERN MAID
　Don Mauro can't make a decision.

DON ROSENDO
　Why drink the house swill when we can have Ribeiro?

THE MARAGATERIAN
　The Castilians make some fine wines!

DON PEDRITO
　The problem with Castilian wines is that they're ruined by the hides they're aged in.

THE MARAGATERIAN
That's not an issue for me.
DON FARRUQUIÑO
Each wine has its advantages, depending on the occasion. For example, white goes well with a chorizo omelette. Espadeiro de Salnés is refreshing when you find yourself in the mountains, or en route to a holy festival, or playing bowls. Rivero de Avia complements fish pie and Lugo pork. Each wine has its companion in life, just like everything else. The world is composed of harmony and Pythagorean consonance. And let no man who is not an ordained theologian claim otherwise!
GOLDEN BOY
It's clear that you run with a clerical crowd!

FILTHY FUSO, with his ragged cassock exposing his hindquarters and his cap full of pebbles, curses and pontificates in the church's courtyard.

FILTHY FUSO
The world is doomed! Doomed! Why change anything, why start any new enterprises? I've been ordained a bishop! There are few real theologians, and those few live in sin with the objects of their lust!
THE BLIND MAN OF GONDAR
Mouths tire of eating! The body tires of sleeping! Only the eyes never tire of taking in the world.

DON MAURO MONTENEGRO, a belligerent, red-headed giant, exits the tavern counting his money, his spurs jangling. He holds a cattle prod and is surrounded by his greyhounds.

DON FARRUQUIÑO
They dealing cards inside?
DON MAURO
Some small-stakes action.
GOLDEN BOY
Who's dealing?
DON MAURO
The Abbot of Lantañón.
GOLDEN BOY
I'm going to take him for all he has.
DON MAURO
You stopped him on the road but don't assume you can stop him at cards.
GOLDEN BOY
I'll clean him out.
DON FARRUQUIÑO
He can work miracles when he's dealing cards.

THE MARAGATERIAN
He doesn't cheat, but he's lucky.
DON FARRUQUIÑO
A lifetime of piety confers some advantages.
DON PEDRITO
If only his theology were as solid as his double-dealing...
THE MARAGATERIAN
I didn't see him pull any tricks, and I was keeping a close eye.
GOLDEN BOY
I'll break his bank!
DON PEDRITO
Don't leave us out, we can all throw something in the pot. It's father's money!
PICHONA
Golden Boy, sir, do buy something off me. This choker, there's no shortage of ladies you could give it to.
GOLDEN BOY
I give it to you, then — though I won't pay you for it.

Wine in hands, the Montenegro brothers enter the tavern. GOLDEN BOY *waits for a moment by the door, listening to* THE PENITENT *and* THE MARAGATERIAN.

THE PENITENT
The Devil himself spruced me up and convinced me to quit my parents' house and see the world. I fell in with bad company. I hit all the fairs as I honed my card-sharping. And with a woman of easy virtue I came to suffer all manner of disgrace. I took so many wrong turns! I was warned by so many signs and portents!
THE MARAGATERIAN
Enough with the drama! That hair shirt you sport conceals the lazy, phoney king's life you live!
THE PENITENT
For my own salvation I do penance.
GOLDEN BOY
And what is it you're guilty of?
THE PENITENT
Of murder. Of a crime worse than Cain's! I raised an axe over my father's head!
GOLDEN BOY
So, you butchered your own father?
THE PENITENT
He dropped dead from fear when he saw me. With an axe of air I killed my father! My anger was enough to kill him! I was an only child, my parents

spoiled me and started me down the road to perdition. I grew up untamed and irreverent.

GOLDEN BOY

What is your name?

THE PENITENT

My name be damned! A man evil in thought and deed, from the blackest Hell — call me the issue of Satan himself!

GOLDEN BOY

I call you a fraud.

Adding a magnanimous touch to the insult, GOLDEN BOY *places a silver coin in the beggar's hand. His final word hangs in the air as he gracefully crosses the tavern's threshold, his saddle draped rakishly over his shoulder.*

FILTHY FUSO

Jealousy and rage at your front door. You killed your father and got off scot-free. Too-porroo-too! It's one of the Devil's own miracles. Are you in league with him? Fine! You two are acquainted? His plan for ruling the world is well known. He won't go easy on the priests, and pious women will give in to concupiscence, shed their clothing, and run headlong into a bonfire.

THE MARAGATERIAN

Maybe if the Devil had a bath and a shave, he wouldn't prevail after all!

FILTHY FUSO

Do you know who I am? The knowledge I possess? And you would gainsay me? Don't even try! It's all going wrong! The world is hopelessly misguided. In a blink of an eye it will burst into a thousand pieces.

A MERCHANT'S CRY

Get your *Ciprianillo* here! A book for everyone, for every household!

ANOTHER CRY

Leeches from Limia! Leeches!

PICHONA

Rose-water for the eyes! Tobacco pouches from Ceuta prison! Something for everyone on the Wheel of Fortune! Yours for a quarter! For just two bits it's yours!

Scene Two

Vines hang in the orchard behind the tavern. Off to the side, traders, muleteers, cattle wranglers, herdsmen and ruddy men of the cloth play monte, the classic game of Spanish fairs.

THE ABBOT

An ace!

THE INDIANO
   He wins again. Never seen anyone deal himself so many face cards.
A HERDSMAN
   I didn't see anything fishy.
DON FARRUQUIÑO
   Who cut the cards?
PEDRO ABUÍN
   I did. Is there a problem?
DON FARRUQUIÑO
   Blessed be your hands!
PEDRO ABUÍN
   You're making out well?
DON FARRUQUIÑO
   Oh yes, wonderfully.

Slowly and slyly THE ABBOT *stacks the money, shuffles and offers the deck to be cut. The cleric watches as* DON MAURO *lays a giant hand over the cards.*

THE ABBOT
   The chaplain of Lesón has offered to cut the cards.
THE CHAPLAIN
   I cede the honour to Don Mauro.
THE INDIANO
   What a game! Now he wins with a king! Son of a bitch!
THE ELDER OF CURES
   Remember the proverb: No point getting sore at sissies and whores. With a king don't get funny or bet all your money.

DON MAURO *stews in silence, his eyes burning into the card, a king, on which he bets his money. Wiry and bent,* THE ABBOT, *with his crooked nose and stony mouth, takes it all in and officiates slowly and dramatically.*

DON MAURO
   If this king fails me I'll be cleaned out.
DON FARRUQUIÑO
   It will!
DON MAURO
   I'm all in with him.
GOLDEN BOY
   How much money in the pot, dear Abbot?
THE ABBOT
   Rogue!
GOLDEN BOY
   How much?

THE ABBOT
   Your discourtesy deserves no answer!

THE ABBOT squints and mutters obscurely. His hands are crossed over the cards which now lie face down on the table. Fair-haired and handsome, GOLDEN BOY laughs as he leans against his cattle prod, his saddle dancing gently on his shoulder.

GOLDEN BOY
   My dear Abbot must know how deep my love is for him!
THE ABBOT
   I know its depth precisely!
GOLDEN BOY
   Which is backed up by my father's prized cattle, worth these thirty Portuguese gold coins here. Which I intend to wager.
THE ABBOT
   You've lost your mind.
GOLDEN BOY
   I want you to have something to remember me by.
THE ABBOT
   Rogue!
GOLDEN BOY
   Perhaps you will win these thirty gold coins? I bet them all.

Briskly and happily the young man tosses the jangling sack of coins on the table. The tonsured dealer weighs it over in mind and in hand.

THE ABBOT
   Is it all here?
GOLDEN BOY
   You're welcome to count it.
THE ABBOT
   You cannot be allowed to play. You're barely off your mother's tit.
GOLDEN BOY
   It's not a matter of age.
THE ABBOT
   Miscreant!
GOLDEN BOY
   Deal.
THE ABBOT
   I'm at your service then.
GOLDEN BOY
   All thirty on the double, spades.

DON MAURO
My money's still on the king.
THE ABBOT
Here we go! A king at the door!
THE INDIANO
That asshole king was eavesdropping.
GOLDEN BOY
Spades. I don't win and I don't lose. Deal again.
DON MAURO
Recall the Oracle of Cures: no point getting sore at sissies and whores.
GOLDEN BOY
Let's see.
THE ABBOT
There's still time to back out.
DON FARRUQUIÑO
Well look here! The king of cups!
GOLDEN BOY
Nothing but kings in this damned deck.
THE ABBOT
I warned you. You can't claim that I stole your money...
DON MAURO
No, but I can. You're dealing marked cards.
THE ABBOT
Impertinent boor!
DON MAURO
Swindler!

The ginger haired giant grabs the pouch of coins, and all the players around the table start back. The cacophony of voices and movements produces a jarring effect. The holy man draws a flintlock pistol. GOLDEN BOY *comes between them and takes the bag of money from his brother.*

GOLDEN BOY
The Abbot has won.
DON MAURO
By cheating!
THE ABBOT
I won't hesitate to blast you, Goliath!
DON MAURO
Cheat!
THE ABBOT
Judas!

DON MAURO *brings down his riding crop. The gun goes off, the flash from the flintlock, bringing forth the smell of gunpowder, barking dogs, insults, frightened shouts.* DON MAURO *is restrained by some clerics and herdsmen who try to calm him.* THE ABBOT, *his robes torn and pistol still smoking, steps backward carefully, groping the handle to the back door through which he escapes. A sudden calm descends on the group. On his forehead* GOLDEN BOY *has been grazed by the bullet. One side of his face is blackened from the shot. He washes himself with wine, and his brothers, grumbling indistinctly, stand around him.*

Scene Three

Lush vegetation encroaches onto the Manor of San Clemente de Lantañón. Its rectory is off to the side. THE ABBOT, *a black robe over his gaunt frame, is bidding farewell to three obsequious old men in the golden, sun-drenched ecclesiastical courtyard. Their figures framed in the pungent verdure, the three men with their long capes, walking sticks and cloth caps, execute synchronized, compass-like genuflections.*

THE ABBOT
  God be with you!
SEBASTIÁN DE XOGAS
  And good health to you!
THE ELDER OF CURES
  And may the King of Heaven protect us from the belligerent and the proud!
THE DEACON OF LESÓN
  We need more good laws!
THE ABBOT
  And fewer bad judges!
THE ELDER OF CURES
  Then perhaps there wouldn't be so many hardened criminals running free in the streets! But let us leave all this grousing about judges and verdicts to those who have nothing better to do.
THE ABBOT
  And if you are called in to testify…
THE DEACON OF LESÓN
  It's unlikely that we would be…
THE ABBOT
  But if you are…
SEBASTIÁN DE XOGAS
  In that case… we didn't see anything!
THE DEACON OF LESÓN
  Speaking for myself, I definitely didn't see anything!

THE ELDER OF CURES
   It's not like there was anything we could see anyway!
THE DEACON OF LESÓN
   That's the idea: we don't know anything because we didn't see anything.
THE ELDER OF CURES
   If we stick to the truth, there's no case against us.
THE ABBOT
   I don't expect servants of the law to come knocking on my door.
SEBASTIÁN DE XOGAS
   The curia is the worst of the worst![9]
THE DEACON OF LESÓN
   Like they say: justice swings to the side of the king!
SEBASTIÁN DE XOGAS
   Gold is our master now. These days coin is king.
THE ELDER OF CURES
   May God be with you, Abbot.
SEBASTIÁN DE XOGAS
   Let's hope the case never comes to trial!
THE DEACON OF LESÓN
   The Montenegros! Barbaric savages!

They set off, their conversation larded with Latin archaisms as old as the stones of the Quintana. They have already disappeared when the crow of a SEXTON *starts calling from the bell tower as he regards the setting sun.*

THE SEXTON
   No doubt about the weather!
THE ABBOT
   I don't know… those clouds over there…
THE SEXTON
   They're passing. We will have nice weather.
THE ABBOT
   Blas, fetch some leeches so I can have some blood let.

On wooden chairs the Abbot's sister and niece sit face to face just inside the door and work the spindle, enjoying the sunshine.

DOÑA JEROMITA
   Nothing good comes with hellspawn!
SABELITA
   Horrid!

---

[9] The implication is that the Abbot will have to face the ecclesiastical as well as secular courts.

THE ABBOT
Get down, Blas!
THE SEXTON
Presently! Sabelita, lovely jewel, tomorrow there is a mass in San Martiño. While we still have some sunlight, would you care to go there to lay out the altar cloth and change the candles?
DOÑA JEROMITA
Change the candles again?
THE SEXTON
They burn away into the air.
DOÑA JEROMITA
Cursed air, you always knock the candles over, but you will not blow them out!
SABELITA
Where do you keep the candles?
DOÑA JEROMITA
In the Pedrayes sisters' old trunk.

THE ABBOT *paces back and forth, his gaunt black-robed figure muttering Latin phrases from his missal. His niece, her arms full of wax candles, crosses his path and brushes him with her shawl.*

THE ABBOT
And where are you going?
SABELITA
To Freyres.
THE ABBOT
Make sure to return before nightfall.
DOÑA JEROMITA
Yes, don't tarry.
THE ABBOT
If I cannot tame that damned family, I will tear off this collar!
DOÑA JEROMITA
Calm down, brother.
THE ABBOT
I had the prayer book with me… imagine if I had been carrying the Eucharist!
DOÑA JEROMITA
The horror!
THE ABBOT
And the sacrilege!
DOÑA JEROMITA
The Montenegros and their coal-black souls!

From the sacristy, jangling his keys, THE SEXTON *of San Clemente emerges. He is fond of telling tall tales and bald lies. His face is like rancid tallow, and he has a wide toothless mouth, no eyebrows and beady eyes; he is an inveterate blackguard. His tonsured superior meets him on the steps to the yard and takes his keys.*

THE SEXTON
The Montenegros! A pack of rabid wolves!
THE ABBOT
I am more rabid than any of them!
THE SEXTON
That's an impressive case of rabies then!
THE ABBOT
They will admit their wrongs eventually. They will eat their humble pie or go straight to Hell!
THE SEXTON
They're already on their way!
THE ABBOT
Bound by a double set of chains!
DOÑA JEROMITA
Chains of fire and serpents!

A horseman gallops toward the church, his silhouette against the setting sun. DOÑA JEROMITA *rises from her chair, her arms outstretched, cackling with an ascending scale of abusive expressions.*

DOÑA JEROMITA
That villain!
THE ABBOT
He wants to provoke me!
THE SEXTON
For three nights straight I've been dreaming of fried mackerel!
DOÑA JEROMITA
And our niece still has not returned.
THE SEXTON
I will go and warn her.

With lupine dexterity THE SEXTON *hops over the wall to the road, turning his head back periodically to see what is happening in the Quintana.* THE ABBOT, *his gaunt figure clothed in the robes of his office, his biretta cocked to one side, enters the house and takes cover in an attic window, aiming a gun outside.*

THE ABBOT
Proud Absalom, keep coming! I have some lead here with your name on it,

ready to send you to Hell!

GOLDEN BOY

Respected Abbot, I come in peace!

THE ABBOT

Reprobate! Your afflicted conscience will bring you no peace!

GOLDEN BOY

I have brought you the thirty gold pieces!

THE ABBOT

With some perverse ulterior motive, no doubt.

GOLDEN BOY

My motive is only to perform good works and earn my place in Heaven. Dear Abbot, come down and take your thirty gold coins.

THE ABBOT

I don't want them! Keep the money and go to Hell!

GOLDEN BOY

Dear Abbot, enough cursing. Let's put our quarrel behind us!

THE ABBOT

It is clear that this smooth talking does not come from the heart! Some foul intent lies behind it.

GOLDEN BOY

Most holy Abbot, take what is rightfully yours and then offer me some wine!

DOÑA JEROMITA

Step away from our door, Satan! Get back, enemy of mankind! Your false humility won't win you our pure niece. Get thee hence! Go on! The virtuous will not be tempted, Satan!

GOLDEN BOY

May lightning strike me dead if I don't ride into that house and take what you deny me!

THE ABBOT

Tarquin the Proud here needs to be on his way if he wants to live![10]

GOLDEN BOY

Damn you, dear Abbot! Here is your coin purse. One! Two! Three!

Standing in his stirrups, the handsome youth brings his arm back and hurls the coin purse at the four-winged biretta peeking out of the window. The purse flies through the night sky like a black bird, and the cleric grunts and lifts his arms from the shadows to catch it.

THE ABBOT

Come back here, you arrogant bastard! Take your bag! My pride is no less

---

[10] Tarquin the Proud, last king of Rome (d. 495 BCE), whose tyrannical reign led to the establishment of the Republic.

than yours! You won't come back? I'll toss it into the road! It can lie there and rot! Come back and pick it up, you barbarian! Ten thousand reales![11] May the executioner forge them into the axe that takes your head!

DOÑA JEROMITA
    The end days are upon us!

THE ABBOT, quivering in a hoarse rage, throws the bag of coins onto the road down which GOLDEN BOY gallops away. DOÑA JEROMITA falls to her knees with her arms outstretched as the four horn-like wings of her brother's biretta glower from the little window.

Scene Four

The sun's waning light mingles with the budding stars, and among four cypress trees perch the Romanesque stones of the chapel of San Martiño de Freyres. Twilight outlines the summits, and violet symphonies cascade down the hillsides. The wind wafts through the cornfields like a prayer, and the cadmium clay hues of the roads are gradually empurpled in the setting sun. San Martiño de Freyres in the twilight is a place of supplications, miracles and funereal votives. Women's hands light the lamps of the chancel. An owl takes fright and flies off into the night. From the shadow, SABELITA appears under the lamplight, and at the door of the chapel GOLDEN BOY reins in his horse.

GOLDEN BOY
    Isabel!
SABELITA
    Do not call my name!
GOLDEN BOY
    Look at me!
SABELITA
    I would rather not.
GOLDEN BOY
    You hate me that much?
SABELITA
    You're scaring me!
GOLDEN BOY
    Do you know where I was just now?
SABELITA
    Up to no good, I'm sure.
GOLDEN BOY
    I offered the olive branch to your uncle.

---

[11] The real (pl. reales) was something like the Spanish silver dollar.

SABELITA
You are too arrogant to do anything of the kind.
GOLDEN BOY
It's not arrogance but love that moves me.
SABELITA
Love comes to you too late! And my uncle, was he moved by your offer?
GOLDEN BOY
Just as Christ turned water into wine, the Abbot made a gun appear out of his holy vestments.
SABELITA
A shame he did not kill you!
GOLDEN BOY
Are you so eager to don the black veil?
SABELITA
I'd dress in scarlet on that occasion.
GOLDEN BOY
You lie, Isabel. Think of the wounds our wedding would heal!
SABELITA
You are dead to me!
GOLDEN BOY
It's only because we stand on consecrated ground that I don't grab you by the waist and throw you over the saddle.
SABELITA
Pirate!
GOLDEN BOY
Farewell, Isabel!
SABELITA
Farewell, little Golden Boy.

FILTHY FUSO with his cap filled with pebbles enters through the sacristy door as the hoof beats of GOLDEN BOY's horse fade away.

FILTHY FUSO
Too-porroo-too! I'm gathering pebbles. But seven thousand capfuls wouldn't be enough! Not nearly! I need to build a house, and soon: I've got a girl coming from America. Too-porroo-too! I knocked her up! I haven't seen her yet, but her and me have been busy every night, sinning in the dark. You have to sin! He who is without sin is damned!
SABELITA
Show some respect on these holy grounds, Filthy Fuso.
FILTHY FUSO
I do. Wait until I've built the house, then we can be together. Too-porroo-too!

My other girl's pregnant: thirty-seven studs and thirty-seven fillies in her belly! Tonight I'll conjure a mare from the wind, you and me can get busy and then slit her throat.

SABELITA

Stop frightening me, Filthy Fuso! What is your business here?

FILTHY FUSO

Getting an eyeful of you!

SABELITA

Get out!

FILTHY FUSO

How about a coin or two for a drink?

SABELITA

Out!

FILTHY FUSO

If you won't give me the money for a glass, you can at least show me your legs…

SABELITA

Filthy Fuso, stop frightening me now!

FILTHY FUSO

Too-porroo-too! Ah, my sweet, just enough for one glass.

SABELITA

I don't have any money on me.

FILTHY FUSO

Here's a great idea: pour all the wine in the world into one fountain with a hundred thousand spouts! A wonderful idea! And the cows, instead of dung they could drop bread! Another fine idea! Laudatory, truly! As it is, the world is a mess! But I know the remedy, as do a few others. Yet no one will reveal it. The first to open his mouth gets four shots in the head, courtesy of the goddamned government. Satan could rule the world and see to everyone's needs. Too-porroo-too! With his wiles he can get on with most anyone.

SABELITA

Respect this holy place! Go away! You're scaring me, Filthy Fuso!

FILTHY FUSO

If Satan were running things, women would be nude all the time. Eating, drinking, fornicating — seven days a week. Since the world is already such a mess, this would be a great way to go indeed. Come on, angel face, show me your legs!

SABELITA

Go away!

FILTHY FUSO

Don't want to.

SABELITA
  Go away, or I'll scream!
FILTHY FUSO
  Damn you, show me your legs!
SABELITA
  Don't frighten me, Filthy Fuso!
FILTHY FUSO
  Too-porroo-too! How fair you are! Give us a goddamned look! Your virgin honey pot must be as pure as our Holy Mother's!

Beneath the romanesque portico, amidst the stone statues of saints: a triumphal erection, insane laughter, fiery eyes, wild matted hair. SABELITA *screams, trying to attract the attention of a distant passerby on the twilit road.*

SABELITA
  Help!
FILTHY FUSO
  Goddamn you, I'll bite off your tongue!
SABELITA
  Help!

A black rider radiating violence and malediction suddenly spurs his horse, which jumps the atrium wall. The dishevelled, terrified madman now finds himself beneath its hooves, cowering like a Moor before Saint James Matamoros.[12] The young girl, quivering and pale, is lifted onto the saddle and collapses on the shoulder of DON JUAN MANUEL.

SABELITA
  Godfather, where are you taking me?
DON JUAN MANUEL
  To be with me forever!
SABELITA
  Forever!

On the road a long-skirted old woman is nearly run down by the horse. She makes the sign of the cross.

Scene Five

LUDOVINA'S *tavern, tucked into the hillside and facing the sea. A lighthouse in the distance flickers in time with the stars in the sky. These faint nocturnal lights*

---

[12] Saint James (Santiago) is the patron saint of Spain. He is usually portrayed striking down or trampling his Moorish enemies.

shine into the cracked open Dutch door. An old brass lamp illuminates the bar, which reeks of homemade wine and spirits. Behind the bar there are candles, a basket of figs, various bottles, spices and tin cups. LUDOVINA *dozes behind the counter with a cat in her lap. She is roused by hoofbeats approaching from the distance. 'Moaning'* PICHONA, *half dressed, peers out of the curtain that hangs above the tiered doorway. The cat jumps up, and* PICHONA *shuts the door and hides. On the road outside is a lone horseman.* LUDOVINA *rubs her sleepy eyes and sees* GOLDEN BOY *entering the tavern, still mounted on his horse. The noble youth is agitated but no less comely for it. He leans forward but his head still grazes the ceiling.*

LUDOVINA
Holy Mother of God!
GOLDEN BOY
A glass of brandy.
LUDOVINA
Strike me dead if I didn't recognize you right away!
GOLDEN BOY
Strike you dead then!
LUDOVINA
And the rest of your crew, where are they?
GOLDEN BOY
No idea.
LUDOVINA
They ordered some fish pies.
GOLDEN BOY
They can choke on it!
LUDOVINA
If you plan to stay, at least tie up your beast outside.
GOLDEN BOY
I've ridden him hard; he's not going anywhere.
LUDOVINA
I need to close up. There're some guests playing cards and they want it quiet. You going to try your luck?
GOLDEN BOY
Another glass.
LUDOVINA
Lucky in love, unlucky at cards, no?
GOLDEN BOY
Bad luck follows me everywhere!
LUDOVINA
Fine, just go tend to that horse of yours! …

GOLDEN BOY
  In time. Say, who is that laughing behind the door?
LUDOVINA
  Someone with a mouth.
GOLDEN BOY
  Is it a woman?
LUDOVINA
  I haven't examined the body, so I couldn't tell you.
GOLDEN BOY
  Why's she hiding?
LUDOVINA
  Perhaps she suspects something.
GOLDEN BOY
  Is she a virgin?
LUDOVINA
  My dear Golden Boy, we ran out of virgins and good wine here long ago!
GOLDEN BOY
  Another glass.
LUDOVINA
  That's three for you. Isn't your head spinning?
GOLDEN BOY
  The world's spinning! Pour another glass.
LUDOVINA
  I'm not pouring you anything.
GOLDEN BOY
  That… curtain's starting to annoy me!
LUDOVINA
  Then don't look at it.
GOLDEN BOY
  Who's in there?
LUDOVINA
  A scorpion.
GOLDEN BOY
  I'm going to drag it out by the ears.
LUDOVINA
  Holy Mother of God, smite down and humble this Antichrist!

The horse rears. Its shoes shine in the shadows of the hallway and clack against the wooden floorboards. PICHONA, *wearing only her slip, opens up the curtain which had concealed her. A kerchief tied 'round her neck accents bare, nacreous shoulders.*

PICHONA
   Can I help you?
GOLDEN BOY
   Show me your face.
PICHONA
   It's not much to show…
LUDOVINA
   Ha! It hits men like a cloud of stone!
GOLDEN BOY
   Come share a glass with me, Pichona.
PICHONA
   No thank you.
GOLDEN BOY
   You drink or I baptize you in it.
PICHONA
   All right, fine! Don't be angry, sweet Golden Boy! I'll take a glass and drink to your health and to the love you try to hide.
GOLDEN BOY
   It's not love.
PICHONA
   Jealousy then!
GOLDEN BOY
   Two more, Ludovina.
PICHONA
   Make it just one.
GOLDEN BOY
   No, you drink too.
PICHONA
   I don't want to drink any more.
GOLDEN BOY
   Drink!
PICHONA
   My head's already spinning.
GOLDEN BOY
   Drink!
PICHONA
   What do you say about him forcing me to have more, Ludovina?
LUDOVINA
   I say drink and be merry!
PICHONA
   Some help you are against this King of the Moors here.

GOLDEN BOY
You'll be stripping off your clothes and dancing before the night is through.
PICHONA
Spoken like a true Montenegro!
GOLDEN BOY
Drink!
PICHONA
Only for the sake of peace.
GOLDEN BOY
Do you enjoy life, Pichona?
PICHONA
Walking the streets? I guess it depends on what you have in mind by 'enjoyment'.
GOLDEN BOY
And what are your thoughts?
PICHONA
To enjoy life, my dear Golden Boy, means not looking back. And making sure you've always got some coin in your pocket.
GOLDEN BOY
How about you and I set off together to travel the world?
PICHONA
You might not believe me, but I've been asked that before. And by men who weren't trying to make fun of me!
GOLDEN BOY
Make up your mind so we can pool our resources.
PICHONA
You're going to contribute a lot of money then?
GOLDEN BOY
Everything you can lend me.
PICHONA
And what do you bring to the table?
GOLDEN BOY
The pleasure of my company.
PICHONA
Ah, now that's enjoyable!
GOLDEN BOY
I'll pitch in what I have.
PICHONA
And I'll receive it as if it were lottery winnings.
GOLDEN BOY
I'll set you on my horse and parade you through the fairs.

PICHONA
  I'm not the kind of woman anyone wants to show off.

LUDOVINA *dozes off behind the bar, the cat once again nestling in her skirts and purring.* PICHONA *laughs, her cheeks flushed, and adjusts the kerchief around her neck.* GOLDEN BOY *lays his hand on her breasts.* LUDOVINA *rubs her sleepy eyes, yawns, and leaves the room.*

GOLDEN BOY
  What's this body of yours for?
PICHONA
  Don't start with that!
GOLDEN BOY
  How firm they are.
PICHONA
  Hands off them!
GOLDEN BOY
  What's this body of yours for?
PICHONA
  I'm sure you have an idea.
GOLDEN BOY
  But I don't!
PICHONA
  I'm a woman you can call on for a year and a day if it pleases you — for as long as it lasts. All the time and money I have, we can spend together. But I won't have you shouting in the streets about it.
GOLDEN BOY
  Why did you hide when I came in?
PICHONA
  So as not to be blinded.
GOLDEN BOY
  Give me a kiss.
PICHONA
  Not here. At my humble abode in Cures. If you come I'll lay out the special lace-trimmed sheets.
GOLDEN BOY
  No one goes anywhere until you dance a fandango.
PICHONA
  To do it here would be a sin.
GOLDEN BOY
  Ludovina, another round so she can dance.

PICHONA
>   Golden Boy, don't force me to drink more. I've been in the sun all day and my head is reeling.

GOLDEN BOY
>   Drink so that you can dance.

PICHONA
>   I will dance if that pleases you.

GOLDEN BOY
>   Nothing pleases me.

PICHONA
>   Poor dear!

GOLDEN BOY
>   To Hell with you!

GOLDEN BOY, *slouching in the chair, suddenly goes out to the road and disappears into the night.* PICHONA *and* LUDOVINA, *who has returned, exchange the mischievous glances and smiles of those who share a great secret.*

PICHONA
>   I'm going home, while the moon can still guide my way.

LUDOVINA
>   Who's waiting up for you there?

PICHONA
>   Just my cat.

LUDOVINA
>   You never told me whether that Indiano was treating you…

PICHONA
>   He was good for a bit of coin!

LUDOVINA
>   Maybe he'll be good for a bit more!

PICHONA
>   That holier-than-thou devil-dodger, scared out of his mind by the thought of death! He went bone white when I turned up the three and seven of cups!

LUDOVINA
>   You read the cards for him?

PICHONA
>   He asked me to.

PICHONA *prepares to leave. Her head is already wrapped in her scarf as she utters these final words. Her black silhouette fills the doorway. One step out the door and she feels a jolt of fear. Down the road, in a sudden burst of violence, a horseman flies by, a black spark which prompts the young fortune-teller and croupier to cross herself.*

LUDOVINA
Pichoneta, that horse is out of control!
PICHONA
It certainly seems that way! It's like the entire road was on fire!
LUDOVINA
Who was the rider?
PICHONA
A man with a woman who seemed to have fainted!
LUDOVINA
Mother of God!
PICHONA
Get thee behind me, Satan!
LUDOVINA
Did you recognize either of them?
PICHONA
I can't say for sure. The Vinculero could have been the rider.
LUDOVINA
That dirty old tomcat!
PICHONA
God forbid father and son run into one another on the road!

Scene Six

The Rectory. By the light of a single candle, in the whitewashed hallway, which is bare except for some antique chests on the floor and some black ceiling beams, the cleric paces back and forth with his blunderbuss, cassock and winged cap. In the candlelight, shadows play against the wall — an indication of how windy it is outside. A zucchetto hangs by a nail on the wall, and a little dog wags its tail and yawns atop the chest containing the tithe money. The place is quiet and enshrouded in night, and the Abbot's sister waves her arms frantically outside by the light of the moon. The candle trembles in the wind, making the shadow of the priest's cap dance against the white wall.

THE ABBOT
Does that devil intend to drag himself back here?
DOÑA JEROMITA
The only thing he's dragging is his tail!
THE ABBOT
God smite him down!
DOÑA JEROMITA
And that sack of coins lying right there on the road! Sweet Jesus!

THE ABBOT

May his haughty gesture land him in the poor house!

DOÑA JEROMITA

If haughty gestures are the crime, my brother, you are guilty as well! You're driving me to an early grave! The first passer-by will pick up the sack! The cursed moon shines its light right on it!

THE ABBOT

Enough with your miserly whinnying. Get inside, I want to lock up.

DOÑA JEROMITA

O moon who desires nothing, conceal thyself in some dark cloud! Schismatic moon!

THE ABBOT

You will cut short these witch's orisons!

DOÑA JEROMITA

And not a living soul in sight! Sweet Jesus!

THE ABBOT

And this pains you?

DOÑA JEROMITA

This shock will be the death of me! So much money! Brother, consider for a moment that you condemn your own soul!

THE ABBOT

Shut up, you serpent!

DOÑA JEROMITA

Did not Justice herself give you that sack? Did she not deal you the fateful card?

THE ABBOT

The card was marked!

DOÑA JEROMITA

You clutch at your precious scruples, yet you allow your arrogance to condemn your very soul. It is pride which gnaws away at you!

THE ABBOT

Perhaps...

DOÑA JEROMITA

In no dispute can you allow anyone to get the better of you. Brother, the grey hairs on your head should keep you from throwing away money like that young fool!

THE ABBOT

I am above him. Get inside now and drop the subject!

DOÑA JEROMITA

You can kill me if you want, but I must defy you! I will pick up the sack and keep it.

THE ABBOT
　Then I will shoot you dead!
DOÑA JEROMITA
　For this small thing you are prepared to murder your own sister! The horror of it!
THE ABBOT
　Inside now and shut your mouth!
DOÑA JEROMITA
　This really will be the death of me!
THE ABBOT
　Of me as well! But this devil will not prevail over me. Inside, so I can lock up.

In the bright moonlight DOÑA JEROMITA *falls to her knees in a pose of supplication, arms outstretched. The stooped and black figure of* THE ABBOT *stands at the door: cap, gun, cassock. The road is browned by the shadow of an old woman.*

THE OLD WOMAN
　Sabeliña! Sabel! Come out for a moment, my dove! Is Sabeliña not here?
DOÑA JEROMITA
　What are you up to? I don't want to hear your gossip. I know your evil ways.
THE OLD WOMAN
　Holy Mother of God, I'm not some busybody!
THE ABBOT
　Why are you looking for the girl?
THE OLD WOMAN
　I'm not looking for her.
DOÑA JEROMITA
　You were calling for her.
THE OLD WOMAN
　I just wanted to make sure.
DOÑA JEROMITA
　Make sure of what?
THE OLD WOMAN
　If it really was her I saw. I think I saw her on the road, so I came here straightaway... Isn't this information worth something to you? Even a cup of flour for tonight's soup?
DOÑA JEROMITA
　Where did you see the child? Sweet Jesus!
THE OLD WOMAN
　The end days are upon us!
DOÑA JEROMITA
　Do not try to frighten me. Answer!

THE OLD WOMAN
   When you've lived as long as I have, your eyes sometimes deceive you.

THE SEXTON *appears in a gap in the Quintana's stone wall. He looks frightened and alert in the moonlit fog.*

THE SEXTON
   Just as my dark dream foretold: sin is omnipresent! That dark dream!
THE ABBOT
   My niece, where is she?
THE SEXTON
   Sin is omnipresent! Black-hearted Satan himself swept her away on his horse!
DOÑA JEROMITA
   Sweet Jesus!
THE OLD WOMAN
   Sabeliña in the arms of that Turk, like a disheveled Magdalene!
DOÑA JEROMITA
   The depraved child planned this all along! I was blind to it!
THE ABBOT
   What a dark hour indeed!
THE SEXTON
   The furies of Hell are unleashed!
THE OLD WOMAN
   Corrupting virgins is the Devil's favourite pastime!
THE ABBOT
   The little black sheep will be back tonight, even if I have to drag her myself. With me, Blás!
DOÑA JEROMITA
   And tomorrow she goes to a convent for good, my brother!
THE SEXTON
   Requies in pace![13]
THE ABBOT
   Which way were these miscreants heading?
THE SEXTON
   Towards the estate, I suspect.
THE ABBOT
   That's our destination then!
DOÑA JEROMITA
   Do not stray from the righteous path, my brother!
THE OLD WOMAN
   Perhaps a husband may yet be found for her? Respected Abbot, is my information worth a little something to you?

---

[13] The Sexton mangles the Latin phrase, which should be *requiescat in pace* (rest in peace).

THE ABBOT
   May your tongue fall out!
DOÑA JEROMITA
   Sweet Holy Virgin! Brother! There! The coin purse! This is killing me! My precious thirty Portuguese coins!

DOÑA JEROMITA raises her arms to heaven, and her shout pierces the stars' nocturnal silence. In the moonlit fog along the silver road appears FILTHY FUSO. *Too-porroo-too! He stumbles upon the coin purse, grabs it and runs off.* THE ABBOT *fires his gun. Hounds bark in the distance.*

Scene Seven

Moaning PICHONA *tosses and turns in her bed to the sound of nearby laughter, song and dance. Her eyes are large and radiant, her hair spreads over the pillow, and her neighbours' cavorting in the night keeps her from sleeping. A single lamp stands in the corner. There is a hen under the bed, and in the shadow a cat stirs. At the sound of hoofbeats approaching,* PICHONA *sighs, the hen scratches the dirt floor, the cat arches its back and runs off to transform into a pair of glowing green eyes in the darkness by the wall. A knock on the door.*

GOLDEN BOY
   Open the door, Pichona!
PICHONA
   I'm undressed and in bed.
GOLDEN BOY
   Less work for me then.
PICHONA
   Oh, you're a slippery one! Who are you really?
GOLDEN BOY
   You know who I am.
PICHONA
   Honestly, I have no idea.
GOLDEN BOY
   Open up!
PICHONA
   Wait a minute while I slip something on. Don't break down the door, my sweet!

GOLDEN BOY *replies with an impious laugh. He stops banging on the door. Half-dressed,* PICHONA *hurries to release the stick that she'd propped against the door. On the deserted moonlit road, against the distant background of trembling stars, the handsome youth holds his horse's reins.*

PICHONA
At this moment, in this light, your face really does look as though it's made of gold.
GOLDEN BOY
You were expecting me?
PICHONA
Kind of. Come inside and take me if you want. But be gentle, sweetheart.
GOLDEN BOY
Step aside!

GOLDEN BOY *shoves the girl out of the way and enters the house, his hand still clutching the reins. The cat hisses, the hen clucks, the lamp gasps and the horse shrinks in fear, its eyes dilating.*

PICHONA
Where do you plan to put the horse?
GOLDEN BOY
Under the bed.
PICHONA
The liquor's gone to your head.
GOLDEN BOY
I'll tie him to the door so the whole world knows I'm here!
PICHONA
What's to announce? That my bed is occupied? We are young and we are enjoying one another's company. Get inside and shut the door.

The handsome youth bends down to enter the doorway. PICHONA *puts the door-stopper back in place, and the horse neighs outside.* GOLDEN BOY *walks over to the shabby bed and takes a seat. The nearly naked girl, tawny and white, turns and smiles at him.*

GOLDEN BOY
Pichona, take off my spurs and shut up. Shut up, goddamnit!
PICHONA
You can tear up the bedspread with your spurs, then move on to my body, if that's what you like. Hit me! Enjoy yourself!
GOLDEN BOY
I don't enjoy myself like that!
PICHONA
What, I don't appeal to you?
GOLDEN BOY
You're amusing. I should laugh, yet I can't.
PICHONA
Something's making you sad, that's why you were drinking so much at

Ludovina's. Do I guess right? Won't you respond?

GOLDEN BOY

I don't know what you're talking about.

PICHONA

Shoo away those dark thoughts and take me in your arms. Whatever's troubling you will pass, and then you will be the first to laugh over it. That's the way of the world! Nothing sad lasts forever. You carry the chill of death on your lips!

GOLDEN BOY

Your talk is getting old.

PICHONA

You can rid yourself of this sadness. The wheel of fortune keeps turning. Do you want me to read yours?

GOLDEN BOY

What witch taught you these skills?

PICHONA

It wasn't a witch. I was taught by a colleague at Madame de la Montforte's house.

GOLDEN BOY

A fine school!

PICHONA, *her gown slipping off her shoulders, riffles through the chest nearby and then turns to the foot of the old bed, holding an oil lamp and a Vilham deck.*[14] *Three times she hands the cards to the handsome youth to cut. Then she lays the deck on the floral-patterned bedspread.*

PICHONA

Tell me the secret, Vilham, bring us some calm, don't make me resort to reading palms. Show us the roads, shine light on our fates... like unto Moses, give us both good and bad signs with your power so great.

GOLDEN BOY

Smooth work so far.

PICHONA

Lift your left hand. Flip over the card. I will read the deck in the Portuguese way. Rings followed by swords. Jealousy and rage. Notice the three of cups below the seven of swords: cups here mean bells and swords point to the agony of death. Does any of this ring true?

GOLDEN BOY

It's damned gibberish!

---

[14] Refers to a common deck of cards (not Tarot), which Vilham invented in early modern Spain. Card suits consist of swords (spades), coins or rings (diamonds), cups (hearts), and clubs or sticks.

PICHONA
> This two, this four, this six — this pattern of evens — represents the lights at a funeral wake. This knight of rings is a person in love. If it's not you, I don't know who it could be. This queen of swords, face down, is a weeping Magdalene. That's the way I see it! And this five of cups is depravity and sin, with the king of cups on top. Now here there are three aces. They are potent, and then three knights of clashing suits. The knights are suitors. Does this explain anything to you?

GOLDEN BOY
> Not a thing!

PICHONA
> I'm going to deal them again face down to see if it's any clearer.

PICHONA *begins to gather up the cards which fan out across the bedspread. She picks up the knight of swords, which she holds and ponders.*

PICHONA
> Have you ever considered killing someone?

GOLDEN BOY
> If I'd thought of it, I'd have done it already.

PICHONA
> You're another Diego Corrientes.[15]

GOLDEN BOY
> I'm more than him.

PICHONA
> But you don't rob and steal! The cards link you with a dead man. He is represented in the two of cups even though that's not usually an important card. But I know it because it was followed by the knight. And that knight of rings, the infatuated young gallant, is you. For certain!

GOLDEN BOY
> Finish the reading!

PICHONA
> I'm finished! Take me in your arms, sweetheart. Take me, my Castilian Moorish king! Finally, you notice me! What is it that makes your blood boil? Your mouth is cold! Darling, take me in your arms!

---

[15] Diego Corrientes Mateos (1757-1781) was a bandit in Spain with something of a Robin Hood reputation.

Act Three

Scene One

A large darkened room in the estate of Lantañón. Against the shadow of the whitewashed wall, Christ in his tattered loincloth expresses the livid tragedy of the Passion. The oil lamp's piercing yellow light casts a hypnotic spell around the room. Through the vaulted opening in the wall a table set for dinner can be seen. Cats and dogs are everywhere. In his armchair DON JUAN MANUEL MONTENEGRO *raises his glass like the feudal lord he is.* SABELITA *stands at the far end of the room near the door, covering her face. How pale her hands!*

DON JUAN MANUEL
  Lower your arms and look at me.
SABELITA
  I cannot.
DON JUAN MANUEL
  Do what I say, Isabel!
SABELITA
  Godfather, return me to San Clemente.
DON JUAN MANUEL
  We will depart after dinner. Sit down.
SABELITA
  Allow me to serve you.
DON JUAN MANUEL
  Stop crying and obey.
SABELITA
  It is my lot to cry.
DON JUAN MANUEL
  Take my glass and drink.
SABELITA
  I am ashamed, godfather!
DON JUAN MANUEL
  To Hell with your shame!

DON JUAN MANUEL *smashes his glass and rises violently from the table, nearly knocking it over. The sudden jolt shakes the tableware, spills the wine and extinguishes the candles. The newborn moon sends silver beams through the window. The figures fade into the darkness; their voices and shadows assume even more gravity.*

SABELITA
Godfather, allow me to return to San Clemente.
DON JUAN MANUEL
The door is unlocked. Go, and never return!
SABELITA
That cursed Filthy Fuso!
DON JUAN MANUEL
Why haven't you left?
SABELITA
I'm frightened of him!
DON JUAN MANUEL
Go!
SABELITA
Calm down, my anxious soul! Begone, fear! Do not bind me to these shadows, this antechamber of Hell!
DON JUAN MANUEL
God strike me down! Run away then! Don't delay!
SABELITA
Lord of Heaven, set me free, save me from perdition!
DON JUAN MANUEL
You're not going?
SABELITA
I cannot.
DON JUAN MANUEL
You belong to me.
SABELITA
My soul is damned!
DON JUAN MANUEL
Give it to me then!
SABELITA
Why do you want my soul?
DON JUAN MANUEL
Because I want it. Give it to me!
SABELITA
I will give it to Satan.
DON JUAN MANUEL
It is mine!
SABELITA
Godfather, save me from perdition!
DON JUAN MANUEL
I am Satan and I say perdition is upon you already!

SABELITA
   Godfather!
DON JUAN MANUEL
   Call me a beast out of Hell. Accursed a thousand times for not even respecting the flower of your innocence.

In the moonlit doorway the stooped black figure of THE ABBOT *appears, followed by* THE SEXTON *of San Clemente who cowers, miming a gesture of terror and lust.*

THE ABBOT
   I have come for my lamb, Pharaoh king!
DON JUAN MANUEL
   Here she is!
THE ABBOT
   I've always thought the worst of you, barbaric Montenegro, you and your foul deeds! But I never imagined you could sink as low as inviting your sons' mistresses over to dinner!
DON JUAN MANUEL
   You knave of a cleric, my god-daughter is no whoreson's mistress!
THE ABBOT
   What do you have to say, impudent harlot?
SABELITA
   I am guilty of nothing.
THE ABBOT
   Who brought you here? Somebody saw you being carried off on a horse. Confess to your turpitude!
DON JUAN MANUEL
   I brought her!
THE ABBOT
   Vade retro![16]
DON JUAN MANUEL
   What is it you fear?
THE ABBOT
   You took her?
DON JUAN MANUEL
   Yes.
THE ABBOT
   What for?
DON JUAN MANUEL
   To keep me company in my solitude.
THE ABBOT
   Montenegro, I ask you to return my lamb to her flock.

---

[16] Back! (Latin). The equivalent phrase in English would be 'Get thee behind me, Satan!'.

DON JUAN MANUEL
She came of her own accord.
THE ABBOT
Montenegro, I come in peace.
DON JUAN MANUEL
I have not declared war.
THE ABBOT
We were once friends, we treated one another as family. And yet you denied me passage through your lands when I needed to administer the last rites.
DON JUAN MANUEL
That was not me. It was one of my boys.
THE ABBOT
But you backed him up.
DON JUAN MANUEL
I was obliged to do so.
THE ABBOT
That sinner died without benediction. We can only assume he now suffers Hell's torments.
DON JUAN MANUEL
Then the Devil owes my son a favour.
THE ABBOT
Blasphemy!
DON JUAN MANUEL
Sacrilege! You want the girl for your own pleasure! We understand one another!
THE ABBOT
You barbarian, Montenegro, you have indeed declared war, and war you shall have! I will trample your lands and collect my wayward lamb.
DON JUAN MANUEL
She is yours, I peacefully surrender her to you. Isabel, you are free to go or stay as you please. Decide.
SABELITA
I choose death!
THE ABBOT
Shut up, you rotten slut! Draw no attention to your licentiousness! Follow me!
SABELITA
My feet won't budge. I can't walk. An evil force restrains me!
THE ABBOT
Come with me!
SABELITA
I am shackled. My feet won't budge!

THE ABBOT
I will drag you out by your pigtails.
SABELITA
Godfather, release me from these chains! Dispel the dark force that binds me here! Let me go! Free me!
DON JUAN MANUEL
You are free.
SABELITA
Begone, fear! Be brave, soul of mine! Overcome! Godfather, release me from this miserable captivity! If you cannot release me, if perdition be my fate, then command me to stay.
DON JUAN MANUEL
Let the sin fall on my conscience. Stay!
THE ABBOT
Montenegro, use your black magic while you can! You don't frighten me, Montenegro! We will settle this later! We will meet again!
DON JUAN MANUEL
Devil take you!
THE ABBOT
Just to punish your arrogance I will happily light a candle to that devil of yours. Tremble!

In a burst of black, the tonsured ABBOT *departs through the moonlit door. The Mayorazgo raises his glass and, kneeling, offers it to the shadow of his new mistress.*

Scene Two

The crossroads at San Martiño de Freyres. Stars fill the sky, wind whispers through the wheat fields. Through a cluster of trees, the moaning of the windmill amplifies the timorous vocalic sounds. The moon moves in a silver fog across the pond. At the pale crossroads the elongated figure of THE ABBOT *stands out. Under the starry firmament his peaked cap of office flaunts its horn-like wings, and his arm outlines dark traces of malediction and anathema. In the cleric's elongated shadow,* BLAS DE MÍGUEZ *cowers like a dog.*

THE ABBOT
Damn that arrogant tribe!
THE SEXTON
The Vinculero is quite the man!
THE ABBOT
Barbaric Montenegro, I will slap you in the face, like this!

THE SEXTON

His just desserts!

The man of the cloth slaps his own cheek, and THE SEXTON *crosses himself several times, groaning and pounding his chest. Distant barking of dogs from a neighbouring village.*

THE ABBOT

Satan, I will trade my soul for help in this hour. Sacrilege does not frighten me!

THE SEXTON

Holy Abbot, do not petition Hell for assistance!

THE ABBOT

Today I wager my soul!

THE SEXTON

If you make that wager, you will lose.

THE ABBOT

And you along with me!

THE SEXTON

Just why do you require a companion?

THE ABBOT

Your fate is bound to mine.

THE SEXTON.

I'd prefer to leave my fate up to St Peter to decide.

THE ABBOT

You will do what I tell you.

THE SEXTON

As long as my soul is safe!

THE ABBOT

When you reach home, you must pretend to be dying.

THE SEXTON

Sweet Holy Mother!

THE ABBOT

On your deathbed you will say farewell to your wife and children. Then you will ask for confession!

THE SEXTON

I begin dying and yet I don't die; got it.

THE ABBOT

What ails you?

THE SEXTON

A pain in my side!

THE ABBOT

As soon as you reach home, you say that you're in insufferable pain. And you beg for the holy sacraments.

THE SEXTON
Your plan gives me the shivers.
THE ABBOT
I require blind obedience from you.
THE SEXTON
So I commence dying... I receive confession and communion — which is never a bad idea. Got it. But I won't go beyond than that. I must protest against actually dying.
THE ABBOT
You will obey!
THE SEXTON
And if my wife senses that something's not right ...
THE ABBOT
Go!
THE SEXTON
... I'll have to smack her around a bit.
THE ABBOT
If necessary, you will die.
THE SEXTON
With one eye open. I can't promise more than that!
THE ABBOT
Off with you!
THE SEXTON
Any more and I must protest.
THE ABBOT
You will obey!
THE SEXTON
I won't even think about dying.
THE ABBOT
You will start to die, and if necessary you will die. That is the plan and you will see it through.
THE SEXTON
Plan be damned! I already told you I refuse to actually die!
THE ABBOT
Then you put yourself in Satan's hands.
THE SEXTON
Yeah right, he'll roast me on a spit! No thanks, I reject him!
THE ABBOT
Go!
THE SEXTON
Shit! We may well be opening the very doors to Hell!

THE ABBOT

I've a mind to plant my fist between the horns on your head. Idiot, open your eyes! Don't you see Hell yawning before you already?

THE SEXTON

We'll be excommunicated! We are profaning the sacraments!

THE ABBOT

Go on, recoil in horror! Tremble!

THE SEXTON

Dies Irae! Dies Illa![17]

The sacrilegious cleric howls and slaps his own face, while the cowering, terrified SEXTON *turns away and runs off in his wooden shoes as if performing a village dance by moonlight. As he enters the churchyard full of haystacks and moonbeams, the shouting begins.*

THE SEXTON

I'm dying! Death is upon me! This sudden pain is killing me! Killing me before I might atone for my sins! Life, do not leave me! Let me see the light of day!

THE ABBOT

Satan, come to my aid and my soul is yours! Come to my aid, King of Hell and lord of all evil! I call on you, Satan! For you I will recite an entire Black Mass! I renounce Christ and put my trust in you! King of Hell, unleash your bitter north winds! Release your serpents! Rouse your demons! Heed my call, Satan!

FILTHY FUSO

At your service, my Captain!

Along the white road the madman dances his wild dance, the sack of money nestled within his tattered schismatic cap. In a flurry he whisks by the sacrilegious ABBOT *of San Clemente.*

Scene Three

Quintán de San Mariño. Hayricks and moonlit rooftops. Dogs' distant barking. Grapevines cast purple shadows before the doorway. A lone house at the far edge of town. Against the blackened bricks of the hearth a half-naked old woman delouses herself. The odour of burning pine needles and grilled sardines wends its way through the roof tiles. The old woman continues her grooming as her

---

[17] Day of wrath (Latin). Something like 'Judgment Day is upon us!'.

young child cries and her eldest daughter, GINERA *Fat-Hussy, sits under the lamp mending some clerical robes.*

THE SEXTON'S WIFE
  I must be hearing things! The wind seems to carry along your father's voice!
GINERA
  No way!
THE SEXTON'S WIFE
  Listen! Can't you hear it? The voice of someone in distress. Can't you hear it?
GINERA
  It's the wind blowing through the roof.
THE SEXTON'S WIFE
  It doesn't sound like a voice to you?
GINERA
  How many have you had, mother?
THE SEXTON'S WIFE
  On that note, time for a little nip!

The half-naked old woman reaches for a greasy tankard from the kitchen shelf. A trivet comes crashing down, frightening the cat. The rickety old bed creaks under the weight of three young children who peer out from under a ragged blanket. The old woman guzzles the tankard's contents, savouring every drop.

THE CHORUS OF LITTLE ONES
  Give us a sip, mama! Give us a sip!
THE SEXTON'S WIFE
  I'll tie you a noose if you don't shut up!
THE CHORUS OF LITTLE ONES
  Just a sip!
THE SEXTON'S WIFE
  Celonio! Gabina! Mingote! You little snakes! You'll get sick and need a visit from San Benitiño de Palermo![18] You like a sip, Ginera?
GINERA
  I don't want the boys to smell it on my breath.
THE SEXTON'S WIFE
  That won't happen if you shut your mouth, you shameless hussy! If you get too close with the boys, you'll find yourself in trouble. Ah, you're hopeless! If you get knocked up, you're out of the house. This anisette is damned good stuff! Take a sip, young lady!

GINERA *Fat-Hussy decisively grabs the tankard the old woman offers her and, having taken a gulp, she wipes her lips with the mantilla draped around her shoulders.*

---

[18] St Benedict, popularly invoked as a last-resort saviour from a dire situation.

GINERA
   It really is good stuff!
THE CHORUS OF LITTLE ONES
   Give us a sip, mama! Give us a sip!
THE SEXTON'S WIFE
   Give those little shits a sip!

From under the ragged blanket THE CHORUS OF LITTLE ONES *continues to beg.* CELONIO, GABINA, MINGOTE *fight tooth and nail over the tankard.* GINERA *hands over the tankard, which falls to the ground and breaks as the many little hands grab for it.*

THE SEXTON'S WIFE
   Oh, you little snakes! May lightning strike you down! You'll end up on the gallows! Unruly shits! Leeches!
GINERA
   Put on your shirt, mother.

Like a conductor, the old woman with her tongs directs the children's squealing, their frightened heads no longer forming a perfect altarpiece. She then returns to her place at the hearth. Among a pile of clothing she searches for her purse from which she counts out a few one-bit coins.

THE SEXTON'S WIFE
   That was the good stuff! Top shelf, the Queen of Spain drinks no better! Ginera, tie up your petticoat and go fetch me another glassful.
GINERA
   The Dutch or the anisette?
THE SEXTON'S WIFE
   The anisette, you simpleton! Always with boys on your mind! The anisette, you stupid cow! The anisette! Take a torch with you.
GINERA
   There's a full moon out!
A FARAWAY VOICE
   I'm dying! This is the end!
THE SEXTON'S WIFE
   Jesus! There's the voice again! The whispering wind! It sounds a lot like your father's bitching and moaning!

A skittish GINERA *opens the door, and under the moonlit vines appears the shadow of* THE SEXTON *who kneels and raises his arms in a crucified pose.*

THE SEXTON
   Where am I? The pain clouds my vision and I can't recognize this place!

THE SEXTON'S WIFE
  What's gotten into you?
THE SEXTON
  The last rites! I need to confess my sins!
THE SEXTON'S WIFE
  A bit early for all that!
THE SEXTON
  No, my vital humours conspire against me. Beloved daughter, don your scarf and go to San Clemente to spread word of my imminent demise!
GINERA
  You sound ridiculous, father!
THE SEXTON
  This sudden pain heralds my death!
THE SEXTON'S WIFE
  Not sudden enough if you ask me.
THE SEXTON
  Sudden pains of this nature can be fatal.
THE SEXTON'S WIFE
  It's getting less sudden by the second!
THE SEXTON
  Argh, you'll croak before me, you bitch!
THE SEXTON'S WIFE
  You drunk!
GINERA
  Go to bed, father!
THE SEXTON
  I give you my blessing, beloved daughter!
THE SEXTON'S WIFE
  How magnanimous of you!
GINERA
  He's delirious.
THE SEXTON'S WIFE
  Delirious from drink!
THE SEXTON
  Wicked woman, show some respect for our connubial bonds at the moment of my departure from this world!
GINERA
  Father's never sounded so learned and wise!
THE SEXTON
  I give to you my blessing, beloved daughter, to you and to these three young

ones. Orphans from this day forward!
THE SEXTON'S WIFE
Celonio, Gabina, Mingote! You little snakes! On your knees!
THE CHORUS OF LITTLE ONES
Our father Blas! Our father Blas!
THE SEXTON
Mother of God, give succour to your devoted servant who's soon to appear before the Supreme Tribunal! This pain that came on so suddenly, it gnaws at me like a rabid dog. Mother of All Sinners! The pain gnaws at me from both sides, Mother of All Mothers! We refer to it as a sudden paroxysm, *Mater Inmaculata*!
THE SEXTON'S WIFE
Shut your mouth, you inveterate liar! How many mothers are you going to call? Should I give you a rubdown?
THE SEXTON
With the holy oil of the final sacrament!
THE SEXTON'S WIFE
Oh, you moron, you're not leaving this world; you're still needed here!
THE SEXTON
The Lord is calling me. I'm truly dying. Tell our daughter to hurry up.
THE SEXTON'S WIFE
Dying seems to agree with you.
THE SEXTON
I meet death in the manner of all good Christians.
THE SEXTON'S WIFE
Oh Blas, never have you shown such wisdom! Now I see that you really on death's door! Oh Blas, don't depart this life! Blas de Míguez, do you know what awaits you in the afterlife?
THE SEXTON
No talk of that until I've been anointed with the holy oil.

BLAS DE MÍGUEZ screws up his eye, twists his mouth, sticks out his tongue, making a thoroughly grotesque, carnivalesque expression. The balding old woman makes the sign of the cross and with trembling hands adjusts her minimal clothing.

THE SEXTON'S WIFE
O Death, why could you not have stayed far away from our home?
THE CHORUS OF LITTLE ONES
Our poor papa! Our poor papa!
GINERA
Blas, my father, do not depart this world which still needs you!

THE SEXTON
  Don't upset me!
THE SEXTON'S WIFE
  Blas, don't go! Insatiable death, why are you taking him?
THE SEXTON
  Too much talking!
THE SEXTON'S WIFE
  Has this life with me been so terrible? Answer me, you old bastard!
THE SEXTON
  You would insult me at this fatal moment, old cow?
THE SEXTON'S WIFE
  Answer me!
THE SEXTON
  I acknowledge your merits, so I bless you as well!
THE SEXTON'S WIFE
  He's really delirious! Get moving, Ginera!
THE CHORUS OF LITTLE ONES
  Our papa! Our papa!
THE SEXTON
  Shut your mouths, blessed angels! Begone, Death!
GINERA
  Truly delirious!

GINERA dons her cloak, grabs a small oil lamp, and leaves the house. The sound of her lamentations can be heard down the road.

GINERA
  Farewell, my father! Never again will I benefit from your upbringing!
THE SEXTON
  You ninny, I'll beat you!
THE SEXTON'S WIFE
  Why do you threaten her at this moment, wicked man? What happened to the wise resignation of a few moments ago?
THE SEXTON
  With death so near at hand, it is no surprise that I would rave a bit.
THE CHORUS OF LITTLE ONES
  Poor papa! Poor papa!
THE SEXTON
  Shut up, you thieving runts!

In a sudden rage and wearing only one shoe, BLAS DE MÍGUEZ, hobbles forward and motions to grab the little ones by the hair. They recoil in terror and race toward their mother for protection.

THE SEXTON'S WIFE

Calm down, Blas! What devil possesses you? Say a prayer and cast him out! Save your soul, you sinner!

THE SEXTON

Shut up, God damn you!

THE SEXTON'S WIFE

Stop cursing! Think of your salvation!

THE SEXTON

You're worried about me dying when you should be thinking of the thrashing I'm going to give you! I'm going to pull through!

THE SEXTON'S WIFE

Don't contravene the Lord's will!

THE CHORUS OF LITTLE ONES

Poor papa! Poor papa!

THE SEXTON

I'll slit your throats, you little bastards! Brew me some wine and cinnamon, sweet, pious, mourning spouse of mine.

THE SEXTON'S WIFE

Your soul's true wisdom returns! The evil power that had possessed you took the form of a cat and scurried off.

THE SEXTON

Poppycock! Don't make up stories! Shut up, you incurable sinner! You are a world of perdition, a bitter font of venom, rotten to the core! Whenever my number is called, I'll have no regrets leaving you. Farewell, my angelic children!

THE CHORUS OF LITTLE ONES

Papa, papa, papa!

THE SEXTON'S WIFE

Shut up, you thieving runts, and fall to your knees! He's trying to impart some paternal wisdom to you!

THE SEXTON

Orphaned children! Delicate saplings!

THE SEXTON'S WIFE.

Pull yourself together, you big jellyfish! You need to be a man in these final moments!

THE SEXTON

Tender babes, in this vale of tears our sole safe haven is the Holy Roman Church! Never forget! This life is transitory!

FILTHY FUSO

Too-porroo-too!

FILTHY FUSO cautiously appears at the doorway. His shadow has a stealthy, lupine quality. Wild laughter. Under his shirt he clutches the disruptive sack of gold Portuguese coins.

THE SEXTON
Get out of here, Filthy Fuso!
FILTHY FUSO
Presently.
THE SEXTON
I don't want you at my door.
FILTHY FUSO
Can I have Ginera? I'll give you her weight in gold.
THE SEXTON'S WIFE
Out of here, you villain! Don't make light of death!
FILTHY FUSO
Do you have any fresh pork rinds then?
THE SEXTON'S WIFE
The holy lights, look at them! Look at them gather in the courtyard! Listen to pealing of the bells!
THE SEXTON
I refuse to die!

A dishevelled BLAS DE MÍGUEZ *jumps off the old bed. Wearing only one wooden shoe, he limps forward. His wife stands in his way, the three children clutching at her skirts.*

THE SEXTON'S WIFE
Back to bed, Blas.
THE SEXTON
I refuse to die. What was the deal again? To close just one eye, that was it! This needs to be underscored! I don't want any lights! Blow them out! May the wind extinguish them all! I refuse to die. The lights! I won't follow the candlelight procession! Let me go! Out of the way, you hag!

Scene Four

PICHONA's *bed. Silence punctuated by sighs and cooing. The mattress shifts merrily on the makeshift bed frame.* GOLDEN BOY *and little* PICHONA *enjoy themselves in the paradise under the Portuguese quilt. Knock! Knock! Knock! A stone rolls down the roof. The busy lovers' mouths stop working and take notice.*

PICHONA
Don't go! Kiss me! Don't dwell on your quarrels!
GOLDEN BOY
Shut up.

PICHONA

Maybe it's the wind rattling the bars on the windows?

GOLDEN BOY

It's not the wind.

PICHONA

What do you think it is?

GOLDEN BOY

A goblin in wooden clogs.

PICHONA

My sweet, don't frighten me, you know how gullible I am! Kiss me! Don't take that mouth away! Kiss me!

The goblin's clogs now break the roof tiles. Laughter mingles with the black smoke and snakes its way down the chimney. Ashes scatter and the trivets dance.

VOICE FROM THE CHIMNEY

Too-porroo-too!

PICHONA

Is that what you heard, my lord?

GOLDEN BOY

I believe so.

VOICE FROM THE CHIMNEY

What bastard did you let into your bed, Pichona?

GOLDEN BOY

Come on down, little man, and let's get properly acquainted.

PICHONA

Don't provoke him, we don't want trouble. Take me in your arms, my treasure!

VOICE FROM THE CHIMNEY

Kick that crab louse out of your bed, Pichona!

PICHONA

Away with you!

VOICE FROM THE CHIMNEY

I've got a sack of shiny gold coins for you. Hear them jingle jangle!

PICHONA

Sounds fishy to me.

VOICE FROM THE CHIMNEY

Now's the time for fun! The pig's tail dancing in the pot! Pichona, you want I should heat up those legs of yours? Between one bout and the next, we'll share some nice fish pie!

GOLDEN BOY

And Ribeiro wine.

VOICE FROM THE CHIMNEY
　Bastard, you seem to be in the know.
PICHONA
　Filthy Fuso, if that's you I'm going to geld you like a pack horse. Quit breaking my roof tiles, you shit!
VOICE FROM THE CHIMNEY
　Too-porroo-too! This sack is just for you, you lordling's whore! Can't you hear it singing?
PICHONA
　A song of chicanery.
GOLDEN BOY
　Little man, you found that sack lying on the road.
VOICE FROM THE CHIMNEY
　Ah, so you see the cat's eye beneath its tail!
GOLDEN BOY
　Such insight is not yours alone.
PICHONA
　Drop dead, you demon!
VOICE FROM THE CHIMNEY
　Too-porroo-too! This treasure makes me richer than the Pope!
GOLDEN BOY
　Definitely.
VOICE FROM THE CHIMNEY
　I could stay in the convent and have threesomes — nay, holy sevensomes! — with the blessed nuns.
GOLDEN BOY
　You could!
VOICE FROM THE CHIMNEY
　You're a real theologian!
GOLDEN BOY
　Weren't you about to get married, little man?
VOICE FROM THE CHIMNEY
　Too-porroo-too! By my four-horned cap! You black she-goat, if we can get past this misunderstanding and be legally wed, I'll lock your chastity belt and throw away the key!
GOLDEN BOY
　Who took your girl, little man?
VOICE FROM THE CHIMNEY
　A Turkish cock came between us.
GOLDEN BOY
　You couldn't scare him off?

VOICE FROM THE CHIMNEY
No, he came on like a black spark.
GOLDEN BOY
And all your learning and lore, little man?
VOICE FROM THE CHIMNEY
That archfiend spits on lore. Too-porroo-too! How clear the moonlight! Come on up, Pichona, and let's tango!
PICHONA
I need to daub a little something on my armpits.
VOICE FROM THE CHIMNEY
Daub it behind your ears too, Pichoneta, and get up here and tango with me under the moonlight. Too-porroo-too! Don't bother dressing!
PICHONA
Time to change your tune, you fat capon!
VOICE FROM THE CHIMNEY
Too-porroo-too! I'm all naked and ready to dance the fandango!
PICHONA
It's like a carnival in here!
VOICE FROM THE CHIMNEY
Too-porroo-too!
PICHONA
The chimney's going to collapse from all your hollering!
VOICE FROM THE CHIMNEY
Listen to the gold coins calling to you!
PICHONA
You've come too late, little man.
VOICE FROM THE CHIMNEY
Throw that faggot out of your bed!
PICHONA
He's a king!
VOICE FROM THE CHIMNEY
Off with his head!
PICHONA
I am bound to him.
VOICE FROM THE CHIMNEY
If you wet the bed you can break the bond.
PICHONA
Now there's a home remedy for you!
GOLDEN BOY
Little man, that sack of coins does not belong to you!
VOICE FROM THE CHIMNEY
Who says?

GOLDEN BOY
You owe the moon that sack!
VOICE FROM THE CHIMNEY
Pitiful lies!
GOLDEN BOY
It sprouted up on the road.
VOICE FROM THE CHIMNEY
You're making that up because you want it!
GOLDEN BOY
Night had already fallen when you stumbled upon it at the Quintana de San Clemente.
VOICE FROM THE CHIMNEY
Who are you that knows so much?
PICHONA
Return the sack to its owner, little man.
GOLDEN BOY
Its owner doesn't want it.
VOICE FROM THE CHIMNEY
Bastard! Who's that in your bed, Pichona?
GOLDEN BOY
Come on down if you'd like to get acquainted.
VOICE FROM THE CHIMNEY
My singed ass cheek still itches. In the flash of gunfire, I recognized the hidden cap lying in wait. Aiming his gun and waiting.
GOLDEN BOY
Come on down, little man!
VOICE FROM THE CHIMNEY
No thank you! I already had a brush with death at the Quintana. When the gun went off I saw a blood-red face and the four-winged cap.
GOLDEN BOY
And was that my face?
VOICE FROM THE CHIMNEY
Too-porroo-too! Holy Abbot, stop fondling that black nanny-goat. Consider your soiled habits!
GOLDEN BOY
You're way off the mark, little man!
FILTHY FUSO
Too-porroo-too! I can see the cap and its horns well enough! That little sunflower on your patio, a Turkish cock is about to peck at it. Too-porroo-too! Hark at the screams piercing through the night! The virginal niece whisked off by the brigand Vinculero!
GOLDEN BOY
What's this awful news you bring to me?

FILTHY FUSO
   Naked, hair down, crying and covering her breasts in a cave at Lantañón. The Turkish cock will have his little white hen!
GOLDEN BOY
   What black light glows before me? My father is the brigand who would steal what is mine!
VOICE FROM THE CHIMNEY
   Bastard! Just who are you anyway?
GOLDEN BOY
   Satan protect me!

With a deafening roar and eyes full of fury, frenzy and fire, GOLDEN BOY *grabs the axe from the chopping block and kicks open the door. He then races off into the starry night.*

PICHONA
   What dark thought takes hold of you? Wait! Don't go! Don't leave my arms only to raise yours against your own father! Remain mine and I will serve you for life! I'll be your slave! Don't make me wear black again! I am the one over whom Benitiño the Penitent murdered his father! Exactly the same rage tore him from my arms! Stay, my love! I'll be here praying for you!
VOICE FROM THE STREET
   Night so dark, night so black
   A fine night for a ride through the air
   On a witch's back!

Final Scene

The courtyard of the estate, redolent of lemon trees. Moonlight on the arches and a still black cypress at the foot of the stairway. The remorseful shadow of DON JUAN MANUEL *crosses the scene. His bowlegged fool tails after him, accentuating his limp with buffoonery.*

DON GALÁN
   Juju! For an old man who's lovestruck, his heart's out of luck!
DON JUAN MANUEL
   Shut up, idiot!
DON GALÁN
   Thus says the wise man!
DON JUAN MANUEL
   Thus says the villain!
DON GALÁN
   Aging bodies ought to stay on Saint Peter's good side.

DON JUAN MANUEL

Don Galán, I'm tempted to set off and become a hermit.

DON GALÁN

I can come with you and carry your saddlebags.

DON JUAN MANUEL

A saint can't have a servant.

DON GALÁN

We'll be equals.

DON JUAN MANUEL

You can't be a saint.

DON GALÁN

All are equal at our Heavenly Father's table.

DON JUAN MANUEL

Don Galán, to become a saint one has to pass through Hell. Seeing as you don't know how to be a sinner, it follows that you can't know how to be a saint. I do!

DON GALÁN

Indubitably!

DON JUAN MANUEL

But is it worth repenting and living a saint's life just now, when the World, the Devil and the Flesh conspire to offer me so precious few opportunities to sin? If only I'd set off down the righteous path thirty years ago! To do so now seems like the moralizing of a proper Pharisee! It's not worth it! Tonight, I drain the cup to the dregs! Don Galán, you don't understand a word I'm saying.

DON GALÁN

I get the gist.

DON JUAN MANUEL

Never in my life have I been dealt such a black card!

DON GALÁN

Black as coal!

DON JUAN MANUEL

An abomination!

A muddle of footsteps and prayers. THREE OLD CRONES, *like three owls with lanterns and cloaks, hunch down and shuffle through the archway. In San Clemente de Lantañón the liturgical bells toll. Distant lights.*

THE VOICE OF A CRONE

Ave María! The moon shines and seizes — it seizes the lord of the manor! To the moon its prize! From here it seems an apostle clothed in silver.

DON JUAN MANUEL

Where are you bound?

THE VOICE OF A CRONE

We accompany the Holy Eucharist needed to perform a man's last rites.

DON JUAN MANUEL

That pointy-capped Abbot is hell-bent on provoking me to sacrilege! Don Galán, unleash the hounds and fetch my gun!

DON GALÁN

Beloved master, do not fly on Satan's wings!

Galloping hoofbeats gather in intensity. A dishevelled, frenzied GOLDEN BOY *bursts into the atrium. Moonbeams make a bright helm of his hair, the axe in his hand a black bolt of lightning.*

GOLDEN BOY

Father, I have come to kill you!

DON JUAN MANUEL

Don't stop now, you brigand! Bring down your arm, open Hell's doors to me!

GOLDEN BOY

Where is Isabel?

DON JUAN MANUEL

Locked away safely.

GOLDEN BOY

Isabel is mine!

DON JUAN MANUEL

Really? And just when did you win her heart?

GOLDEN BOY

Do not invite my wrath, father!

DON JUAN MANUEL

Boy, at your age love comes along often enough. If one woman won't have you, there are a hundred others who will. There are women born every minute, but you only have one father.

GOLDEN BOY

And there is only one true love!

DON JUAN MANUEL

Women! If they don't die young and beautiful, they grow old. Wayward son of mine, blinded by delusions and dreams, regard those points of light coming our way! Can you see the band of hags with their cloaks and lanterns? The Holy Sacrament accompanies this procession with all the pomp that my sins deserve. You cannot be executioner when the condemned must still confess and receive absolution. I can still set a fine example for you.

Under the stone archway from which the heraldic symbols hang by chains, there is a slow procession of cloaked figures bearing torches. Beneath the canopy borne by his fellow clerics strides the sacrilegious ABBOT *of San Clemente, wearing his four-winged cap and the golden mantle reserved for the most solemn occasions. His black hook-like hands hold aloft the silver chalice with the sacramental bread.*

DON JUAN MANUEL
Not another step!
THE ABBOT
Montenegro, the Church requests passage through with the Body of Christ!
DON JUAN MANUEL
And just who is it about to croak?
THE ABBOT
Blas de Míguez!
DON JUAN MANUEL
Let the Devil take him! I see through you, you tonsured fraud!
THE ABBOT
Pharaoh, bow your proud head before the King of Kings!
THE CRONES' VOICES
Montenegro, you of the pitch-black soul, blackened with sins! Black as the cauldrons of Hell itself!

DON JUAN MANUEL restrains his leonine hounds and descends the grand stone stairway. He walks between the lights in the tenebrous silence. THE ABBOT of San Clemente reaches into his cloak and draws and raises the silver chalice. DON JUAN MANUEL, dour, sardonic, enigmatic, kneels on the ground and commands the dogs to do so as well.

DON JUAN MANUEL.
Sacrilegious Abbot! What do you seek?
THE ABBOT
A sinner who lies at death's door.
DON JUAN MANUEL
And here you have him! A master of depravity for whose head the executioner's blade thirsts. This villain of a son of mine plots my death, and to absolve me of my sins you in your priestly bonnet have fallen from grace. I confess my sins here and now for all the world to hear. I'm the worst sort of man. No one rivals me for love cards, wine and women. Satan himself is my patron saint and always has been. My vices are entrenched and ineradicable. They scald my very being. I've never acknowledged any power other than my own. As a boy I took issue with a man at the gaming tables and I murdered him. I dragged one of my sisters to the nunnery. Affairs with hundreds of women add to my wife's indignity. That is the kind of man I've been! And I'm not about to change now! Miracles and saintly acts of repentance are the stuff of yore. Grant me absolution, bonnet!

THE ABBOT
   Step aside, blasphemous knight!
DON JUAN MANUEL
   Sacrilegious cleric!
A CONFUSION OF VOICES
   Montenegro! The pitch-black brand of excommunication is yours!

Someone in the crowd hurls a stone from a sling. It ricochets off the tower wall, frightening off an owl. DON JUAN MANUEL *stands with proud resolve and seizes the chalice from the cleric's hands.*

DON JUAN MANUEL
   Away with you!
THE CRONES' VOICES
   Christ! Christ! Christ! Blessed Christ of the scourges! Oh Night, fall now and veil this obscenity!
DON JUAN MANUEL
   Golden Boy, turn 'round your steed and run down that assemblage of hags!
GOLDEN BOY
   Where is the thunderbolt that should incinerate the lot of us?

GOLDEN BOY *regains the reins from the mane of his spooked mount and tears off through the archway. The pious procession yields, hooded cloaks and lights moving aside. Fatalistic voices. Fleeting shadows. Holy dread.* DON JUAN MANUEL, *silver chalice in hand, takes a seat on the stairway.*

DON JUAN MANUEL
   Perhaps I really am the Devil incarnate!

The Blazoned Eagle

Dramatis Personae

DON JUAN MANUEL MONTENEGRO, aka the Lord of the Manor, the Mayorazgo, the Master, the Vinculero
BROTHER JERÓNIMO ARGENSOLA
AN OLD WOMAN
AN OLD MAN
A GIRL
AN ALTAR BOY
A VOICE FROM THE SHADOWS
SABELITA, aka ISABEL
DOÑA ROSITA
ROSITA MARÍA
ANOTHER OLD WOMAN
Ginger-MICAELA
THE SHEPHERD BOY
DON GALÁN, Don Juan Manuel's Fool
THE GANG LEADER
A NEIGHBOUR
A THIEF
A SECOND THIEF
THE MASKED MAN
VOICES OF THE THIEVES and THE SERVANTS
PEDRO REY
LIBERATA
DON PEDRITO
THE SOOTHSAYER
A YOUNG MAN
AN OLD WOMAN

AN OLD MAN
A YOUNG WOMAN
A SAILOR
THE CAPTAIN
ANOTHER SAILOR
MANUEL TOVÍO
PEDRO ABUÍN
MANUEL FONSECA
A TINKER
A SIEVE-MENDER
A RIBBON MAKER
A MENDICANT FRIAR
DOÑA MARÍA
THE CHAPLAIN
TAINTED JUANA
ROSALVA
BIEITO
ANDREIÑA
THE BAILIFF and THE SECRETARY

Don Juan Manuel's sons:
DON GONZALITO
DON MAURO
DON FARRUQUIÑO
DON ROSENDO
GOLDEN BOY, aka DON MIGUELITO
SEÑOR GINERO
THE VOICE OF A DRUNKARD
TWO LADIES and A SERVANT
THE CHORISTER and THE DEACON
THE GRANDFATHER and THE BOY
THE PREGNANT WOMAN
THE HUSBAND
THE MOTHER-IN-LAW
BABY JESUS

PICHONA

JUANA CREEPY-FINGERS and CROSS-EYED ANDREA

THE FERRYMAN

THE PILGRIM

THE MULETEER

A BLIND OLD WOMAN

Act One

Scene One

BROTHER JERÓNIMO ARGENSOLA *of the Franciscan order hurls anathemas from the pulpit, and in the hazy light of the church his voice inspires terror and dread. He is a burly, ruddy figure with a luxuriant chestnut beard. The main altar glows in the candlelit space, and an old sexton, in his cassock and rochet, passes by and trims the candles. It is a baroque cruciform, scholastic and grandiloquent, calling to mind the rhetoric and postures of the seventeenth-century court. There are various chapels, each established long ago by a guild or a noble house. The altarpieces and sepulchres are emblazoned with the names of these ancient institutions. It is winter. Clogs clack on the floor. Old women cough. Following the novena of Our Lady of Mercy,* BROTHER JERÓNIMO *delivers his sermon.*

BROTHER JERÓNIMO
You reek of sin! Death walks in your shadow, and you don't even know he is there! Each night the fires of iniquity sear your flesh. And the lubricious retinue lining up at your bedside, seeking shelter in your fine linen sheets, whom you rock to sleep in your arms — this is the serpent of sin who tempts you with its ludicrous gyrations. Every night your sin-starved lips lock with the pestilent maw of the Antichrist!

His words elicit heaving sighs from the congregation. One woman faints. Other pious women rush to her aid, and fluttering, agitated white kerchiefs pierce the darkness and disperse perfume over her unconscious form. Whispering voices slice through the shadows.

AN OLD WOMAN
Who is that?

A GIRL
I don't know, Grandma.

AN ALTAR BOY
She's the Mayorazgo's girl...

ANOTHER OLD WOMAN
What business can a woman of such repute have in the church!

A VOICE FROM THE SHADOWS
Perhaps she wishes to repent, Señora Juliana.

Irreverent laughter. The murmur of gossip fades and transforms into the murmur of prayer.

BROTHER JERÓNIMO
> Look! Above your heads... no innocent dove, no bearer of divine grace descends from the Empyrean! It is the black-winged raven, the incarnation of Satan himself! You know how delicate is the clay from which our Lord fashioned you, but yours is a pagan knowledge: you fear the chill of the grave and the mantle of worms which waits to cloak your rotting flesh. Your bones ache at the thought of the coffin's black embrace, your skull anticipates the filth crawling through its empty sockets! It is because your soul lacks a strong foundation, lying in the dark dilapidated prison of sin!

Two ladies, mother and daughter, help the distraught woman exit the church. She has regained her senses and now begins to weep. Supported by the two ladies, she crosses the atrium and a narrow street. Some seminarians walk in pairs past the arched supports: strapping young men who dominate the walkway with their peasant slang and their impoverished student attire of tricorn hats and shabby cloaks. At the end of the street there is a deserted square which, like the ancient cemeteries, is shaded by cypress trees. The three ladies enter an old mansion. Nightfall. The air is thick with the odour of freshly pressed grapes.

Scene Two

A grand house: one of the seats of the local nobility. The three ladies whisper in the receiving room. A balcony opens onto a large part of the square, where DON JUAN MANUEL MONTENEGRO *appears. He is one of those despotic, lusty, short-tempered yet magnanimous noblemen preserved in old portraits scattered about the spectral townships, the villas that evoke with their feudal names the clanking of rusty armour.* DON JUAN MANUEL *approaches with a shotgun on his shoulder, surrounded by greyhounds and retrievers who mill around and break the afternoon silence with their barking and their jangling collars. From the distance he shouts for his mistress. His majestic, cavernous voice penetrates the depths of the room and disturbs the ladies' pious and hushed conversation about the sermon of* BROTHER JERÓNIMO. SABELITA *stands, wipes her eyes, and exits onto the wide stone balcony where the sweet smell of ripening quinces fills the air.*

DON JUAN MANUEL
> Isabel! Isabel!

SABELITA
> Here I am!

DON JUAN MANUEL
> Tell Don Galán to come fetch the shotgun.

SABELITA
> You're not coming up, Godfather?

DON JUAN MANUEL
No... I'm off to see my nephew Bradomín's chaplain. This evening he's uncorking a new wine that he feels especially sanguine about.

DON JUAN MANUEL fires his shotgun in the air and leans it against the wall. He leaves without waiting for DON GALÁN. The smell of gunpowder excites the hounds, who run around and fill the square with their frantic yelping. The mistress sighs and walks back inside. On cue, the other two ladies, mother and daughter, emit sympathetic sighs and renew their whispered, solemn conversation.

DOÑA ROSITA
Ah, I can't help but recall when you lived respectably in your godmother's house! The Devil beguiled you and made you fall in love with Don Juan Manuel.

SABELITA
He treats me like a slave, offends me with countless women, yet I can't help loving him. And for this my soul is damned!

ROSITA MARÍA
Don't think that way. You are too hard on yourself.

SABELITA
Brother Jeronimo gazed right at me from his pulpit. I could feel his fiery eyes fixed on me!... I keep hearing his words. I am committing cardinal sin and consigned to a sinner's death... Those burning eyes!... His words pierce my heart like the blades surrounding our Holy Lady of Sorrows.[1] Holy Mother, how you test me!

DOÑA ROSITA
No one lacks for trials and tribulations, Sabelita!

ROSITA MARÍA
Sabelita, we were all of us on this earth born to suffer!

SABELITA
Forever locked in this prison, too ashamed to be seen in public! If I do step out, it is only to church after I have donned my hood... Now even there I am shunned!

Mother and daughter try to comfort her, their monotonous tones falling like the waves of a gentle sea against the beach. Then a long silence. Darkness steals into the room. The three silhouettes silently share the memory of the friar and his anathemas. Breaking the silence come the footsteps of an old woman who approaches through the corridor. It is Ginger-MICAELA, who served her master's parents and has remained in that noble house ever since. She enters slowly,

---

[1] The Holy Lady of Sorrows, or Seven Sorrows of Mary, is a common Catholic image depicting the Virgin Mary in a sorrowful pose, with seven long knives or daggers piercing her heart, which is often bleeding.

carrying a tray of steaming hot chocolate in glass cups which rattle in their cup holders.

MICAELA

God watch over you this night!

DOÑA ROSITA

Keep God in your heart at all times, Sabelita!

DOÑA MARÍA

But what about our fast?

SABELITA

There's no way you're keeping a fast.

DOÑA MARÍA

Alright, I give up!

DOÑA ROSITA

The Devil wins this round!

In a gesture of amicable resignation, they scoot their chairs toward the snack-laden table, and with an elegance only pious women possess, each dips into the bowl of chocolate her biscotti baked by the blessed nuns of San Payo. Outside they can hear the bells around the sheep's necks and the calls of THE SHEPHERD BOY *beneath the windows.*

THE SHEPHERD BOY

Open the gate!

MICAELA

The boy's already back with the cattle.

THE SHEPHERD BOY

Open the gate!

MICAELA

What's your damned hurry? It's not as if there's a wolf at your heels.

The old woman leaves. The sound of her clogs and her raspy voice gradually fade as she disappears down the long hallway.

DOÑA ROSITA

How well this Ginger-Micaela is preserved! Must be as old as the century, but holding up remarkably well...

ROSITA MARÍA

One of those rare servants who's lived through at least three generations of her master's house.

DOÑA ROSITA

Ginger has witnessed the birth of all Don Juan Manuel's sons — all good-for-nothings who, it must be said, have brought disgrace to his line. From their father they've inherited only despotism, nothing of his nobility. Don Juan Manuel has a kingly nature.

SABELITA
One of them is not like others.
DOÑA ROSITA
Miguelito, the one they call Golden Boy.
SABELITA
Yes, ma'am. I came across them one afternoon in the church atrium, and Golden Boy stopped them from dragging me in the mud for sport.
DOÑA ROSITA
The eldest is the worst of all, an utter bandit. No respect at all for his mother. Because of him that saint of a woman lives like a pauper! Just recently I found myself on hard times and I paid the lady a visit. Nothing doing! She is as poor as I am. Her sons sold off all the crops before they'd even been harvested.
SABELITA
Poor godmother!
DOÑA ROSITA
She asked me about you, and her voice was more full of pity than blame. Doña María can't imagine a woman immune to Don Juan Manuel's charm.

Having savoured their chocolate, mother and daughter stay to pray the rosary. The servants arrive one by one from the kitchen, and they kneel at the periphery of the room. The wooden clogs of MICAELA *are again heard in the corridor. She leads in* THE SHEPHERD BOY, *who has his cap in hand and fear in his eyes.*

MICAELA
Listen to the boy's story. He says that some men lurking about Friar Pines were following him.
DOÑA MARÍA
Good Lord, they must have been thieves!
DOÑA ROSITA
Could it be Juan Quinto's gang?[2]
MICAELA
Take his stories with a grain of salt. I think he lost a sheep and now tells tall tales to escape the blame…
THE SHEPHERD BOY
You don't have to believe me, but I'm telling the truth, Micaela ma'am. There were seven men with blackened faces.
MICAELA
Oh, my son, it looks to me like you have a yellow streak!
SABELITA
Who put out the holy lamp! Was it the wind?

---

[2] The bandit Juan Quinto appears elsewhere in the 'Valle Universe'. He is the protagonist of one of the stories in the collection *Jardín Umbrío* (1914).

MICAELA
No wind, my lamb. The oil burned out.

Scene Three

SABELITA, *half asleep at the foot of the brazier, waits for* DON JUAN MANUEL. *The curfew bell rings at the seminary. An oil lamp illuminates the room, which is large and bare, yet its creaking chestnut floorboards are cluttered. The shadow of servants shucking corn into baskets flickers against the wall. One voice begins a tale. Suddenly there is a loud knocking, and the mistress awakens with a start.*

SABELITA
The master is here!... Open the door.
MICAELA
That's not the master's knock.
SABELITA
Who else could it be at this hour?
DON GALÁN
Maybe it's a goblin!
MICAELA
You are the goblin, Don Galán!

Dumping her corn into the basket, the old woman gets up and looks out the window. The moon clearly illuminates the figure of the master, who waits at the door with two unknown men whose faces are painted black. She also makes out some shapes to the side. With vague unease, she leaves the window open a crack.

MICAELA
Who's there?
DON JUAN MANUEL
Don't open the door!... Shine a light on these bandits.
SABELITA
What's going on?
MICAELA
The master! The master, surrounded by a bunch of cutthroats!
SABELITA
What are you saying? Is he hurt?
MICAELA
He's bound and tied up like Christ Our Lord!

The old lady recoils in terror, and the other servants cower, invoking all of the saints. The quivering SABELITA *rushes to the window.*

SABELITA
Godfather, are you alright? Have they hurt you? Christ in Heaven!
DON JUAN MANUEL
Don't open the door! These thieves want to enter the house.

THE GANG LEADER *steps into view. His visage is darkened by coal, and he speaks in measured and courteous tones.*

THE GANG LEADER
Ma'am, allow us to enter, otherwise we'll be forced to slit his throat…
SABELITA
Don't hurt him! We'll open up.
DON JUAN MANUEL
Cut off the hands of whoever opens this door.
THE GANG LEADER
You're talking too much, Don Juan Manuel!
DON JUAN MANUEL
Shut up, you spawn of a whore and a hundred friars!
THE GANG LEADER
Shut him up, goddamnit!
SABELITA
Please don't harm him!…
DON JUAN MANUEL
Isabel, shine the light outside.

These last words are barely audible. The bandits gag the struggling lord and his voice is muffled by the kerchief they tie over his mouth.

SABELITA
Don't hurt him! Don't hurt him, for the love of God!
THE GANG LEADER
The last thing we desire is to harm him, my lady. Please know that the kerchief which currently impedes his speech happens to be woven of the finest silk. But if you do not open the door soon and allow him to receive the help he needs, be advised that we will depart — with his head.
SABELITA
The key! Where is the key?

With surprising alacrity SABELITA *goads the quivering servants, who proceed clumsily to search the room. As they cannot locate the keys, the thieves grow restless and curse outside the door. When the key is found,* SABELITA *descends the staircase holding a candle. She places it on the floor to free her hands for opening the heavy door. The thieves enter stealthily. There are seven, all with blackened faces except one who instead wears a black mask. Once they are all inside, they cautiously leave the door open a crack and take the key. Hands on their pistols, the bandits surround the old nobleman.* SABELITA, *pleading with them, tries to get closer.* THE GANG LEADER *bars her way. All a-tremble, she walks up the stairs, her candle illuminating the pale and frightened group of servants waiting at the top.*

Scene Four

Back in the large, bare anteroom SABELITA *places the candle on a chest of drawers and collapses, shutting her eyes as if about to faint. The eyes of* DON JUAN MANUEL *bore into her threateningly, and through the gag he emits muffled and unintelligible growls.*

DON JUAN MANUEL
    I'll cut off your hands!
SABELITA
    Forgive me!
DON JUAN MANUEL
    Slut!
SABELITA
    I was scared!
THE GANG LEADER
    My lord Don Juan Manuel, we have no wish to harm you, but you must let us know where you keep your gold.

DON JUAN MANUEL *remains silent.* THE GANG LEADER *gestures for the gag to be removed. The lord stands in the middle of the room. His hands are bound and his face is pale with rage, his eyes glow with violence and ferocity beneath his furrowed white brow.* THE GANG LEADER *addresses him.*

THE GANG LEADER
    My lord Don Juan Manuel, do you wish to respond now?
DON JUAN MANUEL
    Untie me.
THE GANG LEADER
    We will untie you — after you answer me.
DON JUAN MANUEL
    What do you want to know?
THE GANG LEADER
    Where do you keep your money?
DON JUAN MANUEL
    I have no money.

THE GANG LEADER
 Just a few days ago you sold four head of cattle at the Barbanzón market.
DON JUAN MANUEL
 Some other thieves got to me before you did.
THE GANG LEADER
 You lie, Don Juan Manuel!
DON JUAN MANUEL
 Untie me, you sons of bitches, then I'll tell you if I'm lying!

The band of thieves bristles, hissing invectives and fingering their weapons. The man in the mask raises his voice and demands silence. On the blackened faces eyes shine with strange ferocity, and mouths growl in mute fear. THE GANG LEADER *approaches* SABELITA.

THE GANG LEADER
 Revive yourself, my lady, and be so good as to guide us.
SABELITA
 I do not know... We don't have any money...
THE GANG LEADER
 Fine. We will search the house. Take up your candle and lead the way.

As he speaks, he forces her up, grabbing her roughly by the shoulders. SABELITA *holds back her tears and repeatedly raises her hand to her forehead, fearing both her captor and her lover,* DON JUAN MANUEL, *whose eyes she does not dare to meet. Contrite, she tries to approach him. In his crudely chivalrous manner* THE GANG LEADER *keeps her back, the lascivious smile on his blackened face belying his courtesy.*

THE GANG LEADER
 Light the way, sweet thing.
SABELITA
 No!... No!...
DON JUAN MANUEL
 Go with them, Isabel.
SABELITA
 Are you injured?
DON JUAN MANUEL
 No.
SABELITA
 Forgive me!
DON JUAN MANUEL
 Go with them.

Trembling, the mistress picks up the candle and walks off. The thieves tread carefully, following her through the darkness. When they fade away down the hallway the lord shouts imperiously.

DON JUAN MANUEL
  Sabelita! Blow out the candle!
THE GANG LEADER
  Careful, my lady!
THE MASKED MAN
  Damned old fool!

SABELITA shakes spasmodically as the tyrannical voice hits her like a gust of wind. As if moved by a supernatural force, she blows out the candle and slips away in the darkness before the thieves can stop her. DON JUAN MANUEL *cries out the window for help, and his voice races off into the night, pursued by the frantic yelping of stray dogs.*

DON JUAN MANUEL
  Fire! Fire! Help!…
A NEIGHBOUR
  Where is the fire?
DON JUAN MANUEL
  In my house! The house of Don Juan Manuel!

Fearing thieves, the NEIGHBOUR *peers out of his house and, finding his suspicions confirmed as no flames are visible, yields to caution and prudence as he again locks his door. The thieves run toward the source of the voice and find the window open and the room empty. A deep starry sky gleams outside.* DON JUAN MANUEL *has disappeared. Moonlight fills the room with a weak glow. At the far end of the room, under pale silver light, the thieves speak in hushed tones.*

A THIEF
  What's our next move?
THE GANG LEADER
  Damn this luck!
A SECOND THIEF
  If they come for us, we can escape over the garden walls.
A THIRD THIEF
  Are we giving up?
THE MASKED MAN
  Giving up? No way! Listen!…

They quiet down and listen. They can hear the servants' faint voices calling for help, so they scatter to get their bearings in the dark rooms of the house.

Scene Five

On the balcony where the quinces ripen, a woman cries — the old woman who can recall the time of Don Juan Manuel's sires. It draws the attention of one of the thieves, who drags her inside.

MICAELA
  Fire!... Help us!... Fire!...
A THIEF
  You're going to die!
MICAELA
  Receive my soul, Holy Mother of God!
A THIEF
  You'd better talk! Or else!
MICAELA
  What do you want me to say?
A THIEF
  Where does Don Juan Manuel hide his money?
MICAELA
  It's buried.
A THIEF
  Where?
MICAELA
  Far from here! I can take you there.
THE THIEF
  Liar! You die.
MICAELA
  What do you expect? For fifty years I've eaten his bread!
A THIEF
  You'd better talk!

MICAELA leans over and tries to rise to her knees but is beaten down again. THE THIEF takes her braids and wraps them around her throat. Suddenly the door bursts open and DON JUAN MANUEL appears. The old nobleman's hands, now untied, hold two flintlock pistols. He fires a shot, and THE THIEF collapses next to the old woman, who crawls off to hide. THE GANG LEADER and the other thieves rush in, one of them holding a lantern they found in the kitchen. DON JUAN MANUEL sees them approach, and immediately any thought of caution gives way to rage: he raises the other pistol, and the bluish flash of the powder illuminates his face, giving it the look of an antique portrait. His bullet breaks the lantern. The thieves shoot wildly into the darkness and, realizing that the shots will attract attention, flee through the garden. Servants scattered throughout the house run from window to window, crying in alarm.

THE SERVANTS' VOICES
  Help!... Help!...
SABELITA
  Save us! Save us!
THE DOGS
  Woof! Woof! Woof!
THE THIEVES' VOICES
  Which way do we go?... This way?... Shut up!... This way!...
THE GANG LEADER
  Damn the luck!
THE THIEVES' VOICES
  What about the dogs?... Who has some meat for them?
THE MASKED MAN
  The dogs know me. I'll calm them down.
THE THIEVES' VOICES
  We'll hop the wall... Are we all here?
THE GANG LEADER
  Damn it all, what're the odds!... This moonlight's getting brighter!
THE THIEVES' VOICES
  Someone's missing... No... Roll call...
THE GANG LEADER
  To Hell with anyone not here!
THE DOGS
  Woof! Woof! Woof!
THE MASKED MAN
  Whitey! Blackie! Down, boy!

The barking stops, and the moon, rising above the clouds, illuminates the room where DON JUAN MANUEL *confronted the thieves. He lies wounded in the doorway. His old servant leaves her hiding place, approaches and touches his cold hands. He kneels and puts his head on her lap, crying out in pain.*

MICAELA
  Master, beloved master! What draws the life from your body? You will not say! Because it was my fault, beloved master!

Scurrying servants cast ghostly shadows in the hallways. SABELITA *enters and, seeing the body on the ground, embraces it, emitting the moans of a bereaved lover. All of the servants arrive, kneel around the pair, and begin muttering lamentations.*

THE SERVANTS' VOICES
  May we soon see the perpetrator of this foul deed swinging on the gallows!...

The master was the patron of the poor!... He was an example to the rich!... He was the noblest gentleman in the world!... A great bastion of goodness!... Resplendent star!... A high-flying eagle!...

SABELITA

Don Juan Manuel! Godfather!

DON JUAN MANUEL

Shut your mouth, daughter of Satan! Enough with the tears, I'm not dead yet!

He slowly opens his eyes, then closes them again. Although slightly delirious, his voice still retains its lordly majesty. Blood streams over his forehead and pools in his eyes, making them difficult to open. His laboured breath heaves. Painfully he again forces his eyes open, his vision clouded, and stands up. Groping around for support, his hand rests on the shoulder of the old woman who, fearing she will collapse under his weight, experiences at once sadness and joy.

Act Two

Scene One

A room in the ancestral house. Beneath a purple canopy an oil lamp illuminates the hanging crucifix, highlighting Christ's blue-white and bloody feet. Dawn breaks outside. MICAELA *completes her night's vigil in a chair at the doorway.* SABELITA, *wrapped in a shawl, enters silently. In the eaves the birds sing. In the barn a cow moos. Softly the church bells summon the people to mass.*

SABELITA
Is he sleeping?

MICAELA
His thoughts torment him. Though he won't say it aloud, he knows the identity of the Cain whose gang tied him up and tried to rob him.

SABELITA
He will not complain. He will accept no one's pity.

MICAELA
Right you are, my lamb! Last night as Don Galán and I watched over him, I heard him sighing. Mother of God! I dared ask him what was wrong, and he told me to go to Hell!

SABELITA
I would never dare to ask him anything. Wait, what's that noise?

MICAELA
It's the wind at the window.

SABELITA
The dogs have been barking all night, as if someone was lurking outside the house. A little while ago I glanced outside the window and thought I saw shapes moving in the garden. They could have been men.

MICAELA
The trees can cast life-like shadows, especially when you're already jumpy — your eyes make things more frightening than they are. Sometimes when I think of the dear departed, I feel icy breath on my face.

SABELITA
Me too… And sometimes, I feel as though a door were opening behind me, and a shadow bending over my shoulders.

MICAELA
Let's not speak of these otherworldly matters, my lamb.

SABELITA
You are right.

MICAELA

The bells ring for matins.

SABELITA

For the third time. I got up to go the first time, but then I saw those frightening shapes in the garden.

MICAELA

We will go together — safety in numbers.

They leave. The maid, cloaked and hooded, enters holding a lantern. Stars still shine in the morning sky.

Scene Two

DON JUAN MANUEL lies in bed, recovering from the many wounds he received the previous night. At the door dozes a servant who has spent the night apart from the ferrets and greyhounds with whom he usually keeps company. He is DON GALÁN, hideous and old, deceitful, fearful, and a teller of ribald tales. In the master's house he also plays the role of fool. A cock crows.

DON JUAN MANUEL

Don Galán!

DON GALÁN

He lives! You were dead to the world!

DON JUAN MANUEL

What's that you say?

DON GALÁN

Welcome back to the land of the living.

DON JUAN MANUEL

Is the sun up?

DON GALÁN

The cocks crow, but the stars still shine in the sky.

DON JUAN MANUEL

I cannot sleep!

DON GALÁN

I can — if I could! Do you require anything, my lord?

DON JUAN MANUEL

Yes. For you to go to Hell.

DON GALÁN

Woohoo!... I'll wait to be relieved. Don't want to leave you all alone.

DON JUAN MANUEL

In the meantime, you can spin a yarn for me, Don Galán.

DON GALÁN
'Hares in the sea, fish in the mountains…'
DON JUAN MANUEL
Shut your mouth, you moron!
DON GALÁN
My mouth was shut.

The buffoon yawns, revealing an enormous mouth, and crawls under the table to go back to sleep.

DON JUAN MANUEL
Don Galán!
DON GALÁN
At your service.
DON JUAN MANUEL
I could swear that I put down one of those thieves!
DON GALÁN
Folks say he's risen from the dead.
DON JUAN MANUEL
I saw him fall!
DON GALÁN
Maybe the shock knocked him over.
DON JUAN MANUEL
Nonsense, I shot him! But his accomplices took away the corpse in order to conceal their identities.
DON GALÁN
Sorcerers, all of them — they blew on his tail, and up he pops and runs off. Woohoo!
DON JUAN MANUEL
Shut your mouth, you idiot!
DON GALÁN
My mouth was shut.

The new sun's rays strike the windows. The contours of an antique carved walnut bed are etched into the background. The nobleman's head rests on pillows, his eyes open beneath their sallow lids, and a bloody bandage covers his forehead. Under the table the fool snores.

DON JUAN MANUEL
Don Galán!
DON GALÁN
At your service.
DON JUAN MANUEL
No rumours in town about who broke in?

DON GALÁN
   The talk is that they weren't bandits at all but my lord's very own sons. That's what they say in town!
DON JUAN MANUEL
   Enough with your insolence!
DON GALÁN
   My mouth was shut!

Under the table DON GALÁN *puffs up his cheeks with a clownish grimace, while the master, with eyes closed and tearing up, heaves a sigh. His gaunt hand wipes his tears, then suddenly his expression merges with that of his fool, although his laughter drips with fierce irony and bitterness.*

DON JUAN MANUEL
   Don Galán, what does a father do with children who would steal from him?
DON GALÁN
   Distribute their inheritance now so we can die in peace.
DON JUAN MANUEL
   And then?
DON GALÁN
   Woohoo! Then we beg for alms.
DON JUAN MANUEL
   That's all well and good for you with your peasant blood, Don Galán. But you don't realize that we would then have to steal back from them.
DON GALÁN
   Better to retire to a monastery.
DON JUAN MANUEL
   Like the Emperor Charles V after he abdicated.[3]
DON GALÁN
   And at night we can hitch up our cassocks and chase girls.
DON JUAN MANUEL
   We'll think about that, Don Galán. Now open the window and let's see if the sun is up.
DON GALÁN
   It is, master.
DON JUAN MANUEL
   Clear skies?
DON GALÁN
   A beautiful sunrise.

---

[3] Charles V (1500–1558) reigned as King of Spain from 1516 and Holy Roman Emperor from 1519. He abdicated in 1557, retiring to a monastery in Yuste, Spain after passing on the crown to his son, Philip II.

SABELITA and old MICAELA return from church. They peer into the bedroom. SABELITA approaches, gentle and timid.

SABELITA
Why are you up so early, godfather?

DON JUAN MANUEL
What a night!... Was it all a dream?... Even now I am not sure! Are we dreaming or are we awake, Don Galán?[4]

DON GALÁN
I know only that I'm sitting here, my lord, taking refuge from the woes of the world. How long have we wandered this earth, master!

DON JUAN MANUEL
Neither sitting nor sleeping can provide respite… Only death has that power. This thought accompanies me day and night… My mind can imagine all the things my hands are no longer capable of — old age binds them far more tightly than those bandits did. If these hands were in tune with my mind, I would have already hanged them all.

SABELITA
Why are you so dismayed? Why don't you tell me what pains you, godfather?

DON JUAN MANUEL
I have no pains, and if I had any, Don Galán would scare them away. Why are you crying, Isabel? If you can't learn to laugh like that fool, go away and wipe your tears somewhere else. Don Galán, tell them to prepare my breakfast.

DON GALÁN
What shall I have them cook?

DON JUAN MANUEL
Ask if there are any curds and corn bread. Then some French toast in white wine, cooked golden brown, and fetch me a jug of wine from the cellar. And if there are fresh eggs, I'll have an omelette as well.

DON GALÁN
And if there are no eggs, we kill and eat the cock for not doing his job! Woohoo!

DON GALÁN, already at the door, capers and roars with the grotesque, bawdy laughter of a crude cardboard mask. The morning sun penetrates the bedroom, gilding the window panes. Grape vines swaying in the wind climb the trellis, providing sustenance for the clustering sparrows.

---

[4] A reference to Calderón de la Barca's classic play *La vida es sueño* [Life is a Dream] (1635).

Scene Three

The Mayorazgo's bedroom. In the late afternoon comes THE MILLER, *who rents the mills of Lantañón. As an offering to his landlord he brings a pot of honey, although the reason for his visit is to find out how the Mayorazgo is faring. He is a spiteful old peasant married to a young and voluptuous local beauty, whom he has left at home. He makes his entrance, with cap clutched obsequiously in his fingers and a psalm on his lips.*

THE MILLER
  The Blessed Virgin Mary has not left the poor without a father and benefactor! Our Divine Lady will bring these bastards to justice, and they will pay for their crime on the gallows!... I had heard that those cunning foxes were lying in wait, biding their time for an opportunity! Would that Our Lord had smitten them with a bolt of lightning and fried their flesh!... A pity my master could not identify the culprits!... For if he knew who the ringleader was, he wouldn't need to wait for the arm of justice to lower the axe: he could tell me, and eventually I'd come across the villain on the road, and with St Peter's help I'd cut him down with my shotgun!

DON JUAN MANUEL *cuts him short with a gesture of authoritative familiarity, and the wily old* MILLER *slowly passes his cap from one hand to the other.*

DON JUAN MANUEL
  Enough of your babbling! Why are you here?

THE MILLER
  We were concerned about your well-being.

DON JUAN MANUEL
  And your wife, why did she not come?

THE MILLER
  We did not want to leave your property unattended.

DON JUAN MANUEL
  Why did you come and not she?

THE MILLER
  My wife is unwell... When she heard the news, she took to bed. By our account, we will be baptizing the little one she carries in July, around St Santiago's.

DON JUAN MANUEL
  Tell her to come see me. Saddle the mule with her condition in mind.

THE MILLER
  Straight away, master!

DON JUAN MANUEL
  Make sure she doesn't come on foot!

THE MILLER

Of course, master. I love her like the king loves the queen. And she will be delighted, as she was sorry she couldn't make it today! As an offering to the master, she put a pot of honey in my saddlebag. As my late mother used to say, honey is as good on a wound as it is on the lips.

DON JUAN MANUEL

I will try your honey, and you tell your wife how much I appreciate her visiting me.

THE MILLER

You do us great honour by accepting our humble gift.

DON JUAN MANUEL

Don Galán! Don Galán!

He shouts, and smiles with the magnanimity of a prince receiving his subjects' offerings. Under flour-caked brows THE MILLER's *eyes glow maliciously, green and transparent, like the river around the mill.*

DON JUAN MANUEL

Don Galán! Don Galán!

DON GALÁN

At your service, my lord!

DON GALÁN *shouts in response from the other end of the hallway. Eventually he shows a face that shines with honey-smeared bread crumbs.*

DON JUAN MANUEL

I will have some of that honey brought by Pedro Rey.

DON GALÁN

Woohoo! There is none left, master. My lady Sabelita ordered it thrown to the dogs, so I helped them polish it off. My lady Sabelita wants no gifts from these people whom she would prefer not to admit into the house.

DON JUAN MANUEL

I am the sole master of this house, and mine is the only voice of authority. Isabel! Isabel!

DON JUAN MANUEL *waits a moment, pale with anger.* DON GALÁN *and* THE MILLER *steal wily, uncouth glances. The veins on old* MONTENEGRO's *bare forehead bulge, tracing out blue branches beneath the ivory skin.* SABELITA's *soft footsteps are heard. The mistress is smiling as she enters the room, but a shadow of fear shows in her tearful eyes, and her trembling lips hold the smile in place.*

SABELITA

What is your command?

DON JUAN MANUEL

I would know who is the master of this house!

SABELITA
   The same as ever.
DON JUAN MANUEL
   Then how is it that someone other than I would dare order the door closed to my favoured servants!
SABELITA
   I would not close the door on anyone, and today I will leave this house forever…

Her hoarse voice resounds solemnly beneath a veil of tears, at which the nobleman laughs with cruel and despotic disdain.

DON JUAN MANUEL
   Isabel, you will do what I say, like everyone else! Pedro Rey, tell your wife to come and see me tomorrow, and I will forgive you this year's rent. Isabel, bring a jug of our best wine for Pedro Rey and me to share.

Barely suppressing her tears, SABELITA *departs.* MICAELA *enters a moment later with a jug overflowing with foaming red wine.*

DON JUAN MANUEL
   It was not you I ordered to serve us.
MICAELA
   My lord, do not humiliate she who humiliates herself already by living with you in sin. She is a shining example of goodness and virtue! Not everyone will say so, but that is only because the truth is foreign to their venomous natures. The truth blinds them! After Doña María, first among the saints and my supreme mistress, Sabelita is purest of motive and heart, having no interest in your riches! Alas, my king, do not lend your ears to perfidious, deceitful talk — sugary words that cannot hide the bitterness underneath!
DON JUAN MANUEL
   Pour some wine for Pedro Rey.
PEDRO REY
   To your health! May this be the first of many occasions we raise a toast!
DON JUAN MANUEL
   Now get out.
DON GALÁN
   We'll see you a year from now, Pedro Rey.
PEDRO REY
   May God bless you, master.

He departs to the accompaniment of DON GALÁN's *protracted, carnivalesque courtesies.* DON JUAN MANUEL *stands pensive, tears welling up in his dark, puffy eyes.*

DON JUAN MANUEL
> I am surrounded by the ungrateful and the treacherous. Do you imagine that the hearts of these people are opaque to me? They all, my sons first and foremost, want me dead! Wicked scions who have turned against me, who would convert my forefathers' home into a den of thieves. In my veins runs the last drops of truly noble blood; in yours, the last of the true and loyal servants'.

MICAELA
> My king, may the hour of death cleanse us of all sin. Curse not those whom you have begotten. The young are unaware of the wrongs they commit against old age; youth demands our forbearance.

DON JUAN MANUEL
> Ginger, you know as well as I who tied me up and tried to rob me!

MICAELA
> Don't think such things, my lord. Sometimes the Enemy deceives us in order lead us to perdition.

DON JUAN MANUEL
> I recognized the one in the mask.

MICAELA
> Just because you recognized one, would you accuse them all? My angels? How could you imagine them capable of such evil?

DON JUAN MANUEL
> You didn't recognize any of them?

MICAELA
> Not a one, thank the Lord.

DON JUAN MANUEL
> And have you seen my sons since then?

MICAELA
> Every day I run into dear Golden Boy, who asks me for news of your recovery.

DON JUAN MANUEL
> I hope you told him that I'm not dead yet, that he and his brothers will inherit from me nothing but stones, that if they cross the threshold of this house, I will strike them all dead and bury their corpses in the entryway.

MICAELA
> Master, do not torment yourself! Heed not these nightmares! Do not condemn your soul to Hell with these evil notions! They are your children and as such I must respect them as my masters. You must know they are part of you, blood of your blood.

DON JUAN MANUEL and the old woman are silent for a moment. Then with a trembling hand the Mayorazgo beckons for the jug and fills his glass, fully resolved to drown his sorrows in wine.

Scene Four

The mill of PEDRO REY *rises out of the green meadow. Outside the door grapevines wend their way from rough stone benches. The young leaves seem even more delicate in contrast to the centuries-old vines and the coarse Celtic stones forming the benches. A flock of sparrows orbit wildly the top of a fig tree on which is perched a hideous scarecrow dressed as a raggedy old woman with a spinning wheel at her waist and in her right hand a goat's horn for a spindle. The miller's wife sits in the shade of the hanging vines, vivacious and flushed like the cherries of Santa María de Meis.* LIBERATA LA BLANCA *beats cream in a bowl, and from her rosy lips issues the rose of a song. A high-born huntsman approaches: the Mayorazgo's eldest son, whose name is* DON PEDRITO.

LIBERATA
   I see Cangas, I see Vigo,
   I see Redondela too!
   I see the bridge of San Payo,
   The road home, it's true!
   I see Cangas, I see Vigo!
DON PEDRITO
   You have good eyes, little vixen!
LIBERATA
   Oh!... I didn't see you there.
DON PEDRITO
   And where's your sap of a husband?
LIBERATA
   What a way to talk for a gentleman!
DON PEDRITO
   Is it true that my father is injured?
LIBERATA
   That's what Don Galán told us.
DON PEDRITO
   But you haven't seen him?
LIBERATA
   No, sir. Believe what you like. I've been in bed nursing a pain in my side.
DON PEDRITO
   And Pedro Rey?
LIBERATA
   He went to town this morning to see the master.
DON PEDRITO
   I need to speak with your husband.
LIBERATA
   He'll be here soon.

DON PEDRITO
You use the mill practically for free.
LIBERATA
What are you talking about, my lord? Mother of God, 'for free'!
DON PEDRITO
For free, because you give only twelve bags of wheat and twelve bags of corn meal — nothing. And even that you don't pay every year!
LIBERATA
Because the master has forgiven us the rent. Mary Mother of God, for free! For a mill that half the year has water to move one millstone! The other two work maybe until June!
DON PEDRITO
It looks like the three are working fine today.
LIBERATA
That's because today they're not irrigating.
DON PEDRITO
Well, seeing as how the mill isn't producing enough for you to pay rent, I will relieve you of this burden.
LIBERATA
What are you saying, sir?
DON PEDRITO
Just that!... You need to leave now, without kicking up a fuss.

DON PEDRITO stands, surveys the scene, and emits lupine laughter. The miller's wife fearfully turns her eyes to the road as well, and sees that it is deserted. She tries to rise and enter the house.

DON PEDRITO
Sit, Liberata la Blanca.
LIBERATA
I'll just go and fetch some figs to offer you. We picked them this morning, some are still green but the sparrows were already at them.
DON PEDRITO
You're lying... Pedro Rey has taught you well.
LIBERATA
Shall I milk the cow?
DON PEDRITO
I just want you to sit down, little vixen.
LIBERATA
Please don't be angry.

DON PEDRITO
You must pay me the rent that my father isn't charging, and if you can't, you have to leave the mill.
LIBERATA
And does the master agree with this?
DON PEDRITO
I don't need anyone's permission... Or you pay me with a hundred sacks of corn, which is traditionally what renters have paid. Or tomorrow you leave and we turn the mill over to its previous tenants.
LIBERATA
You want to give it back to Juan de Vermo because of his two young daughters!
DON PEDRITO
Perhaps some might need to give away mills to win their peasants' favour, but I don't have to be so magnanimous in order to bed Juan de Vermo's daughters.
LIBERATA
If you're referring to me, forget it! I am constant, and only my husband warms my bed! I am more faithful than Vermo's daughters!
DON PEDRITO
How about I fill that rotten belly of yours with some buckshot.

DON PEDRITO *grabs his shotgun, and the miller's wife screams and tries to escape toward the house. She cannot reach it, and with fear in her eyes she looks again to the road. Far off on the river bank a shepherd boy lets his cows drink, and the miller's wife cries harder for help. The shepherd boy shields his eyes from the sun, stands tall and looks toward the mill. Then he walks away, interrupting his cows' refreshment and shooing them away, water still dripping from their snouts.* DON PEDRITO, *with a cruel smile, an expression that evokes a resemblance to his old sire, sics his dogs on the miller's wife. They set upon her and tear apart her dress, leaving her nearly naked. The screaming* LIBERATA *flees under the trellis, her flesh quivering temptingly beneath in the tatters of her remaining clothes. Her eyes still seeking out help, she climbs one of the stone benches to defend herself from the dogs, who howl and tear at her with their ferocious white fangs. Streaks of red drip down the agile legs, which throb between the tatters. Beneath the centuries-old vines is re-enacted the spell of the ancient epics, which sing of blood, rape and power.* LIBERATA LA BLANCA *pleads and cries. A prophetic numen possesses the firstborn son, who acts out the verses that the heroes of old heard in languages now dead. He strides over to the miller's wife, grabs her, throws her down and takes her by force. When he is done with her, he ties her to the bench with strips of her own torn clothing. Then he walks away, whistling to his dogs.*

Scene Five

Evening at the mill. Old folk speak importantly in the light of a lamp which hangs from a smoke-blackened beam, and young men grope the young women against the dark background which smells of hay. Among the company LIBERATA *weeps as she shares her sorrows, and an old soothsayer stands near the fire tending to the wine and rosemary while she prepares mountain herbs known to cure pregnant women of the evil eye.*

LIBERATA
  Why me!
THE SOOTHSAYER
  Have patience, Liberata.
LIBERATA
  I can barely move!
A YOUNG MAN
  That Don Pedrito is rotten to the core.
AN OLD WOMAN
  A soul black as a funeral!
A YOUNG WOMAN
  Last year around harvest time I ran into him one night as I was returning from the fields. He chased me almost up to the church.
LIBERATA
  You were lucky he didn't catch you.
A YOUNG MAN
  He wasn't running very hard.
AN OLD MAN
  Since night was coming on he must have been looking for company.
THE SOOTHSAYER
  The other brothers are no better than Don Pedrito.
THE MILLER
  Sons of Cain, all of them!
LIBERATA
  Worse!
THE MILLER
  People in town say that they were the ones who broke into the estate.
LIBERATA
  Can you imagine, children rising up against their parents like this?
AN OLD WOMAN
  Especially disgraceful in such a distinguished family! Nobility is a thing of the past! Oh, if you had known Grandfather Don Ramon María! He was the foremost knight of these lands, the likes of whom we'll never see again!

THE MILLER
   And what about our master? Was there ever any lord who treated rich and poor alike with such justice? Have we known a greater benefactor?
AN OLD MAN
   In that respect he surpasses his father and grandfather. No king was ever such a benefactor. I recall one year at the town fair he plied all the young men dancing there with food and drink. I was one of them.
A YOUNG MAN
   And what did he do with the young women?
A YOUNG WOMAN
   We don't speak of that.

The fragrance of the rosemary-infused wine spreads among the assembled, the villagers and shepherds who keep the traditions of a remote, disingenuous and happy age. If a girl nods off in the candlelight, a boy gooses her awake. While the old folk talk and laugh, bold hands dart under skirts. THE SOOTHSAYER *blows on the boiling wine, and in the midst of the company* LIBERATA LA BLANCA *weeps and gives voice to her sorrows.*

LIBERATA
   Damn them all! And their dogs!
THE SOOTHSAYER
   You can damn the master but not the dogs, because they have Our Lord's blessing.
AN OLD WOMAN
   Or maybe damn only their fangs.
THE SOOTHSAYER
   Of all animals, only dogs have healthy saliva. When Our Lord Jesus Christ was walking the earth, it happened one day that after a long day in the mountains, the wounds from the nails on the cross were opened on His feet. At the side of the road was the palace of a rich man, whose name was Centurion. Our Lord asked for water to quench His thirst, and the rich nobleman, who was a gentile and practically the same as a Moor, ordered his servants to set the dogs upon Him, and with his hands around his women he intended to watch Our Lord's suffering from the comfort of his balcony. However, the dogs did not bite but instead licked the divine feet, restoring them and healing the wounds of Our Lord who then blessed them. And that is why I tell you that of all the many animals in the world the only ones whose tongues have the power to heal are dogs. The rest — wolves', wild boars', lizards' — are all poison.
A YOUNG MAN
   Wolves too, you say?

THE SOOTHSAYER

Wolf bites are fatal. Only dogs carry with them the blessing of Jesus Christ Our Lord.

LIBERATA

Forget their tongues, then, damn their fangs! My legs are covered with dog bites, and I can barely move.

THE SOOTHSAYER

Well, if they'd been even part wolf, you'd be much worse off. Because when you mix dog and wolf, then the saliva is neither healthful nor harmful, because the two breeds cancel one another out.

AN OLD MAN

Yes, and such puppies can take after either sire or dam — just like we Christian folk.

AN OLD WOMAN

I've heard that sometimes it's not the blood but the quality of the mother's milk that determines how a child turns out. I had a granddaughter raised on goat's milk, and in all my life I've never seen anyone so fond of traversing the hillsides.

THE SOOTHSAYER

Haven't you noticed how these part-wolf dogs look more ferocious in the light of the moon?

THE MILLER

Yes, I have noticed that at the master's house!

THE SOOTHSAYER

Yes, for they were conceived by the light of the moon, and that same light emboldens and enrages them. And if they bite someone during that time, it's because their wolfish nature reigns. But many people don't understand this, and when they see the wound swell and rot, they mistakenly believe the victim's humours to be out of sorts.

THE MILLER

And that's why we need to know the remedy for every malady.

THE SOOTHSAYER

For every malady there is a remedy, a herb.

AN OLD MAN

That's what they said in the old days. The Moors still know all the cures.

THE SOOTHSAYER

Moors know more about poisons and herbs that bring sleep.

The moon rises above the pines and whitens the door of the mill where by candlelight the young people entertain themselves with tales of thieves, elves and spirits. In the fields, dogs bark as if at the creatures conjured by the tales: ghosts wandering the earth and witches riding their broomsticks in the moonlight.

Scene Six

A calm estuary, and a galleon that sails with a brisk north-eastern gale. Viana del Prior, the old feudal villa, is mirrored in the water. Some fishermen stand motionless in the distance. It is the eve of the town fair, and on the decks of the galleon are grouped herdsmen bringing their cattle to market. Oxen yoked together, Merino goats and donkeys bustle under the hatch, their huge, sad and disoriented eyes peering upward.

A SAILOR
 Weather's shifting.
ANOTHER SAILOR
 Seagulls on land mean a good wind's on hand.
THE CAPTAIN
 That's the truth.

The cattlemen, when not talking about other fairs they have seen, discuss the deeds of an infamous bandit. There are three: MANUEL TOVÍO, MANUEL FONSECA *and* PEDRO ABUÍN.

MANUEL TOVÍO
 Juan Quinto made a mess of it this time. He thought that breaking into Don Juan Manuel's home would be like robbing a village priest. But even with a blade at his throat, the Mayorazgo just laughed and didn't tell him where his money was.
PEDRO ABUÍN
 They say that when Juan Quinto witnessed the Don's courage, he ordered him untied and released.
MANUEL TOVÍO
 They say that, but it's a lie.
MANUEL FONSECA
 They also talk about how Don Juan Manuel reminded him of the time he busted him out of jail. Juan Quinto owed him a favour and had to untie him.
MANUEL TOVÍO
 No one knows for certain. People say all kinds of things!
MANUEL FONSECA
 Careful, Doña María's eyes are on us.

With his eyes the herdsman gestures toward a wan, mournful woman wearing a Franciscan habit and sitting in the shade of the mast. The three herdsmen continue talking in low voices, joined occasionally by a village priest.

A POTTER
 We'll see how it is at the fair.

A SIEVE-MENDER
   For the likes of us, all the fairs are the same. We'll still die poor.
A RIBBON MAKER
   We're thankful just to have a slice of bread to eat!… We are arriving at Viana del Prior. The weather spoiled us on the way here, but I fear it won't be so nice for the return trip.

Sailors prepare for the approach. The ship's timber creaks, seagulls float around the masts and leaping dolphins break the mirrored surface of the waters. The salty sea foam breaks against the ship's port side, and the lady in the Franciscan habit prays. An old mendicant collects money to say a mass for departed souls.

THE CAPTAIN
   Do not be afraid, Doña María.
THE MENDICANT FRIAR
   You always say there is nothing to fear, but last time we nearly died.
THE CAPTAIN
   No, it was the same as now.

The lady, without pausing in her prayer, smiles with gentle sadness and gives an offering to the old man. Her mind is clearly somewhere else. The sailors dock the ship and exchange shouted greetings with an old fisherman with a Catalonian cap and sailor's beard who sits on a stone mending his lines and nets. The lady disembarks and with the village priest walks off down the beach.

THE CHAPLAIN
   Does anyone know we're here?
DOÑA MARÍA
   No.
THE CHAPLAIN
   And that woman still lives in the house!…
DOÑA MARÍA
   As payment for my sins, Our Lord God will accept my sacrifice of pride.

They enter the church. The churchyard is full of gravestones and cypress trees that extend to the shoreline. A beggar wearing a short mantle with shells and a long beard stands at the entrance. He resembles the penitents of olden times, a brother to the saints sculpted into church porticos.

Scene Seven

A large room lit by a single candle. The Mayorazgo sits at the table, eating and drinking with great appetite. There is fine silverware and a handmade linen tablecloth with a trim as red as an Azuela wine. The fool sits on the floor facing the nobleman at the opposite end of the room.

DON JUAN MANUEL
Have you been in town?

DON GALÁN
No, master.

DON JUAN MANUEL
You do know that your job is to entertain me while I dine? Tell me what they're talking about in town.

DON GALÁN
Woohoo!… No reason to go to town when the town comes to me, my lord.

DON JUAN MANUEL
What are you saying, you idiot?

DON GALÁN
Only the truth, master. Two distinguished ladies, my sisters, came by to bring me some patched underwear. Juana Creepy-Fingers and Cross-Eyed Andrea — if they don't know something, it's not worth knowing! And that's not family pride talking; they're only my half-sisters. I'm simply telling it like it is.

DON JUAN MANUEL
And what do these princesses have to say?

DON GALÁN
They themselves don't say anything… The poor souls just pass on what they hear… It seems that on the way here they ran into one of my master's sons, who was walking with a limp.

DON JUAN MANUEL
Which one?

DON GALÁN
Don Pedrito.

DON JUAN MANUEL
Does anyone know what gave him this limp?

DON GALÁN
Must be because he's not walking straight. He says a horse kicked him, though others say he was shot in the leg, and still others whisper that he's under the care of Andrea the Bonesaw.

DON JUAN MANUEL *pounds his fist on the table. The fool leaps to his feet and in a gesture of exaggerated fright begins to shake and stick out his tongue out, his eyes blank.* DON JUAN MANUEL *throws his plate at the fool, who catches it mid-air and begins licking it.*

DON JUAN MANUEL
I knew I recognized him! I wish I had slain that son of Oedipus!

DON GALÁN
  Son of whom, master?
DON JUAN MANUEL
  The Devil!

He rises from his seat and walks from one end of the long table to the other wearing a pained but proud expression. The fool remains sitting on the floor with the plate on his head, like the helm of Mambrino.[5]

DON JUAN MANUEL
  What other gossip is there, Don Galán, you moron?
DON GALÁN
  They say, like father like sons.
DON JUAN MANUEL
  That's a lie!
DON GALÁN
  Woohoo!... I agree, master.
DON JUAN MANUEL
  You're gambling with that tongue of yours!

DON JUAN MANUEL *kicks him. The fool rubs saliva in his eyes and feigns a cry of contrition.*

DON GALÁN
  May God grant you the health to kick me again!
DON JUAN MANUEL
  Continue with your account, you idiot Don Galán.
DON GALÁN
  I'm having an attack. Look at me trembling. My master's threats have shaken me to the core. My lips are sealed forever more, master. I don't wish to lose my tongue, even if it is as brazen as a wanton slut, naked and without shame.

With a mischievous grin he pretends to start pulling out his tongue. DON JUAN MANUEL *throws him a bone, and lets loose a kingly and cruel laugh. The fool begins acting like one of the dogs, knowing the master will be amused, and gnaws at the bone.*

DON JUAN MANUEL
  Enough fooling around. Why is my god-daughter Sabelita not serving me?
DON GALÁN
  She's off crying her eyes out.
DON JUAN MANUEL
  Isabel! Isabel!

---

[5] In Cervantes' novel (1605), Don Quixote mistakes a barber's basin for the Helm of Mambrino, the hero of many chivalric romances. The helm was reputed to be made of pure gold and to grant its wearer invulnerability.

AN ECHO
　Sa-beeel!... Sa-beeel!

The mistress looks on from the doorway, a cloud of sorrow covering her eyes, the floral eyes of a pious child.

SABELITA
　Who calls?
DON JUAN MANUEL
　I do. You don't recognize my voice, Isabel? If you serve me, I will eat; if not, the servants can clear the table.
SABELITA
　I am your slave, without a will of my own.
DON JUAN MANUEL
　Don Galán, clear the table.
DON GALÁN
　It's not a fast day, master.
SABELITA
　I've never refused to serve you, godfather.

SABELITA *pours wine into one of those large Portuguese crystal glasses from which the clergy and nobility once drank the fruit of the vine. Under the table* DON GALÁN *licks clean the dishes, and the old lord erupts into roaring laughter.*

DON GALÁN
　Master, now we can drink without fear of falling. We're already on the floor!
DON JUAN MANUEL
　Shut up, you imbecile!
DON GALÁN
　Woohoo! No fair! The master's had nine glasses, and Don Galán only one!
DON JUAN MANUEL
　Didn't you say the wine was a little vinegary?
DON GALÁN
　That was yesterday; today it's fit for a king's table. It tastes like fresh strawberries!
DON JUAN MANUEL
　Like wine, you dunce.
DON GALÁN
　Yesterday I drank from Pedro Rey's glass. No wonder it had a sour taste. One more drop, master, I appeal to your noble lineage!
DON JUAN MANUEL
　I have no wish to see you drunk, Don Galán.
DON GALÁN
　I don't see why not!

DON JUAN MANUEL
   If you get drunk, I'll have your head dunked in the well.
DON GALÁN
   Woohoo! Just like the majestic St Peter during a drought.[6]

As master and servant carry on with their banter, a veil of sorrow covers the loving eyes of SABELITA. *The mistress pales as she hears two murmuring voices in the corridor outside the door. With anguished eyes she retreats slowly backward just a wizened hand raises the curtain at the doorway to reveal the crying old servant woman.*

MICAELA
   Master, my lady has travelled here to see you.
SABELITA
   Doña María! Here?
DON GALÁN
   Woohoo!

The mood of DON JUAN MANUEL *darkens suddenly, and he commands silence with a gesture of imperious anger. A lady, still beautiful but stooped over, appears at the door, where she stops for a moment to wipe her eyes. The Mayorazgo, recovering from the initial shock, pounds his glass on the table with an arrogant blow and raises his voice, which loses nothing of its sovereignty and magnificence.*

DON JUAN MANUEL
   Welcome, my saintly and noble spouse, Doña María de la Soledad Ponte de Andrade!
DOÑA MARÍA
   They told me you were dying. That is the reason for my visit…
DON JUAN MANUEL
   I should be dead, but like a cat I have nine lives.
DOÑA MARÍA
   You never could recognize holy Providence at work!
DON JUAN MANUEL
   I know, I know…!

The old hidalgo nods with a mocking solemnity, his white mane shaking. The lady comes closer to him, followed by her village priest, who serves as chaplain in her house. DON JUAN MANUEL *regards her, an ironic and compassionate affection burning in his eyes.* SABELITA *remains withdrawn in the background.* DOÑA MARÍA, *with her innate nobility, pretends not to notice her.*

---

[6] The fool refers to a folk custom according to which a saint's statue is dunked in a well in order to alleviate drought.

DOÑA MARÍA
I was ill as well, I believe quite close to death… But you never bothered to come to see me.
DON JUAN MANUEL
I did not dare to… I have offended you so deeply!
DOÑA MARÍA
And you forget that I always forgive you!

DON JUAN MANUEL shields his eyes in the tragic manner he learned in his romantic youth, and the lady gives him a look of resigned tenderness that an indulgent grandmother might give to children when they lie to conceal their naughtiness. She smiles a delicate and sad smile, which lends a youthful charm to her withered mouth.

DON JUAN MANUEL
María Soledad, even though I don't believe in God…
DOÑA MARÍA
Do not blaspheme!
DON JUAN MANUEL
I still believe in saints who walk the earth.
DOÑA MARÍA
Quiet! I see that you are nowhere near death… But since I am here, I will not leave without speaking as if it were I about to die.
DON JUAN MANUEL
I know what you wish to speak of, María Soledad.

A long silence. With tear-filled eyes, SABELITA clears the table. An anguish fills her soul in the presence of that aged and long-suffering lady whose smile expresses more sorrow than do tears, and whose eyes are weary from crying over the misfortune the two women share. DON JUAN MANUEL drinks down the last glass, leans back in his seat and feels his eyelids growing heavy from the wine. Wife and mistress look on, sadness in their loving eyes. Then, stepping quietly, they leave the room, turning in opposite directions. DON JUAN MANUEL snores.

Act Three

Scene One

All of the servants have gathered in the main kitchen of the house. From the fireplace lively flames cast trembling red light on the peasants' faces, which are burned by their work sowing and harvesting in the fields. Beneath the canopy of the enormous fireplace the servants sit on wooden benches, and tongues of flame strain desperately upward to hear the wind's fantastic voice. It is a stone fireplace which calls to mind tales of witches shimmying down the chimney and goblins dancing jigs around the hanging smoked blood sausages. The servants sit round slurping up the last bits of bean soup which stick stubbornly to their wooden spoons. There are five of them: ANDREIÑA, *an old woman attached to the house since the days of the master's parents; the fool* DON GALÁN; TAINTED JUANA, *who knows the nuns' ancient recipes;* BIEITO, *a boy who tends the cows; and* ROSALVA, *a girl who works on the estate in exchange for room and board. They speak in hushed voices.*

DON GALÁN
 I don't expect the master's reunion with my lady María to be of long duration.

TAINTED JUANA
 So then why did Doña Sabelita leave?

ROSALVA
 Well, perhaps the master really will return to a Christian life with Doña María.

DON GALÁN
 Woohoo! I'd give it three days, tops. You'll see later the new 'queen' he'll introduce us to! You're new to this house and you don't understand that what's happening now has happened many times before. Doña Sabelita is gone, but my master is not one to wait around with no girl to shoo away the flies while he sleeps. Woohoo! Doña Sabelita's replacement is probably on her way here now!

TAINTED JUANA
 You know who she is, you sly fox.

DON GALÁN
 We all know who she is!

BIEITO
 Good Lord! If he's not going to live like a Christian, why not just stay with Doña Sabelita?

TAINTED JUANA
 I know who you speak of, Don Galán.

ANDREIÑA
: We all know. It's Liberata la Blanca. I tell you here and now that I'll quit this house for good if that wife of Pedro Rey is to be the new lady of the house. At least Doña Sabelita is of good breeding!

DON GALÁN
: Go wash your legs, Rosalva! The next queen of the manor might be you.

ROSALVA
: I'm in no hurry to condemn my soul.

DON GALÁN
: Your term of service will be up well before you die, so there will be plenty of time to repent.

ROSALVA
: You are well versed in these lewd matters, Don Galán!

DON GALÁN
: Woohoo!

ANDREIÑA
: Don't pay attention to him, girl. Tell him that you'll have to marry him. He's such a smooth talker, he can pimp his own wife — just like Pedro Rey.

DON GALÁN
: Hear that, Rosalva? Then there's no shame if your belly swells. Don Galán will take care of everything.

ROSALVA
: How about I throw this bowl at you?

DON GALÁN
: Don't be upset, my dove.

ANDREIÑA
: Leave the girl alone, Don Galán.

DON GALÁN
: Leaving, leaving… left!

BIEITO
: I saw Doña Sabelita recently. Bumped into her in front of the church. I don't think she was on her way home!

TAINTED JUANA
: Well, look at that: such a noble lady ruined by the love of a man!

ANDREIÑA
: Now shunned even by her own kin!

ROSALVA
: Disdained by all the other noble folk!

DON GALÁN
: Still, you'd give anything to walk in her shoes!

ANDREIÑA
: No way!

DON GALÁN
   Have you seen her curves, those arms and legs and those white breasts? Woohoo! She'd make a great housekeeper for some priest!
ANDREIÑA
   Shut your mouth, you lecher!
DON GALÁN
   I'll tell you what. She'll land on her feet and do better than any of us here if one day the master lets us go.
TAINTED JUANA
   True enough! But it looks to me like it's not the master who's chased her away. She left on her own accord because she doesn't want to see the one who's taking her place.
DON GALÁN
   Maybe so.
ANDREIÑA
   See how the Evil One blinds us poor women!
DON GALÁN
   Woohoo! The Evil One should blind men too. Maybe then some of them might sin with you, Andreiña.

The servants guffaw. Then they hear the voice of DON JUAN MANUEL *calling for his dinner.* TAINTED JUANA *places a trivet over the fire, and the servants begin speaking about how in the mountains a cow gave birth to a two-headed calf.*

Scene Two

The Collegium clock strikes two — the traditional afternoon siesta. Riding a mule, Don Ambrosio Malvido, THE SECRETARY, *arrives at the door of the main house and dismounts, assisted by* THE BAILIFF, *who has been waiting for him all morning in the entrance hall. Together they ascend the wide stone stairway. When they reach upstairs* THE SECRETARY *realizes that he still has on his spurs, so he sits and removes them.* THE BAILIFF *bangs on the door with his rod of office.*

THE BAILIFF
   Open up!
DON GALÁN
   Who's there?
THE BAILIFF
   The Law is here, from Viana de Prior. How is Don Juan Manuel's health?
DON GALÁN
   Don Juan Manuel is having his nap. What his health is up to, I cannot say.

The Blazoned Eagle

THE BAILIFF
Has his strength returned?

DON GALÁN
It never left.

THE BAILIFF
Inform him that the honourable secretary Malvido has come to take his testimony.

DON GALÁN
Woohoo!... You're welcome to wait. I'd make yourselves comfortable if I were you.

DON GALÁN goes to rouse the master, and THE SECRETARY and BAILIFF remain in the entrance hall where two hallways cross. Above the door hangs a wicker cage with a singing blackbird. THE SECRETARY looks out the window into the garden.

THE SECRETARY
Such lovely green pears!

THE BAILIFF
Just like the ones in the priory.

THE SECRETARY
Remember that you said you'd give me a graft from your tree.

THE BAILIFF
And I will, honourable Don Ambrosio.

THE SECRETARY
Such excellent fruit trees the Mayorazgo has! Do you know what kind of apples those are? They're pippins. And look at the other pear tree.

THE BAILIFF
Those are different. Delicious, they melt in your mouth!

THE SECRETARY
Mother of God, all the plums on that tree over there!

THE BAILIFF
That's because they're Merryweathers.

THE SECRETARY
No, not Merryweathers, they're Mirabelles.

THE BAILIFF raises his hand to his forehead and examines the tree more closely. His mouth forms a philosophical smile. At that moment the Mayorazgo arrives. The old wood floor trembles beneath his martial, knightly gait.

THE SECRETARY
Lord Don Juan Manuel, a thousand pardons for bothering you today.

DON JUAN MANUEL
One pardon is enough, Señor Malvido.

THE SECRETARY
No need to doff your hat in our presence, Lord Don Juan Manuel.
DON JUAN MANUEL
In my house I carry myself as I please, Señor Malvido.
THE SECRETARY
I realize… I realize…
DON JUAN MANUEL
Let's sit down.

Somewhat short of breath, THE SECRETARY *removes the inkwell from his coat pocket and places it on the table. He looks over the judicial decree and then prepares to write.*

THE SECRETARY
You no doubt realize why we've come, Lord Don Juan Manuel?
DON JUAN MANUEL
I don't realize anything.
THE SECRETARY
To take your testimony…
DON JUAN MANUEL
I have no testimony to give.
THE SECRETARY
You don't know, you have no idea who harmed you to the point where after a week you are still recovering?
DON JUAN MANUEL
Old wounds now reopened: the hazards of advanced age.
THE SECRETARY
So you refuse to bear witness?…
DON JUAN MANUEL
I do refuse, Señor Secretary Malvido.
THE SECRETARY
It is a pity you would not see justice done!
DON JUAN MANUEL
I scoff at your justice.
THE SECRETARY
Your testimony would aid us in ascertaining precisely what transpired.
DON JUAN MANUEL
If I knew who those bandits were, I would not give their names to you to fill your tomes of legal nonsense, Señor Malvido.
THE SECRETARY
And what about punishing the guilty?
DON JUAN MANUEL
I'll see to it with my own hands. Do you know what my grandsire, seven

generations back, the Marquis of Bradomín, did?
THE SECRETARY
 I do not... But those were different times, long ago.
DON JUAN MANUEL
 For me nothing has changed. The Marquis, my grandsire, spent a great deal of time in a dispute with the Dominican friars. One day he decided to put an end to it: he distributed arms to his servants and stormed the monastery. They slew seven friars right in the choir, and he mounted their heads on spikes outside of this very house. When I first heard this story from my mother, who found it scandalous and horrible, I decided once and for all that I would settle all of my disputes in a similar fashion. And there have been thirty-two of them!
THE SECRETARY
 And how many criminal charges have been brought against you?
DON JUAN MANUEL
 Enough to make me laugh each time! I've always taken justice into my own hands — no pity for friend, no fear of foe. This 'justice' of yours — clerks, bailiffs, jails — I'm not saying that it's not a worthy institution which has done plenty of good for women, children and doddering old folk, but Don Juan Manuel Montenegro has found no use for it yet.
THE SECRETARY
 So, we will say that you did not recognize any of the invaders and that you have no idea as to their identities.
DON JUAN MANUEL
 You can say that I have no wish to provide testimony and that I can serve as my own justice, Señor Secretary Malvido.
THE SECRETARY
 But writing that down is out of the question, my lord Don Juan Manuel!
DON JUAN MANUEL
 If you cannot write that, write nothing at all.

Boldly he slams his hand down on the documents, a fleshless hand with blue veins which map out tragic pathways of exaltation, violence and madness. THE SECRETARY *and* THE BAILIFF *exchange frightened glances.*

THE SECRETARY
 My office is sacred, Lord Don Juan Manuel! This is an official hearing, and I represent the judge.
DON JUAN MANUEL
 In this house I am the judge!
THE SECRETARY
 I represent the King.

DON JUAN MANUEL
: I am king here as well!

THE SECRETARY
: My lord Don Juan Manuel!

DON JUAN MANUEL
: Señor Secretary Malvido!

THE SECRETARY
: I have come here in good faith, trusting in your nobility, with no guard, no witnesses, only the bailiff. I hope you will do me no violence!

THE BAILIFF
: Your compromising actions compromise us too, Lord Don Juan Manuel!

DON JUAN MANUEL
: And what does that matter?

THE SECRETARY
: You're not in your right mind, Lord Don Juan Manuel!

DON JUAN MANUEL
: Would you say that of a lion? A tiger?

Standing up with fiery arrogance he tears the documents and tosses MALVIDO's *inkwell out the window. His regal and resonant voice spreads throughout the house and echoes in the hallways.* THE SECRETARY *and* BAILIFF *retreat carefully, like two old foxes.* DON JUAN MANUEL's *choleric eyes burn in tyrannical mockery: cruel, violent and fierce. He then calls for his fool, who appears in one of the hallways, leading the hounds.* DOÑA MARÍA, *accompanied by her chaplain, approaches from another hallway on the way back from the chapel.* DON JUAN MANUEL *stands in the hall, greeting them with his magnificent and lordly laughter.*

DON JUAN MANUEL
: Don Galán, loose the hounds on those fleeing peasants!

DON GALÁN
: They won't catch them! They've never chased hares who run so fast.

DON JUAN MANUEL
: As if the Devil himself were on their tails!

DON GALÁN
: I hope they don't come back with an army! Woohoo!... I'll hide in the stove, and the master can turn fugitive, just like that time when Secretary Acuña paid you a visit.

DON JUAN MANUEL
: You are a misbegotten cur, Don Galán.

DON GALÁN
: Begotten by a woman I was, master.

DOÑA MARÍA *and* THE CHAPLAIN *arrive. An enchanting smile adds youth to the wilted flower of* DOÑA MARÍA's *mouth. She approaches slowly, and* THE CHAPLAIN *rushes ahead to offer her a chair.*

DON JUAN MANUEL
   What are you doing, Don Manuelito?
THE CHAPLAIN
   For my lady to rest…
DON JUAN MANUEL
   That chair just hosted a secretary's buttocks; it is consigned to the fire. By the Code of Chivalry!
DON GALÁN
   The clerks keep coming, though. If we consign every chair they sit on to the fire, we'll have nothing left for our own buttocks to sit on!
DOÑA MARÍA
   Why was the secretary here?
DON JUAN MANUEL
   To take my testimony.

It is as if a dark cloud comes over his proud bearing, aquiline profile and deep-set eyes. DOÑA MARÍA *regards him fearfully as she tries to guess at the thoughts that roil behind these eyes.*

DOÑA MARÍA
   My husband, we need to talk.
DON JUAN MANUEL
   Yes, my lady, we need to talk.
DOÑA MARÍA
   I would very much like to return to my house today.
DON JUAN MANUEL
   I don't dare beg you to stay… But I feel a need I can't explain — the need to have you close to me.
DOÑA MARÍA
   What's gotten into you?
DON JUAN MANUEL
   I'm not sure.

Don Manuelito cautiously walks toward the door, and the lady halts him with a gesture. THE CHAPLAIN *returns to his seat and pats his forehead with a scented kerchief.* DON GALÁN *goes and stretches out along the windowsill.*

DON GALÁN
   Don't mind us dogs, my lady.
DOÑA MARÍA
   As long as you don't bark.

DON JUAN MANUEL

Get out, you idiot… It appears you're not welcome here!

He gestures toward the door, his voice full of paternal affection. DOÑA MARÍA's *inveterate nobility shows itself, and she regards the fool both with compassion and contempt.* DON GALÁN *departs, the hounds in tow.*

DON GALÁN

Let's go, brothers!

DOÑA MARÍA

How do you tolerate so much insolence in a servant?

DON JUAN MANUEL

Don Galán amuses me! But he is also the voice of my conscience!…

DOÑA MARÍA

Don Galán, the voice of your conscience?

DON JUAN MANUEL

Don Galán, with all his jokes and improprieties, edifies my soul, just like Don Manuelito edifies yours with his sermons.

DOÑA MARÍA

Stop it, don't blaspheme, you devil!

DON JUAN MANUEL

I speak no blasphemies. Both tell us the bitter truth. You chaplain sweetens it with holy water, my fool with wine.

THE CHAPLAIN

Don Juan Manuel has such a great wit!

DOÑA MARÍA

You know his wiles, Don Manuelito.

DON JUAN MANUEL's *eyes burn with irony.* DOÑA MARÍA *smiles amiably, looking at the chaplain and crossing herself. Don Manuelito shakes his head reproachfully with the gesture of a resentful commoner. He is old, emaciated and crude, with bony, fleshless, hairy hands. He wears a wide-brimmed cleric's hat and a greenish cassock which tangles with his spurs.* DON JUAN MANUEL *is fond of him because of his two excellent hounds, and the cleric likes the nobleman for the tales based on his many wanderings and adventures. With good humour* DON JUAN MANUEL *interrogates him. The cleric's eyes glow with excitement and vibrancy.*

DON JUAN MANUEL

When do we start the rebellion, Don Manuelito?

THE CHAPLAIN

As soon as I find fifty brave young men, Lord Don Juan Manuel!

DON JUAN MANUEL

There are no men like us anymore, who are prepared to die for an idea. These

days enemies do not hate one another, they shake hands and smile.
THE CHAPLAIN
Our kind are finished!
DON JUAN MANUEL
I wish we were! Better to have finished than to have degenerated so. I begat six sons — six lying thieves!
DOÑA MARÍA
Stop! Stop please! What could make you believe something like that?
DON JUAN MANUEL
I recognized one of them when they bound my hands and mouth. Ten thousand curses upon them! They will not inherit a single penny from me!

DON JUAN MANUEL *stands up. A noble pallor spreads over his cheeks, and his eyes shine under hoary, trembling brows. His kingly voice resounds all over the house.*
DOÑA MARÍA *and* THE CHAPLAIN *exchange a dubious glance.*

THE CHAPLAIN
We cannot believe such calumny, Lord Don Juan Manuel.
DON JUAN MANUEL
It is no calumny!
DOÑA MARÍA
Yes, it is! I must stand up for my sons... I could never have given birth to such monstrosity.

DON JUAN MANUEL *looks at her, his eyes flaring violently, his hands across his proud bare forehead, where all his violent energies are concentrated into both love and hate. A sad and sarcastic smile plays across the ill-tempered mouth.*

DON JUAN MANUEL
María Soledad, forget Don Galán's nonsense.
DOÑA MARÍA
That monster made those accusations!
DON JUAN MANUEL
No, they came from me!
DOÑA MARÍA
I must speak with you about our sons.
DON JUAN MANUEL
I kicked them out of house and heart on the same day. When they were under my roof, I kept my eyes closed and pretended not to see how they stole both wheat and corn from my lands. There were times I did not have enough even to feed the servants! When I tired of their thievery, I offered to support them if they stayed on their own. But like robbers they would break down the door that I closed. If you are here on their errand, return to them and convey my malediction.

The anguished lady, hands on her tear-stained face, tries to rise to the defence of her sons, but the words freeze in her throat as her faith withers and dies. She starts crying again, her sorrowful eyes fixed on the only man she has ever loved, the only man who still ignites in her the fire of youth.

Scene Three

A courtyard. The seminary in the background. Tight against the wall walk DON ROSENDO, DON GONZALITO, DON MAURO *and* DON FARRUQUIÑO, *four of the Mayorazgo's sons.* DON FARRUQUIÑO *wears a tricorn hat and large-collared cape, timeless emblems of the seminary of Viana del Prior.*

DON GONZALITO
 I can't wait to find out!…
DON MAURO
 I can.
DON GONZALITO
 Can mother talk some sense into him?
DON MAURO
 I doubt it.
DON FARRUQUIÑO
 The power of words is great, my brothers. God willing, Doña María will come through.
DON MAURO
 I don't believe in miracles. I'm pretty sure that nothing will come of this.
DON GONZALITO
 Shut your mouth if that's what you think.
DON MAURO
 No man's hand can gag this mouth.
DON GONZALITO
 Maybe not a hand, but a fist…
DON MAURO
 Neither hand nor fist nor air. I say whatever I want, and whoever doesn't like it had better walk away.
DON ROSENDO
 Enough! Why quarrel?
DON FARRUQUIÑO
 Peace and harmony among Christian gentlemen.

The four brothers pace the length of the wall in silence. DON MAURO *is tall, thin, handsome, with hard eyes and a proud aquiline profile. His speech is laconic yet domineering, demanding obedience if not love. The four brothers share a family resemblance.*

DON GONZALITO
The Chaplain will let us know when he finds out something.
DON ROSENDO
Who did he talk to?
DON GONZALITO
Me. We arranged to meet back here.
DON ROSENDO
What time?
DON GONZALITO
Sunset.
DON ROSENDO
He's already late then.
DON MAURO
Maybe he stopped by the tavern.
DON FARRUQUIÑO
We men of the cloth say 'shrine', brother.
DON GONZALITO
Mother wrote her will, which divides her estate into equal portions. Plus something for the servants and a bit for the Chaplain. Her jewellery will pay for room and board in the convent.
DON FARRUQUIÑO
What is the Chaplain's provision?
DON GONZALITO
He'll receive six reales a year to perform a mass for her soul. It will weigh on our consciences not to pay him. Mother was very specific on this point, threatening us with excommunication if we didn't do it.
DON FARRUQUIÑO
Laypersons cannot excommunicate.
DON GONZALITO
Well, that's a relief. Excommunicated or no, I don't think we need to pay him. It's mother's weakness to allow herself to be manipulated by the clergy.
DON FARRUQUIÑO
She should entrust these matters to me once I finish divinity school. But the things I have seen! I'm tempted to go into another profession.
DON ROSENDO
I think your share will be about the same as the Chaplain's.
DON FARRUQUIÑO
We'll see!

DON ROSENDO
  Let's not fight about this.
DON FARRUQUIÑO
  I feel fairly confident! I have a proposition for you. You pay me, then all my property goes to you when I die. If you don't pay me, then everything goes to my housekeeper!

THE CHAPLAIN enters the courtyard and is approached by the brothers whose spirits are still raised by the junior cleric's wit.

DON MAURO
  I don't like that look on his face. The old man must have said no.
DON GONZALITO
  Any good news?
THE CHAPLAIN
  There's no use talking to him.
DON ROSENDO
  Why?
THE CHAPLAIN
  The robbery...
DON ROSENDO
  Does he blame all of us?
THE CHAPLAIN
  All.
DON MAURO
  And mother didn't say...?
THE CHAPLAIN
  What could she say?
DON MAURO
  That we are not all responsible... that it was only one.
THE CHAPLAIN
  How could she accuse any one of her sons?
DON MAURO
  Well, she could defend the others who are blameless. Tomorrow I will go to father's house and proclaim the truth for all to hear.
THE CHAPLAIN
  You know the truth?
DON MAURO
  I do. It was our brother Pedro. He tried to talk me into it but I refused.
DON ROSENDO
  We all refused.

THE CHAPLAIN
Nevertheless, you are his accomplices. Did you fulfil your filial duty to protect your father? What did you do, impious ones? You bound and gagged the one brother who was prepared to stand and do the right thing.
DON MAURO
Lies spun by Golden Boy.
THE CHAPLAIN
I didn't mention a name. Recall what your mother told you yesterday: a Cain who accuses his brother will stand to be disowned. And recall too that we may still all get what we want here.
DON ROSENDO
But didn't mother already go back to Flavia?
THE CHAPLAIN
No, Don Juan Manuel begged her to stay. She assented as a kind of penitence. Tomorrow she will try talking with him again.
DON ROSENDO
Let's wait until tomorrow then.
DON MAURO
Father will only say no again. He needs to know who tried to rob him. We shouldn't take the blame for something we didn't do.
DON FARRUQUIÑO
Right! There's enough blame to go around as it is.

A rider on a wild-maned horse enters the courtyard. It is another one of the Mayorazgo's sons: Don Miguel. Among the townsfolk and villagers his good looks have earned him the nickname GOLDEN BOY. *Incessant gambling and womanizing have left him even more impoverished than his brothers. So deep in debt is he that he roves the Viana del Prior streets on horseback to keep a step ahead of his creditors. But despite the poverty to which his pastimes have reduced him, his aristocratic bearing and magnanimity remain unchanged.*

GOLDEN BOY
What news?
DON MAURO
A lost cause.
DON GONZALITO
Not yet.
THE CHAPLAIN
Tomorrow all will be decided.
GOLDEN BOY
I will sign away my entire share to whoever will give me a coin or two now.

DON GONZALITO

So you too have no faith?

GOLDEN BOY

No trust, no faith. No money either — maybe just enough to buy a rope to hang by.

DON FARRUQUIÑO

Lucky you! Enough money to buy a rope!

GOLDEN BOY

Well, maybe I'll save the money and hang myself by these reins here.

DON FARRUQUIÑO

I have a business proposition for you.

GOLDEN BOY

Any money in it?

DON FARRUQUIÑO

A bit for each of us.

GOLDEN BOY

When do we get it?

DON FARRUQUIÑO

Patience, brother. We'll go over the details later.

GOLDEN BOY

When is curfew at the seminary?

DON FARRUQUIÑO

Eight o'clock... But at nine I'll leave through the window.

GOLDEN BOY

Fine, pick the night and we'll meet at Pichona's place. If I'm not there yet, just wait for me. Hey, look there, it's that Jew I owe money to. Good bye!

The horse rears back but GOLDEN BOY *digs in his spurs and gallops off, nearly running down an old man with spectacles, top-hat and carved cane.*

GOLDEN BOY

Move aside, my dear Ginero! There's no taming this savage beast! I can't control him!...

SEÑOR GINERO

May a bolt of lightning strike you, son of Pharaoh! It's not enough to take my money, you want to take my life as well! No respect for your elders! You liar, you cheat!

DON ROSENDO

Watch your mouth, Señor Ginero.

SEÑOR GINERO

Didn't you see how he nearly ran me down?

DON FARRUQUIÑO

Who did? It was the horse. Save your anger for the horse, Señor Ginero.

SEÑOR GINERO
 I'll never get back the money he owes me!
DON MAURO
 What use can you have for money? You have a foot in the grave already.
SEÑOR GINERO
 I'll live to see many more young people buried!
DON FARRUQUIÑO
 I have a gift for prophecy, Señor Ginero. You will die under the hooves of my brother's horse, just like a Moor before St James.
SEÑOR GINERO
 My family has been Christian for generations, and even without a coat of arms we are of noble blood!... My money is lost, I know it! The poor honour their debts more reliably than the lords... Fine, make fun of me!... All your pride is nothing but smoke and becomes less real with each passing day. The high towers will fall, and the hovels will rise. You wrathful, despotic, mad people — you will witness the downfall of your house!

The old man enters the church as the brothers continue to mock him. THE CHAPLAIN *cautiously implores them not to make a scene right outside the house of God.* DON MAURO *rudely cuts him off, and the others, paying no mind, walk off and continue to discuss the matter that brought them together.* SABELITA *crosses the courtyard, her hood up. It is already dark, and the brothers fail to recognize their father's mistress.*

Scene Four

The receiving room in the mansion. Sunset. The shadowy presence of two women. In the air wafts the balsamic aroma of ripening quinces on the late Gothic balcony with its stone railings. The women's whispering is barely audible.

MICAELA
 So often have I dreamed of seeing the lady of the house return! So often I thought of setting out for Pazo de Lantañón to warm my hands at your hearth!
DOÑA MARÍA
 Micaela, you cannot imagine how sorrowfully the hearth fire burns there.
MICAELA
 It used to be happy, like the fires of San Juan. The servants gathered daily 'round the stove — twelve of us, just like the Apostles. At harvest time or when picking the grapes there were more than fifty. Telling stories, folk laughing, young ones singing and playing without a care!

DOÑA MARÍA

All in the past! My hands and heart have cooled with the ashes of time.

MICAELA

My lady, do not return to your exile.

DOÑA MARÍA

The flames of sin lick at this house.

MICAELA

But she who ignited them has gone away.

DOÑA MARÍA

Do not speak her name!

MICAELA

Won't you forgive her, my lady?

DOÑA MARÍA

She is the cause of my sorrows! She, who forgot that I provided her with food and shelter and raised her as a daughter!

MICAELA

She weeps from the shame of deceiving her godmother. When it's just the two of us, she is humble and contrite! The hawk circles 'round, the dove tries to evade him, but eventually his talons sink into her. He ensnared her, as he has so many others!

DOÑA MARÍA

So many! I hold onto the hope that he will return to me with time, that we will be happy together in our old age… But he has lost none of his vigour and continues to attract women and corrupt their souls.

A shadow noiselessly crosses the door, kneels down and heeds the lady's resigned speech. A kerchief covers her bowed head. It is DON JUAN MANUEL's *mistress.*

SABELITA

Godmother!… My poor godmother, how much you have suffered all these years! Godmother, listen to me.

Still on her knees, SABELITA *moves toward her godmother. Her voice is tepid and dramatic; hers is a guilty soul wishing to unburden itself in confession.* DOÑA MARÍA *turns pale, her eyes boring into her god-daughter.*

DOÑA MARÍA

What do you want?

SABELITA

I've travelled so far. I'd left this house intending never to return, and when I realized how lost and alone I was on the road, I cried my eyes out. I thought I would die. No more wandering. I kneel before you and beg your forgiveness. Godmother, godmother, please allow me to kiss your hands!

DOÑA MARÍA
> Now you ask for my hands; I gave you my heart. I cried over you as for a dead daughter. Not jealousy but pity I felt, a crushing pity, because you betrayed me. Was I not a mother to you?

SABELITA
> Mother, my mother!

DOÑA MARÍA
> I was a mother to you, but not anymore.

SABELITA
> Yes, you are right, mother!

DOÑA MARÍA
> Get up.

SABELITA
> Do not deny me your hands to kiss.

DOÑA MARÍA
> Get up, Sabelita!

SABELITA
> I must kneel as I speak to you, godmother!

DOÑA MARÍA
> I will not listen to you like this.

In the shadow she offers her hands, pale and bewitched by the moon and with an aroma of decaying flowers. A weeping SABELITA *kisses them.*

SABELITA
> You cannot forgive me, godmother!

DOÑA MARÍA
> I can and I do.

SABELITA
> How I have offended you!... Godmother, I wanted to put an end to this sin and leave this house forever...

DOÑA MARÍA
> That is well and good, therein lies your salvation. But I ask nothing of you, my daughter. I know that as soon as you left, another woman, probably not as pure of heart as you, was here to take your place. I am an old woman, and I will never get him back. I could not keep him when I had my youth and looks! You are a good woman, and you love him!...

SABELITA
> If there could be any excuse for my actions, that would be it.

DOÑA MARÍA
> How many girls' hearts he has broken!

SABELITA
> My will is not my own. I truly wished to break the bonds of sin, but I could

not… But as I saw the misfortunes befalling him, the bonds became tighter. I lacked the courage to leave him at those moments.

DOÑA MARÍA
You know the identity of the robbers!

SABELITA
Yes!

DOÑA MARÍA
It's awful!

SABELITA
Awful!

DOÑA MARÍA
I came here thinking that he did not know, intending to ask him permission to retire to a convent and pass my property on to our sons when I die. But I didn't have the courage to ask. I was afraid to see into his heart. He damns them and wishes them only misfortune!

Two sighing shadows and a long silence. DOÑA MARÍA's *hands cover her face and stifle her sobs. A profound darkness permeates the room. Her silver hair is caressed both by the other shadow and the moonlight.*

SABELITA
Godmother, I am leaving. Do not allow that other woman to take your rightful place. It is you, only you, who have the right to live in this house. I am leaving because I wish you happiness, godmother. Deep down in his soul godfather loves only you. As God is my witness, I implore you not to yield your place to another woman. Stay by his side forever and support him!

DOÑA MARÍA
And you, where will you go?

SABELITA
I don't know… I don't know…

DOÑA MARÍA
What will become of you, all alone with no one to support you?

SABELITA
You have forgiven me, and now my soul is free of remorse. Goodbye, godmother.

DOÑA MARÍA
You are truly leaving?

SABELITA
Yes.

DOÑA MARÍA
No, it's not possible.

SABELITA
If I do not leave now, I may not find the courage again.
DOÑA MARÍA
That is true.
SABELITA
Godmother, do not allow another woman to steal your place.
DOÑA MARÍA
It's not my place but his heart that's at risk of being stolen! Embrace me, Isabel!
SABELITA
Goodbye, godmother!
DOÑA MARÍA
Goodbye, my daughter!

The two shadows stand still in a long embrace, weeping audibly. Then the younger phantom departs, and from the darkness of the room the clack of wooden shoes grows louder, foretelling the figure of the old serving woman.

MICAELA
Are you crying, my lady?
DOÑA MARÍA
Where is that girl off to in the night all by herself?
MICAELA
Our Lord will not abandon her.
DOÑA MARÍA
Lost on the road, where can she go?
MICAELA
To where her guardian angel points her. Oh! If only I were younger, she would not need to wander the world on her own, the poor lamb!
DOÑA MARÍA
Call her back!
MICAELA
Her soul is in peril here.
DOÑA MARÍA
Call her back to us! Any misfortune that befalls her will be my fault... All alone, with no one to support her, she might sink even further into iniquity.
MICAELA
Even if I call out to her, she will not return.
DOÑA MARÍA
Isabel! Isabel!
MICAELA
She is out of earshot. Let us pray for her, my lady.

Scene Five

A street. Night. SABELITA, *wrapped in her cloak and hood, walks along, hugging the edge of the walkway and whimpering like an abandoned child. The streets are deserted, the houses full of darkness and gloom.* SABELITA *can hear a cacophony of sailors' voices issuing from the taverns. Frightened, she hurries past the tavern doors which spill quavering light onto the cobblestones, making them appear to move. A drunken man's shadow wobbles on the corner and starts mumbling incoherently.* SABELITA *walks past, wrapping herself even more tightly in her cloak.*

THE VOICE OF A DRUNKARD
  Honey, I'm home... The wind was with us, honey... Sheathe those nails of yours, 'cause any good man needs to share a drink with his pals... Careful, we're sinking, taking on water! Hold on... if you're not my wife, ma'am, hold on a minute. I'm almost ready... You won't wait? We can set sail together...

The drunkard stumbles into the street toward SABELITA. *She walks faster and his drunken rambling fades into the distance. She passes through a square overlooked by a convent. It starts to rain. She comes across two older ladies escorted by a servant with a lamp. The wind whips against their skirts, revealing the contours of their bony legs and their undulating white slips. Their heads are hidden beneath the umbrella that shelters them. The servant looks curiously at the hooded figure crossing the square.* SABELITA, *having reached the other side, perceives their meddlesome scrutiny.*

ONE LADY
  Who was that?
THE SERVANT
  It looks like Don Juan Manuel's mistress.
THE OTHER LADY
  The niece of the late Archpriest of Lantañón?[7]
THE SERVANT
  I can't be certain...

SABELITA *picks up her pace even more. Despite the downpour which beats on their umbrella like a drum, the ladies have stopped in the middle of the square, and* SABELITA *feels their accusing stares. She cowers before the evil eye and then breaks into a breathless run. The clock tower strikes ten, and two priests emerge from one of the buildings, which is illuminated outside by a twisted iron lamp. They are the seminary's* DEACON *and* CHORISTER.

---

[7] The Other Lady refers to the Abbot of *Golden Boy*, the prequel which was written more than a decade after *The Blazoned Eagle* and *Wolves Rampant*.

THE CHORISTER
   It's raining, Don Lino!
THE DEACON
   My leg told me it was.
THE CHORISTER
   It looks like it will rain all week.
THE DEACON
   The new moon will bring a change in the weather.

Wrapped tightly in their mantles, the men of God continue down the street. SABELITA, *concealed in a doorway, watches them pass and gasps as she recognizes them: the great old friends who long ago gathered at the master's house and shared cups of chocolate with him. When they are gone, another figure approaches: the renowned nobleman, the Marquis of Bradomín, accompanied by a servant who carries a glass lantern.*[8] *Fearing recognition,* SABELITA *buries her face into her hood. The nobleman and servant fade into the night, their footsteps lingering just behind them. Time passes. It is still raining, and the clock tower strikes again. Tired, her nerves shot,* SABELITA *passes through other streets. In the doorway of a seedy gambling den, two shapeless masses stop what they are doing and stare at her. Even in the darkness she recognizes them by the horse one of them is leading.*

GOLDEN BOY
   Who could that be at this hour?
DON FARRUQUIÑO
   I don't know… But she looks young and tasty.
GOLDEN BOY
   Did you get a good look at her?
DON FARRUQUIÑO
   Only for a moment.

GOLDEN BOY *walks faster, trying to catch up with her. His mount trots behind him, its horseshoes clacking arrogantly and sacrilegiously in the empty street.* SABELITA *realizes she is being pursued and stops in her tracks.*

GOLDEN BOY
   It is you! Where are you off to, Isabel? Why are you trembling? Why are you crying?
SABELITA
   Why do you follow me? Who is that man behind you? One of your brothers? Leave me alone! Leave me alone!
GOLDEN BOY
   Don't be afraid, Isabel.

---

[8] These figures emphasize Don Juan Manuel's social and familial connections to the local clergy and aristocracy.

SABELITA
I'm not afraid of you. But your brothers...
GOLDEN BOY
You shouldn't fear anyone; I'm here to defend you. Despite all that's happened, I've never forgotten that time... And I don't blame you, because I know what and who led you astray. What's wrong? Tell me, why are you crying, Isabel?
SABELITA
I have left your father's house... I have left it forever... I want to return to you, his true flesh and blood, what I took from you... Don't hurt me. I am a poor fallen woman. I never conspired against you. Don't hurt me. Leave me be! Leave me be!

SABELITA runs off, leaving GOLDEN BOY dumbstruck in the road. After a few moments he resolves to overtake her again, but feels his brother's hand on his shoulder.

DON FARRUQUIÑO
You look petrified. Who was that?
GOLDEN BOY
I didn't recognize her.
DON FARRUQUIÑO
Don't you think she looks a bit like Sabelita? Too bad it wasn't, we could have given her a proper thrashing!
GOLDEN BOY
Spoken like a true peasant!
DON FARRUQUIÑO
Better than you trying to act the knight errant.

The two brothers retrace their steps, and in the doorway of the gambling den they complain about their bad luck and the deck from which a card-sharp inside is dealing.

Scene Six

SABELITA runs through the deserted streets, all the while imagining that she hears sneaking, treacherous footsteps in the dark. In mortal terror of the night, she is convinced her end is near. Leaving the town, she comes to an ancient Roman bridge, and the moon illuminates the stone crucifix in an archway erected long ago by a pious patrician. A dog barks, and two villagers wearing coarse shirts, breeches and berets stop her and doff their hats as a show of respect and a desire to speak with her. One of them is an old man with grey locks, the other, who appears to be his grandson, is a youth, slim as an ear of wheat.

THE GRANDFATHER
Slow down, my lady.
SABELITA
For the love of God, don't hurt me! I have nothing worth taking.
THE BOY
We are not thieves, my lady.
THE GRANDFATHER
We mean you no harm, and you have our deepest respects. I am Juan de Vila, at your service, and this young man is my grandson. We live on the other side of the river, four leagues from San Clemente de Brandeso.

The old man stops talking in order to count the tolling of the bell, which twelve times sends ripples through the night.

THE BOY
Midnight.
THE GRANDFATHER
Pardon us, my lady, but we need you to serve as godmother in a baptismal rite. Someone cast the evil eye on my daughter when she was a young girl, and now she cannot conceive a child. We were told that the only way to break the spell is to come to a bridge with a cross on it and then, after midnight, perform the ritual with river water. We have been coming to this spot three nights running. The first night we didn't encounter anyone who could help with the ritual. The second night a dog ran over the bridge and ruined everything. Neither my son-in-law on one side nor my grandson on the other could prevent this from happening. You must know, my lady, that in order to break the spell, no dog, no cat, no person may cross the bridge before the cleansing ritual is complete.
THE BOY
On my soul, that dog was actually a witch out to test our resolve. She hoped we'd give up and go home.
THE GRANDFATHER
She has her tricks, but we have ours! Witches know a lot, but there are good people who know even more. A wise woman told us how to thwart the demons and witches: at each side of the bridge we placed an old Moorish coin depicting King Solomon's seal.
THE BOY
See, my lady, everything has worked out, thanks be to God.

As they talk they reach the middle of the bridge where the cross hangs in the archway. Two cloaked women huddle below. They stand and mumble greetings. They are the mother and daughter-in-law. The former still has lively eyes nestled in her wrinkly face, the other is like a pale shadow whom pregnancy has given a frail, drawn appearance. The pregnant girl's HUSBAND *approaches from the other side of the bridge. Attached to his wrist is a metal-tipped wooden cane. He too offers a muffled greeting.*

THE HUSBAND
A good and blessed evening to you!

SABELITA
Please don't hurt me!

THE MOTHER-IN-LAW
My lady will be treated like a queen. Just do us this great favour.

THE PREGNANT WOMAN
God reward you here and in the afterlife!

SABELITA
The baby you want to baptize, where is he?

THE PREGNANT WOMAN
The baby hasn't been born yet, my lady. Didn't they tell you what kind of service we require of your kind heart? Poor dove, you're shaking all over! Did you think we would harm you?

THE HUSBAND
We don't bite, I promise!

SABELITA
They told me they needed me to act as godmother…

THE GRANDFATHER
Yes! But the baptism will be performed now with the baby in the womb, so he will be born healthy and on time.

THE PREGNANT WOMAN
An evil woman bewitched me with a poison apple, and I cannot give birth. Oh, Lord!

THE HUSBAND
Damned hag!

THE MOTHER-IN-LAW
We offered her a bag of wheat if she would break the spell, but she wouldn't take it.

THE HUSBAND
Damned hag! Only reason I didn't give her a beating was because I didn't want to deal with the police.

THE PREGNANT WOMAN
Our good Lord will punish her.

THE MOTHER-IN-LAW
Amen!

THE BOY *runs down to the river and returns, bringing a bowlful of water for the baptism. The old woman takes the bowl in her hands, kneels and presents it to* SABELITA.

THE MOTHER-IN-LAW
Bless and sanctify the water, my lady. What name have you chosen for the baby?
SABELITA
The one his mother wants.
THE PREGNANT WOMAN
It should be the godmother's choice.
THE MOTHER-IN-LAW
Why not your name, my lady?
SABELITA
Disgrace follows my name.
THE PREGNANT WOMAN
If it's up to me and it's a girl, let's give her the name of the most holy Virgin, Mother of God, the name I gave to my baby girl who died at three days old.
THE MOTHER-IN-LAW
And if it's a boy, we'll name him after my late husband. Ah, if he could come back from the afterlife he would be so happy to see his grandson!

THE PREGNANT WOMAN, *at the foot of the cross, her febrile eyes burning beneath her hood, lifts up her skirt to reveal her swollen pale belly, her actions so candid and full of conviction that there is nothing indecorous in them — in fact they appear sacred.* THE BOY *makes a torch out of rye straw, and* THE GRANDFATHER *reads in a deep baritone the formula of the ritual.* SABELITA *dips her hand in the river water and makes the sign of the cross over the accursed womb, and the unborn child stirs inside its mother. Night whispers the mystery of life under the red flame of the torch in the child's hand, like in a pagan symbol of love.* SABELITA *repeats* THE GRANDFATHER'S *words: the sacred formula breaks the spell.*

SABELITA
I baptize you with the holy waters of the River Jordan, just like St John baptized our Lord Jesus Christ. I baptize you with the holy name that bestows peace of mind and body. If you be a girl, you will bear the name of the Holy Virgin, and if you be a boy, you will take the name of St. Amaro Glorioso, who shared his table with Our Almighty God Jesus Christ. Amen.
THE BOY
Amen.

Playfully THE BOY *tosses the torch into the river while* THE PREGNANT WOMAN, *realizing that she is unclothed, lowers her skirts and closes her eyes, trembling, transfigured as if in ecstasy. Her lips tremble and she mutters ardently.*

THE PREGNANT WOMAN

The baby's kicking. Kicking in my belly!

SABELITA

Our paths will never cross again. Farewell, good people! Farewell!

THE MOTHER-IN-LAW

Where are you off to unaccompanied, my lady? There are three men here who can escort you.

SABELITA

I don't want anyone to accompany me. I'm travelling very far.

THE HUSBAND

We would accompany you to the end of the world.

THE PREGNANT WOMAN

Allow them to escort you, my dear lady. If you go off by yourself, I will worry myself sick.

THE MOTHER-IN-LAW

The roads are unsafe, all kinds of things might befall you.

SABELITA

Do not try to stop me… Do not follow me… Don't make me kneel down and beg!

THE GRANDFATHER

God forbid!

THE PREGNANT WOMAN

Allow me to embrace you, my dear lady.

SABELITA *approaches* THE PREGNANT WOMAN, *who wraps her arms around her shoulders and with respectful gratitude kisses her on her pale cold face which sorrows have rendered an immobile, tragic mask. The village girl's mystic soul senses the agonies and anguish with which* SABELITA's *heart beats, like a frightened bird in the hand of a child.*

THE PREGNANT WOMAN

Our Lord will watch over you wherever you might travel.

SABELITA

Thanks to you, my good woman!

THE PREGNANT WOMAN

Perhaps one day my eyes will see you again, relieved of all your troubles and burdens.

SABELITA, *breathing rapidly, departs without replying, running wildly once she realizes that she is in the fields in the middle of the night, again all alone. Overhead the distant and miraculous stars flash like thoughts trapped in the darkness of their monotonous, enervating and constant grief.*

THE PREGNANT WOMAN
   Go after her! Go after her!
THE HUSBAND
   We'll follow her, don't worry.
THE GRANDFATHER
   I'll go with the boy. A husband should look after his wife.

The old man and THE BOY *follow the shadow which runs along the riverbank. The rest of the group, silent and serious, return to the inn and from there, at sunrise, to the village. A donkey bears* THE PREGNANT WOMAN. *Her* HUSBAND *and* MOTHER-IN-LAW *walk at her side. Like clear spring water, the image of them on the village path calls to mind the naive, pious memory of the Flight to Egypt.*

Act Four

Scene One

The anteroom where two corridors meet. A mural unfolds on the wall, showing in pictures and text the legend of Señorita de La Valiera.[9] At the rear of the room there is a window at which DON JUAN MANUEL *diverts himself, shooting the swifts that fly around the dark myrtle garden in the blue afternoon. He still wears a bandage on his head. His cheeks are sunken and fever flares in his eyes. However, the real root of his malady is the memory of the loving and gentle figure who tamed the passions and violence of his life, like roses blooming triumphantly in the trunk of an old tree.* DON GALÁN *enters from one of the hallways.*

DON JUAN MANUEL
   Any news of her? I said I did not want to see you until you could tell me if she's alive or dead. So, what information do you have?
DON GALÁN
   I'm sniffing around, master. Like a bloodhound on the trail.
DON JUAN MANUEL
   She did not care that she was abandoning me in my old age and misery! No, she would not have left me if I were ten years younger. Then she would have remained my slave until her knees grew sore from kneeling before me... Other women have gone through that! The feeling that I feel now I have never felt before — it is the sorrow of old age, the chill of the grave. Each day, each hour that passes is another shovelful of earth before my tombstone. Ah, if I were only ten years younger!

DON JUAN MANUEL *stops talking and shoots out at a flock of swifts. The hounds bark in the distance. From one of the hallways come* THE MILLER *and his wife.*

THE MILLER
   Up ahead is the master, Liberata.
LIBERATA
   So wonderful to see you in good health, my lord.
THE MILLER
   May we enter?
DON JUAN MANUEL
   Yes, please. You just arrived?

---

[9] Louise de La Vallière (1644–1710) was a mistress of Louis XIV of France. Celebrated by Saint-Beuve and others as a perfectly selfless lover, she was also very pious. The point here is that, along with the portraits and heraldic symbols that detail Don Juan Manuel's lineage, the ancestral house depicts a version of Sabelita's story as well.

LIBERATA
Yes, my lord.
DON JUAN MANUEL
Liberata, I heard that you were in poor health, and here you are with a wan look to you.
LIBERATA
I had a fright the day before yesterday. I thought I was going to die!
THE MILLER
That is the reason we both came, to ask you to forgive...
LIBERATA
We cannot keep up with the mill, master. Don Pedrito has his knife to our throats.
DON JUAN MANUEL
And who is this Don Pedrito?
LIBERATA
You tell him, husband.
THE MILLER
But you understand the situation better, Liberata.
LIBERATA
He says that we have to pay him rent or else he will take the mill.
DON JUAN MANUEL
And you cower like little rabbits.
LIBERATA
We just want to live in peace, my lord.
THE MILLER
So we are turning over the key to you. Hand it to the master, Liberata.
DON JUAN MANUEL
You keep the key, do not test my patience.
LIBERATA
By all the saints in heaven, do not force me to return to the mill. Don Pedrito wants to kill me, he'll sic his dogs on me and have them rip me apart.
THE MILLER
It is painful to see her like this. Show the master your legs, Liberata.
DON JUAN MANUEL
The blackguard should know that your flesh is not for his hounds to touch.
LIBERATA
I have dog bites on my breasts as well.
THE MILLER
Show him, Liberata.
DON JUAN MANUEL
Pedro Rey, this bastard is not going to have his way. Is it in your interests to

maintain the mill and the Lantañón properties?

THE MILLER
Our duty is to serve the master, Liberata. Since he wants us to keep the mill, we will keep it.

LIBERATA
I am not afraid for myself but for the one I carry in my belly.

DON JUAN MANUEL
Do you want it or not?

THE MILLER
We want whatever you command. We know that you will not overcharge us on the rent.

DON JUAN MANUEL
No rent at all.

LIBERATA
My heart tells me that something bad will come of it.

DON JUAN MANUEL
No more tears! Pedro Rey, return to the mill, and if that upstart shows his face beyond the threshold, you have my blessing to gun him down. I give you my word that you won't go to jail for it. Women only get in the way in such matters; Liberata can stay here on the estate. Hold on a moment, I want it to be my shotgun that brings him down. I'll load it now.

THE MILLER *and his wife exchange happy yet nervous glances.* DON JUAN MANUEL's *hands, trembling with rage, pour the gunpowder in equal amounts into each of the barrels, then pack it down. A redolent breeze from the garden wafts over his hair and beard, which are as luxuriant as those of the three Magi.*

Scene Two

The bedroom of DOÑA MARÍA. *Her first night back at the estate. An antique bed frame, carved from lustrous walnut, looms in the background before crimson damask curtains, which add something liturgical to the room, as they call to mind aged ecclesiastical banners. A* BABY JESUS *in a white tunic embroidered with silver seems to float above the dresser among the lily-laden vases. Outside, hoofbeats resound on the flagstones of the square, and a horse neighs beneath the balcony. Someone raps softly on the windowpane. Shuddering, the lady hearkens even as her withered lips mouth a prayer. The hand knocks again, this time accompanied by a low voice.* DOÑA MARÍA *opens the doors to the balcony. Standing atop the saddle, gripping the window grille,* GOLDEN BOY *appears.*

GOLDEN BOY
Good evening, Doña María!

DOÑA MARÍA
Calm down, son.
GOLDEN BOY
Were you asleep?
DOÑA MARÍA
I was praying. Who's that with you?
GOLDEN BOY
I am alone.
DOÑA MARÍA
And your brothers?
GOLDEN BOY
I haven't seen them.
DOÑA MARÍA
I am not afraid of you. You've always been honourable and I trust you always will be. But don't stand like that on your horse, you will break your neck.
GOLDEN BOY
Death comes to us all, mother dear!
DOÑA MARÍA
Don't be silly.
GOLDEN BOY
Mother, I came to say farewell to you. I'm off to join the Carlists.
DOÑA MARÍA
God bless you! Do you need money?
GOLDEN BOY
Mark my words. Xavier Bradomín claims that men like me have only this one path in life. The day we cannot fight for a king, there will be nothing for us to do other than retreat to the countryside and live as robbers. That will be my brothers' fate.
DOÑA MARÍA
Stop! I can't bear it. You're killing me. What do you need? What do you want? I will sell my last trinket if need be, but don't tell me this is the last time I lay eyes on you!
GOLDEN BOY
Who said I would never return? I too have nine lives, like cats — and like father.
DOÑA MARÍA
But I won't see you again.

DOÑA MARÍA takes her son's face in her hands and kisses his forehead. GOLDEN BOY *respectfully removes his hat. In the distance, behind the cypresses, the sea glistens and beckons the young man to a life of adventure.*

DOÑA MARÍA
It is God's will, I suppose!
GOLDEN BOY
Amen, mother.
DOÑA MARÍA
When do you depart?
GOLDEN BOY
Tomorrow.
DOÑA MARÍA
Without your father's blessing?
GOLDEN BOY
I fear father will try to bless me with his gun.
DOÑA MARÍA
Son, be humble and ask to kiss his hand. I will intercede on your behalf.
GOLDEN BOY
Mother, I was loathe to say it, but yesterday you could have come to our defence. Yet you did not. Or perhaps you weren't able.
DOÑA MARÍA
You know how this whole affair pains my heart!
GOLDEN BOY
I'm well aware that father's love is always tinged with cruelty. He accuses all his sons, yet my mother does not tell him that only one of them was with Juan Quinto's gang when they entered this house.
DOÑA MARÍA
It wasn't any of you.
GOLDEN BOY
It was Pedro.
DOÑA MARÍA
You dare accuse him?
GOLDEN BOY
I do, which is why I'm hesitant to receive my beloved father's blessing.
DOÑA MARÍA
Then receive mine, my son.

DOÑA MARÍA leans over the balcony. Her moonlight-kissed hand traces a cross and falls gently on the handsome young man's arrogant head. GOLDEN BOY *respectfully kisses her hand, and drops back down in his saddle.* DOÑA MARÍA *sobs as she watches him depart, remaining on the balcony until he disappears from sight. Sorrowfully she goes back inside, kneels and prays.* THE BABY JESUS, *dressed in sequins and beads, smiles beneath his glowing nimbus and reaches out his innocent hands to the poor childless mother.*

Scene Three

THE BABY JESUS and DOÑA MARÍA wander in the woods, lost. They sit down to rest on the roadside. A rainbow covers the sky, and twelve black bells toll in the distance. Like hanged men, the twelve bells dangle from the branches of a gigantic tree.

DOÑA MARÍA
  Divine Child, tell me why the bells do toll.

BABY JESUS
  They toll for Sabelita. Hast thou not seen her walking on the other side of the river, and how a black demon pulled her by the skirt, dragging her into the water?

DOÑA MARÍA
  Save her from perishing in sin, Baby Jesus!

BABY JESUS
  If that happens, it will be thou who hast delivered that soul unto Satan.

DOÑA MARÍA
  Let us go help her, Baby Jesus!

BABY JESUS
  We don't know the way and we will get lost in the bush, Doña María.

DOÑA MARÍA
  We must hazard it, Baby Jesus. I will carry you in my arms, Divine Child.

BABY JESUS
  Thou art very old, thou dost not have the strength. Give me thy hand, the white dove will guide us.

DOÑA MARÍA
  Divine child, bless my arms so that they might carry you.

BABY JESUS
  But thou canst barely walk, Doña María!

They walk down the path to the tree from which hang the twelve bells, which as they approach transform into twelve crows who take wing and croak above their heads. DOÑA MARÍA *shudders.*

DOÑA MARÍA
  This murder of crows casts a shadow over my heart! Baby Jesus, allow me to kneel and pray for my god-daughter.

BABY JESUS
  Pray for her and for thyself, for when thou sawest her repent, thou feltest no pity for her in her despondency. If she die in mortal sin, thou wilt accompany her to Hell.

DOÑA MARÍA
Baby Jesus, do not torment my soul.
BABY JESUS
Learn to heed the voice of truth, Doña María. Cry, but do not let thy sobbing drown out my words. Don Juan Manuel doth tolerate the cruel jokes of his servant, yet thou wilt not heed the voice of the Baby Jesus.
DOÑA MARÍA
Forgive me, Divine Child.
BABY JESUS
Thou meanst to say thou did not know that she would be left alone and unprotected in her misfortune? Why didst thou not keep her by thy side and take her to the convent with thee? Thine evil nature prevented thee from protecting her, Doña María. The heavens recoil at this deed: allowing a repentant woman again to fall into sin. Evil is with thee; and evil and death await the best and brightest of your children, he who now rideth to war.

DOÑA MARÍA *halts, crying disconsolately.* THE BABY JESUS *walks along the edge of the path, picking wild daisies, and the lady, after a moment, raises her tearful eyes to him, calls out to him with maternal, pious alarm.*

DOÑA MARÍA
Careful, Baby Jesus! Shepherds set wolf traps along the path.
BABY JESUS
So easily frightened, Doña María!

These words still linger in the air as BABY JESUS *descends into the depths of a cavern. His disappearance is accompanied by a blinding radiance from which* DOÑA MARÍA *shields her eyes. Still seeing spots and shouting in rapturous fear, she then espies in the shadow of the bushes a maiden spinning silver wool on a glass wheel. The maiden lowers her work and approaches the edge of the cavern, where she lets fall the spindle. The pendulous instrument forms a luminous ladder which* BABY JESUS *climbs. Witnessing this miracle, the lady kneels and prays, recognizing the maiden who sat spinning in the bushes as the Blessed Virgin. A ray of moonlight dazzles her, and her star-drunk eyes, full of holy visions, again contemplate the lilies in their vases and the white robe of* THE BABY JESUS.

Scene Four

DON JUAN MANUEL MONTENEGRO, *having dined and drunk heartily while being entertained by his fool, rises unsteadily from the table and collapses onto his bed.* DON GALÁN *moves to take off his boots.*

DON JUAN MANUEL
   What time is it, Don Galán?
DON GALÁN
   Time for bed, master.
DON JUAN MANUEL
   Fetch Liberata.
DON GALÁN
   I'll whistle for her.
DON JUAN MANUEL
   She needs to warm the bed.
DON GALÁN
   Woohoo!!!

DON GALÁN *tucks his master in bed and departs.* DON JUAN MANUEL *has already fallen asleep when his fool and mistress come squabbling into the bedroom.*

DON GALÁN
   I hope you're not the jealous type, Liberata la Blanca! If only Don Galán were your husband! Woohoo!
LIBERATA
   Cut it out, you clown, don't wake my lord!
DON GALÁN
   You are the boss here, Liberata: the lady of the house.
LIBERATA
   I am no such thing!
DON GALÁN
   You are. Don't you know that Sabelita is gone?
LIBERATA
   Gone? I don't think so!
DON GALÁN
   If I'm lying, I'm dying!
LIBERATA
   To Hell with you and your fibs!
DON GALÁN
   Woohoo! As the bearer of good news, I feel I deserve a reward. I could use some new undergarments.
LIBERATA
   Don't imagine I don't know what you mean by 'lady of the house'!
DON GALÁN
   No such insinuation ever crossed my mind.
LIBERATA
   All you do is insinuate!

DON GALÁN
Cross my heart!
LIBERATA
Lying is a sin.
DON GALÁN
Alright, let us speak frankly.
LIBERATA
You say 'lady of the house', but you mean 'mistress in the bed'.
DON GALÁN
Woohoo!
LIBERATA
Am I right?
DON GALÁN
Woohoo!
LIBERATA
There, I can see through your fancy rhetoric.
DON GALÁN
Woohoo! You need to buy me that underwear.
LIBERATA
Oh sure, I'll have it made from the finest silk.
DON GALÁN
So magnanimous! Careful, you'll fall in love with me!
LIBERATA
Don't worry, I'll be sure to shut my eyes when you're nearby.

DON JUAN MANUEL *stirs in his bed, mumbling confusedly and snoring. The fool and the miller's wife pause in their banter. Dogs bark outside.*

LIBERATA
Oh! Hearing the dogs barking like that makes my skin crawl.
DON GALÁN
And such fine skin!
LIBERATA
Don't be an ass, you lecher!
DON GALÁN
If I were a dog, I'd lick you all over... And since your skin is so fair, I'd just have to nibble at it. But don't worry, I'll be gentler with you than Don Pedrito's hounds were.
LIBERATA
On about it again, are you, Don Galán?
DON GALÁN
We can get on about it, but not here... How about behind the door?

LIBERATA
Just think if the master hears you talk like that!
DON GALÁN
He'd have a good laugh.
LIBERATA
Good Lord, you can talk the talk!
DON GALÁN
The talk is my bread and butter.
LIBERATA
Hey, Don Galán, should I wait here until the master awakes?
DON GALÁN
Up to you. He asked me to fetch you; you've been fetched.
LIBERATA
But you know how things work here.
DON GALÁN
I'm still finding my way around.
LIBERATA
What if he sleeps through the night?
DON GALÁN
Get in the bed, it's plenty big.
LIBERATA
Enough with your naughty remarks, Don Galán.
DON GALÁN
But you asked.
LIBERATA
I only asked if you think I should wait or leave.
DON GALÁN
Come now, Liberata, you're new here, but not that new!
LIBERATA
Quiet!... I think he's waking up.
DON GALÁN
If you want him to really wake up, why not tickle him on his favourite spot?
LIBERATA
Again with you.
DON GALÁN
I'll leave you to it then.
LIBERATA
I'll just take a little nap in the corner here until my lord opens his eyes.

LIBERATA prepares to lie down next to the bed. DON GALÁN leaves, his cheeks puffed in a clownish grimace. LIBERATA watches him depart, crosses herself and kneels in prayer. At 'amen', she moves to lock the door and disrobes. Her skin pale and trembling, she pats the pillows and with feline grace slides into bed. The bedroom is silent, and silvery light flickers from the lamp. Beneath the floorboards, mice run about and chatter.

Scene Five

PICHONA's *house. An earthen-floor kitchen. By the light of the oil lamp* PICHONA *knits Camariñas lace. With no chimney in the one-room house, smoke from the fire escapes through the tiles. A wattle screen stands before the pine bed frame, which is painted blue. The bed's thin mattress is stuffed with corn husks, its sheets are burlap, its quilt is a motley assemblage of rags. Surrounded by her chicks, a hen scratches the dirt floor, her foot bound in a red tie made from one of* PICHONA's *old slips. Passers-by often knock at her window, making rude remarks, to which* PICHONA *replies with a litany of counter-insults which fade only as the instigators finally walk away.* PICHONA *is a lusty young woman who is always game for a good time. Someone knocks at the door.*

PICHONA
 Who is it?
DON FARRUQUIÑO
 Open up.
PICHONA
 I'm in bed. Who is it?
DON FARRUQUIÑO
 Ask the Devil to help you open up, Pichona.
PICHONA
 I think the key will be more helpful.

PICHONA *unbolts the door.* DON FARRUQUIÑO *enters in a festive mood and makes to embrace her. The girl pushes him away, and his student's tricorn hat, cocked rakishly on his head, is knocked to the floor.*

PICHONA
 Hands to yourself.
DON FARRUQUIÑO
 No Golden Boy today?
PICHONA
 I haven't seen him all day. He's distracted by something — or someone — else. I'm sure of it! His heart used to be mine, but some witch has put a spell on him, because it's been days since I've had a taste of his good love. Believe me, this bed hasn't seen any action for a month. Have you seen a coal burning hot and bright as the sun? And then you take it out of the flame and

it blackens and cools? Well, that's what's happened with the love of my soul and my body — even though he's not using my body anymore.

DON FARRUQUIÑO
That's no good. You'll dry up, because women, like plants, need watering.

PICHONA
Truer words were never spoken!

DON FARRUQUIÑO
Your grievances move me to offer some consolation. Time for that bed to be put to good use, Pichona.

PICHONA
Don't sow discord now.

DON FARRUQUIÑO
My prudish little Lucretia, you're what? Afraid of incest?[10]

PICHONA
Enough with the Latins, speak Christian.

DON FARRUQUIÑO
It's not Latin, Pichona.

PICHONA
It's all Latin to me, because I don't understand what you're talking about.

DON FARRUQUIÑO
But you're a smart girl; you can figure it out.

PICHONA
I figure it's something indecent.

The girl resumes her position under the lamp, her lacework on her lap, pins in her mouth.

DON FARRUQUIÑO
Pichona, when I am ordained, you can be my housekeeper. We'll have a wonderful life! Your hands were made for three things: making blood sausage, fattening up the cockerels and jarring preserves. This is all you need to be a perfect priest's housekeeper, Pichona.

LA PICHONA
You're not afraid the Holy Father will excommunicate you?

DON FARRUQUIÑO
To obviate such complications, you will call me Uncle.

---

[10] Don Farruquiño (and, thanks to the form of their education, the clergy in general) is clearly fond of classical allusions. Lucretia was a legendary heroine of ancient Rome, the beautiful and virtuous wife of the nobleman Lucius Tarquinus. She was raped by Sextus Tarquinius, son of Lucius Tarquinius Superbus (to whom the Abbot refers earlier), the tyrannical Etruscan king of Rome. After exacting an oath of vengeance against the Tarquins from her father and her husband, she stabbed herself to death.

PICHONA *laughs.* DON FARRUQUIÑO *draws near and pinches her. With a pin she pricks his hand and laughs with still more gusto. Someone from outside knocks at the window, which raises her hackles.*

PICHONA
> You out there, drop dead! Fall down and break a limb, you mangey, scabby, flea-ridden dog!

DON FARRUQUIÑO
> Surely this be one of the Eumenides,[11] not Moaning Pichona.

PICHONA
> Don't give me any nicknames. I bet you wouldn't like it if I called you Don Pockmarks. That name would stick with you your whole life, because your face is covered with the pockmarks the Lord gave you.

DON FARRUQUIÑO
> Pichona, I'm having second thoughts about taking you on as my housekeeper.

PICHONA
> I can do better than that.

Hoofbeats are heard outside, then the unsaddling of a horse. PICHONA *opens the door.* GOLDEN BOY *enters, leading his horse by the reins.* PICHONA *circles around him, submissive and affectionate.*

GOLDEN BOY
> Pichona, you have some corn to feed my horse?

PICHONA
> Not a single kernel.

GOLDEN BOY
> He'll have to fast then!

DON FARRUQUIÑO
> Not to worry, we'll take him to greener pastures. We need to set out for the Franciscan cemetery.

PICHONA
> To the cemetery! Why there? I know you're not going there to pray for your ancestors. Dear God, even for a gold coin I wouldn't set foot there at night! My mother's brother was bold enough to go there to fetch a bone, and he saw the Procession of the Damned! A few days later his jaundiced face drew its last breath!

DON FARRUQUIÑO
> Not to worry, I know how to exorcise the Procession.

GOLDEN BOY
> Let's go then.

---

[11] The Furies of classical mythology.

DON FARRUQUIÑO
    Boil a cauldron of water, Pichona.
PICHONA
    I'll get the one I use for laundry.
DON FARRUQUIÑO
    And give me a sack if you have one.

Taken aback, PICHONA *gives him an empty sack, and the brothers go out into the street without answering the girl's questions, which cease only when she closes and locks the door securely. She is left alone with her fear and curiosity.*

Scene Six

An alleyway. A dog roots around in a stable. It's raining. GOLDEN BOY *leads his horse by the reins and heeds attentively the discourse of* DON FARRUQUIÑO.

DON FARRUQUIÑO
    We'll go to the Venerable Franciscan Cemetery. There we'll dig up a skeleton and sell it to the Seminary. I've already spoken with them, and they support us completely, because at this point the one in the classroom is practically dust. It's a patchwork skeleton, made from a bunch of bones that don't even match. The tibias — one's from a dwarf, the other from a giant. When I was at Santiago Seminary I sold a fresh skeleton to them; theirs was just as bad.
GOLDEN BOY
    And they really gave you some coin for that?
DON FARRUQUIÑO
    One coin. You think it's not worth it?
GOLDEN BOY
    I've had no truck with skeletons, I don't know what to say.
DON FARRUQUIÑO
    O brother of mine, one copper coin is one more than we have now.
GOLDEN BOY
    I'll help you gratis. No point in divvying up a single coin!
DON FARRUQUIÑO
    Croesus could not show greater magnanimity at such a moment. Yet just a few hours ago you would have sold your soul for pennies.
GOLDEN BOY
    Yes, but tonight my luck's changed. Xavier Bradomín's purse is open to me, he's entrusted me with a very important mission to the Carlists' camp. In a few hours' time I'll be on my way.

DON FARRUQUIÑO
Lucky for you.
GOLDEN BOY
I think so. My only regret is leaving behind Pichona.
DON FARRUQUIÑO
Leave her to me in your will.
GOLDEN BOY
I'll need to leave her to my creditors to cover my debts — if her grief doesn't drive her to a convent, that is.

Rain continues to fall. The brothers descend the hill at the bottom of which the Venerable Franciscan Cemetery extends. They halt before the iron bars of a gate topped with a cross. Partially occluded by clouds, the moon illumines the black cypresses, which skirt the cemetery walls, and the ruins of a Romanesque church, which serve as an ossuary. The brothers peer through the iron gate.

DON FARRUQUIÑO
We'll need to hop the wall. I'll go first. Give me a boost.
GOLDEN BOY
And then? Who'll give me a boost?
DON FARRUQUIÑO
Once I'm inside I'll open the gate.
GOLDEN BOY
Maybe on the church side the walls have crumbled?
DON FARRUQUIÑO
They fixed it up.

DON FARRUQUIÑO mounts the wall with his brother's help, and once atop it, jumps to the other side. With the wall between them, they converse.

DON FARRUQUIÑO
I nearly broke a leg.
GOLDEN BOY
If you break it on that side, you'll have to remain there until morning.
DON FARRUQUIÑO
There's a cross half buried in the grass that I couldn't see. If it's a sign from heaven, too late.
GOLDEN BOY
I just hope you can open the gate.
DON FARRUQUIÑO
It's already open.

Through the gate GOLDEN BOY leads his horse, who sniffs the grass growing on the graves. FARRUQUIÑO leaves the gate ajar. As the horse grazes, the brothers inspect the tombstones for a suitable candidate. Behind the church ruins, out of sight, they search for a niche that will be easy to break into.

DON FARRUQUIÑO
  Let's try this one.
GOLDEN BOY
  Maybe this one here. It must be old. I can't make out the epitaph.
DON FARRUQUIÑO
  No wonder. It's been a while since they buried anyone on this side.

Selecting the one with the epitaph, they take hold of the bronze handle and pull away the stone which covers the grave. Slowly they remove it, revealing a cold and pitch-black hole. With one hand, DON FARRUQUIÑO draws out the worm-covered grave slab. Moths flit about his head. He draws forth the disintegrating slab on which lie dusty bones and the yellowed pages of a prayer book.

DON FARRUQUIÑO
  All dust. Let's try another one.
GOLDEN BOY
  How about this one here.
DON FARRUQUIÑO
  It's missing a handle.
GOLDEN BOY
  No matter.

They tug at the single handle, removing the stone cover and casting it on the ground. Within the niche they can make out a casket on the top of which a lizard scurries along. The two brothers heave and, using stones, they set about opening the coffin. Beneath a torn and ragged shroud, the blackened mummy, which still has patches of hair, can be seen.

DON FARRUQUIÑO
  We're in luck this time. Where's the sack?
GOLDEN BOY
  You had it.
DON FARRUQUIÑO
  It's over there on the grass.
GOLDEN BOY
  I hope this fellow fits.
DON FARRUQUIÑO
  We'll make him fit.

They dump the corpse head-first into the sack. When they try to cram the legs in, the makeshift shoes fall off, exposing hundreds of maggots. With the corpse bagged and stretched across the horse, they leave the cemetery. GOLDEN BOY is mounted in order to hold the sack in place. Catching sight of a group of students serenading someone with guitars and garrotes on a street corner, they change their route, taking a long detour to avoid detection.

Scene Seven

PICHONA's *earthen-floored kitchen. The candlelight dies out, and only the water boiling in a large copper cauldron disturbs the night's silence. The lady of the house has nodded off in the cosy warmth of the fire. The two brothers knock, rousing her, and sleepily she rises to unbolt the door.* GOLDEN BOY, *still mounted, hunches down to pass through the doorway, and after him follows* FARRUQUIÑO, *wrapped in his cape and hood.* GOLDEN BOY *pushes aside the corpse-filled sack, which makes a crunching sound as it hits the floor. The corpse's brittle feet poke out of the sack.*

PICHONA
  Sweet Lord!... Who did you kill?
GOLDEN BOY
  No reason to be frightened, Pichona.
PICHONA
  Sweet Jesus! Sweet Jesus!
DON FARRUQUIÑO
  Salt pork to last the whole year for you!

The terrified PICHONA *recoils in fear, moves to the bed and covers her eyes with the quilt.* GOLDEN BOY *moves to her side and pets her soothingly.*

GOLDEN BOY
  Take off my spurs, Pichona.
PICHONA
  God in Heaven, the law will be here any minute!
GOLDEN BOY
  Nothing to fear.
PICHONA
  Who did you murder?
GOLDEN BOY
  The good Señor Ginero. What do you think?
PICHONA
  A God-fearing person!
GOLDEN BOY
  That Jew feared the wrong god, Pichona.

With trembling hands PICHONA *kneels to remove his spurs. Meanwhile* DON FARRUQUIÑO *dumps the corpse into the cauldron, spilling the water which hisses as it drips onto the coals.* PICHONA *shrieks and clutches* GOLDEN BOY's *knees, mumbling incoherently.* GOLDEN BOY *smiles.*

PICHONA
 Why did you kill him? It can't have been you, you're a good person, it must have been your brother, who's as wicked as the centurions who whipped and beat our Lord. It wasn't you, right? Why did you listen to him? Clever as a fox and wily as a wolf, that one.

Ever smiling, GOLDEN BOY *bestows long hot kisses on her eyelids and lips to show his love for her. The girl's breath quickens.*

DON FARRUQUIÑO
 You don't have a bigger pot, Pichona?
PICHONA
 Even if I did, I wouldn't give it to you, you Judas.
GOLDEN BOY
 Easy, girl!… Simmer down.

PICHONA *continues to breathe heavily. Her arms around* GOLDEN BOY's *neck, she draws him to her. Entwined, they fall upon the creaking old bed. With one hand* GOLDEN BOY *caresses her warm white breasts.*

PICHONA
 Wait 'til your brother leaves.
GOLDEN BOY
 Don't mind him.
PICHONA
 It's embarrassing…
GOLDEN BOY
 I can't hold back!
PICHONA
 My king!

Locked in embrace, they start to kiss. DON FARRUQUIÑO *looks back and regards them peevishly.*

DON FARRUQUIÑO
 Any room for me?
GOLDEN BOY
 Your girl's in the cauldron there.
PICHONA
 Sweet Jesus!

DON FARRUQUIÑO

She's a leathery old witch with goat hide for skin. The meat's still not coming off her bones. Go on and entertain yourselves, children, it's going to be a while.

PICHONA

My sweetness, ask him to blow out the light.

GOLDEN BOY

Quit acting the nun!

PICHONA

Tell him.

GOLDEN BOY

Brother, your sister-in-law requests that you blow out the candle.

DON FARRUQUIÑO

Sorry, I'm reluctant to give up the view.

PICHONA

Judas!

The girl, with eyes shining and heaving breasts exposed, removes a shoe and hurls it at the lamp, which sways back and forth. In the chimney's firelight PICHONA's *ash-covered cat rears and hisses. The candle in the lamp is finally extinguished, leaving behind its burning odour. The darkness is punctuated by the cat's meows and the boiling water in which the mummy thumps around, occasionally revealing its still flesh-covered skull and black, claw-like hands.*

DON FARRUQUIÑO

I'll be damned if this isn't a witch's corpse! Skin like beef jerky, impossible to get off the bones. When I hit them with the tongs, it sounds like an old tambourine. Last time we dunked the corpse in boiling water and the bones were clean in just a few minutes. That's how the shepherds prepare bones for their dogs... Devil take me if this isn't a witch!...

Tongs pound against flesh and bone, the girl breathes heavily, and the cat continues to meow.

GOLDEN BOY

Your ablutions are upsetting our hostess, Farruquiño.

PICHONA

Don't go scaring me now, of all times, you fool!

DON FARRUQUIÑO

To Hell with you, Pichona!

PICHONA

It's you who'll be dragged down to Hell.

GOLDEN BOY

Still that tongue of yours, Pichona!

PICHONA
If it sweetens things for you, my love!

The cock crows, followed a few minutes later by the bell tolling for matins. DON FARRUQUIÑO *grumbles and curses, and his brother, now sitting on the edge of the bed, laughs heartily. The rising sun's rays enter through the window.*

DON FARRUQUIÑO
I need to be back at the seminary before sunrise… Damn the luck!
GOLDEN BOY
What's next? You tell me.
DON FARRUQUIÑO
Our only option is to return the witch to the cemetery.
GOLDEN BOY
Then let's go before the sun comes up.
PICHONA
So it wasn't Ginero after all!
GOLDEN BOY
You heard: it was a witch.
PICHONA
Sweet Lord! Sweet Lord!
DON FARRUQUIÑO
You weren't complaining a few moments ago.

Still in bed, PICHONA *covers her face and sobs. The brothers take the cauldron, pouring the water down the drain in the floor and placing the awful withered mummy, now black and bare, back into the sack.* DON FARRUQUIÑO *lays it across the back of the horse, which* GOLDEN BOY *begins to lead away by the reins as he places some coins on the mantle. At the threshold he turns and waves goodbye to the weeping girl.*

GOLDEN BOY
'Bye, Pichona! We might not see one another again. I'm off to join the Carlists.
PICHONA
I knew that.
GOLDEN BOY
Who could've told you that? I decided only last night.
PICHONA
The cards told me.
GOLDEN BOY
Good bye!
PICHONA
Take your money.

The girl, numb and despondent, runs her fingers through her hair and buries her face in the pillow. GOLDEN BOY *shuts the door and as he moves away thinks he hears a wailing voice. He picks up the pace to catch up with his brother. The two walk together in silence, hoping to avoid any pious early risers. When they reach the cemetery gate, they laugh with relief.* FARRUQUIÑO *adjusts his tricorn and cloak, then grabs the sack with the body, spins it around over his head and hurls it over the fence. The sack hits with a thud which echoes throughout the street.*

DON FARRUQUIÑO
   A miserable old she-goat, she was.
GOLDEN BOY
   Maybe it was Aunty Dolores. Damned old bag! She must've left all her money to the maid; nothing for us, not a penny. No love for family at all. She's surely wandering the circles of Hell.

The brothers leave, parting ways at the end of the street. GOLDEN BOY *spurs his horse to a gallop and disappears among the poplars by the river just as the church bell rings in the dawn. Two devout women descend the hill on their way to attend mass at the Venerable Franciscan Church.*

Scene Eight

A living room in the manor. Late morning. DON JUAN MANUEL *has been pacing from one side to the other since sunrise, when he unceremoniously rejected his new paramour. The fool moves aside the curtain and teeters drunkenly inside. His master's downcast expression greets him.*

DON JUAN MANUEL
   Who called for you?
DON GALÁN
   Woohoo! If you had called me, I would've pretended to be deaf.
DON JUAN MANUEL
   Your jokes fail to amuse me. I am too sad, you idiot!
DON GALÁN
   Well, any sad is 'too' sad, no?
DON JUAN MANUEL
   It feels like a worm is gnawing my heart.
DON GALÁN
   But it comes from your head, a stubborn thought that hatched there like a crazy crow, only to fly down and make a nest in your heart.
DON JUAN MANUEL
   I can't get her out of my head!

DON GALÁN
These eyes of mine have seen her — by the banks of the river.
DON JUAN MANUEL
Don't make light about this, Don Galán!
DON GALÁN
Woohoo! She's a shepherdess now! Who would've thought!
DON JUAN MANUEL
You reek of wine.
DON GALÁN
An error of perception, I assure you. I had only one glass for refreshment; I've never been more sober and lucid in my life. Woe is me! Even if I spent my annual earnings on wine, I couldn't get properly drunk anyway!
DON JUAN MANUEL
I could stomp you now like a bunch of grapes. I'm sure it would produce at least a cask of wine.
DON GALÁN
Woohoo! Look before you act. Could a drunkard balance like this?

A wobbling DON GALÁN *executes a number of ballet poses.* DON JUAN MANUEL *regards him with sombre disdain and continues to pace the room, sighing, his head hung low.*

DON JUAN MANUEL
She's dead, I can feel it! Sorrow eats away at my soul, which senses that she is gone.
DON GALÁN
I have seen Lady Sabelita.
DON JUAN MANUEL
It must have been a ghost.
DON GALÁN
Her heart was heavy, and she asked me not to tell anyone where she was… (*aside*) Stop wagging, tongue!

DON GALÁN *covers his wine-stained lips with his hand and laughs his clownish laugh, spraying spittle like a grotesque statue in a baroque fountain.* DON JUAN MANUEL *sighs again.*

DON JUAN MANUEL
Those hands, which so recently served me as if I were a king — they have already grown cold! I've seen her ghost as well. In its hands was a rosary formed from a great chain which it dragged behind.
DON GALÁN
Maybe what I saw was an apparition. If it's a ghost, it needs our prayers in

DON JUAN MANUEL
order to rest in peace.
DON JUAN MANUEL
Tomorrow in my chapel the priest will read one hundred masses.
DON GALÁN
Master, let us pray together for Lady Sabelita.
DON JUAN MANUEL
I forgot how to pray a long time ago.
DON GALÁN
You're no heathen, sire.
DON JUAN MANUEL
Tomorrow Don Manuelito will read a thousand prayers for her.
DON GALÁN
A thousand! Woohoo!
DON JUAN MANUEL
I think his prayers carry more weight than ours, Don Galán.
DON GALÁN
A thousand prayers won't hurt! Still, master, that's no reason for us not to add our own.

DON GALÁN kneels and clumsily, in the somnambulant manner of drunkards, crosses himself. DON JUAN MANUEL regards his fool's reflection in the mirror, which seems to him a chimerical, nebulous dream vision. DON JUAN MANUEL's eyes gradually tear up, adding even more haze to the fuzzy reflected image.

DON JUAN MANUEL
Do you even know how to pray, Don Galán?
DON GALÁN
Like the Pope himself.
DON JUAN MANUEL
Go on then.
DON GALÁN
Master, what if she's not dead? I saw her, and she spoke to me. (*aside*) Be still, my tongue! A prayer for Lady Sabelita's eternal repose, then. Master, we have neither aspergillum nor aspersorium.[12]
DON JUAN MANUEL
Shut up, you drunken oaf. I wish to pray, and you distract me.

DON JUAN MANUEL is deep in prayer, his head bowed and hands clasped. DOÑA MARÍA enters silently and approaches her spouse, who is engrossed in his rusty orisons.

DOÑA MARÍA
You are praying?

---

[12] The liturgical implements used to sprinkle holy water.

DON JUAN MANUEL

I'm praying for her!... María Soledad, shall we pray together? I'm at a loss...

DOÑA MARÍA *kneels and leads the Our Father. The lord and his fool do their best to follow along. At the prayer's conclusion* DON JUAN MANUEL *rises to his feet.*

DON JUAN MANUEL

María Soledad, you must pray on your own because my prayers count for nothing. The heavens do not heed them. I am a great sinner and I fear that the saints will stop their ears at the sound of my voice. But you are a saint yourself. Pray for her!

He strokes the head of his silver-haired spouse. DON GALÁN *makes a clownish grimace, mumbling incoherent prayers behind* DOÑA MARÍA.

DON GALÁN

My master says she is a lost soul. Woohoo! But I saw her recently in her cloak and clogs.

DOÑA MARÍA

You have seen my god-daughter?

DON GALÁN

My master said, 'Find her, Don Galán'. So I told the hounds, 'Come on, my brothers, let's sniff out the trail'. Woohoo!

DOÑA MARÍA

Where did you see her?

DON GALÁN

My master will find her and bring her back to the manor! Woohoo!

Seated before the lady, DON GALÁN *laughs heartily.* MICAELA *appears at the doorway to scold him with the authority of chief servant.*

MICAELA

What's this drunkard doing here? Off to bed, Don Galán!

DOÑA MARÍA

It's true what he said? It's possible that he saw my god-daughter?

DON GALÁN

(*aside*) Not a word, my lips are sealed!

MICAELA

Yes, he claims he saw her and that she was walking on her knees like a penitent, shouting that if the master went off to look for her, he'd find her dead. The poor lamb is afraid of falling back into sin!

DON GALÁN

(*aside*) She even kissed your hands, Don Galán! Your blackened peasant hands which didn't deserve the touch of her blessed lips.

DOÑA MARÍA
   Last night I had a vision that filled my soul with regret. A dream that was certainly a sign from Heaven.
MICAELA
   We are all sinners, incapable of understanding the motives of the spirits who visit us in our dreams. Nor can we comprehend their messages.
DOÑA MARÍA
   Sometimes when we dream, our soul can hear and understand them, but then we wake and forget it all.
MICAELA
   The day is for our fallen natures. It plays tricks on our senses…
DOÑA MARÍA
   Micaela, I will go find this sweet creature. I will tell her that she can be daughter to me once again.
MICAELA
   Doña María, my lady, my great lady, whom I love as both mistress and daughter! You are a saint on earth!
DON GALÁN
   (*aside*) Not a word, my lips are sealed!
MICAELA
   Up with you! Sober up, you drunkard, you're in the presence of our lady. Sober up, you need to lead her to Lady Sabelita.

The fool again laughs his drunken grotesque laugh, sliding around on the floor to avoid the wooden shoes which kick at him. DOÑA MARÍA *sits in an armchair engrossed in thought.*

Act Five

Scene One

A grand anteroom in the manor. The windows are shut against the scorching afternoon sun, and in the hazy unlit rooms one can feel the heat that signals siesta time. A saddle is perched atop a large trunk next to which lies a skein of half-wound linen. Two turtle-doves confined in a wicker bird cage outside sing in the shadow of the grapevines. LIBERATA *spins in the shade of the open door.*

LIBERATA
Rosalva!... Juana! What are you doing in the kitchen? Come here.
ROSALVA
We're coming.

The serving women take the spinning wheel and pull up stools to sit beside the miller's wife, just like two ladies-in-waiting at the foot of their queen. LIBERATA *looks at them cheerfully.*

LIBERATA
Doña María already left?
TAINTED JUANA
Yes. I knew she wouldn't be here for long.
ROSALVA
You're the lady of the house now, Liberata.
TAINTED JUANA
And may your reign be a long one. I must confess that at first I didn't really like you, but after a couple of days with you around, I've changed my mind.
ROSALVA
Same here.
TAINTED JUANA
Well, you'd be ungrateful to say otherwise. After all, who gave you that lovely shawl, and the jerkin and blouse? You might well have been naked before, and now you dress like a princess.
LIBERATA
I will give you a coral necklace that the master bought for me when I was younger.
TAINTED JUANA
As long as you're not the jealous type, your reign will be a happy one.
LIBERATA
I am no queen! I'm a servant just like you two. You have no idea how the master pines for Lady Sabelita! Tomorrow if not today we'll see her come

back through this door. He's been bewitched; his heart is hers forever.

TAINTED JUANA

For every spell there is a counter-spell, and one clever witch is no match for two.

ROSALVA

Spells can be broken.

TAINTED JUANA

Why not call on the Enchantress of Celtigos? She knows spells and has remedies for all kinds of ailments of the heart.

LIBERATA

I already went to see her.

ROSALVA

And what did she tell you?

LIBERATA

She told me that for any spell she'd need a scrap of one of Sabelita's favourite garments. Since I didn't have anything like that with me, she said she'd drop by the manor to pick it up.

ROSALVA

She's coming today?

LIBERATA

I'm waiting for her now. I don't suppose you can fetch me an article of her clothing?

ROSALVA

I have an embroidered kerchief that she gave me. I'll let you take it, but I'm afraid of something bad happening to her.

LIBERATA

Mother of God, girl! Why would something happen to her?

ROSALVA

I've heard things about that old woman of Celtigos! A girl from my town went to ask her for a spell to win the heart of a married man. The witch gave it to her, and the next day the man's wife died in a fire.

They hear a knock at the kitchen door. LIBERATA *rises to her feet and listens: more knocking, timid and peculiar. The three women exchange apprehensive glances, the spindles trembling in their hands.*

LIBERATA

She's here already! Rosalva, you won't deny me that kerchief?

ROSALVA

I just hope nothing bad happens!

From a pouch tied around her waist ROSALVA *pulls out medallions, scraps of bread and finally the folded handkerchief in question.* LIBERATA *walks to the door* and opens it cautiously. *The Enchantress of Celtigos appears wrapped in a shawl. Witch and mistress walk in silence across the room. As they leave,* TAINTED JUANA *and* ROSALVA *exchange frightened glances.*

TAINTED JUANA
Girl, I wouldn't do what you've just done, not for all the money in the world.
ROSALVA
Something bad's going to happen to Lady Sabelita?
TAINTED JUANA
Just the possibility is too terrible to think about.

Scene Two

A farmhouse near one of the old roads near Viana del Prior. Two women chat in the back of a hallway under the dark chestnut roof boards. Prodigious bunches of grapes hang from a beam. The open door allows for a view of the hills where the shepherds tend their flocks, and from another corner of the house one can hear the clacking of a loom. The two women chatting are THE PREGNANT WOMAN *and* THE MOTHER-IN-LAW.

THE PREGNANT WOMAN
Father is working fast with the loom.
THE MOTHER-IN-LAW
He needs to get some fabric to the Archpriest's maid.
THE PREGNANT WOMAN
I thought he was going into town.
THE MOTHER-IN-LAW
Seems he changed his mind, and it'll be me going to see Don Juan Manuel. I'm a compassionate woman, but she can't stay here forever.
THE PREGNANT WOMAN
Has she mentioned her plans at all?
THE MOTHER-IN-LAW
Not a word, and she's given no hint as to when she's leaving. A little charity's all well and good, but we can't have her here indefinitely. There's not enough to go around, and another mouth to feed amounts to less bread, less soup for us.
THE PREGNANT WOMAN
Good thing she doesn't drink wine!
THE MOTHER-IN-LAW
I can see that the girl doesn't want to be a burden. She says she's never tried wine, but I know she's just being polite. It's hard to hear her night after night tossing and turning and sighing. Believe me, if I had the means to follow my

heart and help her, I'd never allow her to leave.

THE PREGNANT WOMAN

What will happen to the poor girl? Father says that when my boy caught up with her, she knelt down by the river bank and begged him to just let her die because her sufferings eclipsed the brightest stars in the heavens.

THE MOTHER-IN-LAW

To see her wandering the roads like a homeless pilgrim, it's too much… If father won't do it, I'll go into town and seek help from Don Juan Manuel. The lady lived for a long time with him, and I seem to recall her having a son who lives in San Clemente de Brandeso.

THE PREGNANT WOMAN

A nobleman like him wouldn't leave her in such a pitiable state. I just don't get why she hasn't sent word to him before now. It seems like she'd prefer to die before he finds out where she is.

THE MOTHER-IN-LAW

I'm sure her jealousy's to blame. She was used to being queen of the castle and didn't want to share Don Juan Manuel's affections with the wife of Pedro Rey. This advice I gave to her: you need to be patient in this world. The worst is over; you're an adulteress, and your soul is already lost.

A long silence follows. THE PREGNANT WOMAN *raises her head and assumes an ecstatic pose. She whispers an account of the babe kicking in her womb, which seems like a cloister full of sacred, mystical virtue. The dark room with its chestnut ceiling is replete with rustic charm. It is like the smell of fresh autumnal apples ready to be preserved for Christmas jam.*

Scene Three

Celtic stonework festooned with thousand-year-old lichen casts its soothing shade on SABELITA. *From the threshold of the house, she is seen tending a cow atop the druidical hill the shape of a woman's breast.* SABELITA *has changed almost beyond recognition. She is now wearing peasant's clothing, a tow-colored shirt, a simple patched skirt and wooden shoes. Marela the cow pulls at her lead as she nibbles the grass which grows in the shade of those sacred stones. Suddenly, two dogs appear in the thicket. They are the greyhounds which are usually chained up in front of the manor.* SABELITA *pales when she recognizes them. With frightened eyes she stares toward the road. The dogs race forward and jump to lick her hands, barking with the joy of recognition. A man climbs up the slope of the hill: it is* DON GALÁN *who arrives, panting.*

DON GALÁN

Made it! Thank God! I've been running all the way from town.

SABELITA

The dogs scared me!

DON GALÁN

Woohoo! You were worried it was Don Juan Manuel? You thought that I must've told him how I spied you by chance by the river?

SABELITA

I don't know what I was afraid of!

DON GALÁN

It's my lady who's coming to visit you.

SABELITA

You told her where I was?

DON GALÁN

No. If I'm lying, I'm dying!

SABELITA

Then how did she find me?

DON GALÁN

Not a clue! She must've had a vision because at the crack of dawn she called for me and said, 'Don Galán, you have seen my god-daughter, and you must lead me to her so that my soul can be unburdened of this great sin. Go and ask the servants to saddle my mule.' Woohoo! So I began to wonder if it truly was a holy revelation or if it was Micaela. That wily woman was trying to wheedle it out of me, offering me French toast and a bottle of Arnela wine to loosen my tongue.

SABELITA

And you, you nincompoop, you told her everything!

DON GALÁN

Woohoo! It wasn't me, it was the bottle. But don't worry, her visit won't bring you any harm. Doña María is coming to fetch you and free you from this peasant business. Woohoo!

SABELITA

It is important that she cannot see me.

DON GALÁN *sits on the grass and nods his head gravely and sadly. He removes his knapsack and hands it to* SABELITA. *A timorous, tender flame flickers in the fool's eyes.*

DON GALÁN

My lamb, I've brought you some delicious pigeon stew. Woohoo! An abbot doesn't dine on anything better. I've also brought you two juicy red apples, the first ones we picked this season. Look at what beauties they are!

SABELITA

Doña María must not see me.

DON GALÁN

You are a dove of the royal dovecot, you were not born to eat peasant gruel.

SABELITA *sighs and stops talking, her eyes welling up with tears.* DON GALÁN *spreads a napkin over the grass and pulls the food out of the knapsack.*

SABELITA
Please put that away. Take the cow to the stable. I'm going to greet my godmother.

DON GALÁN
Please don't refuse a poor man's offering, Lady Sabelita. At least take this apple.

SABELITA *takes a rose-red apple and breathes in deeply the balsamic, floral scent. Her affectionate gaze turns to Marela the cow who grazes next to her, dragging her lead around the grass.*

SABELITA
I wish I could forget about all of life's sorrow and just be like you, poor Marela!... Take her to her owner, Don Galán.

DON GALÁN *winds up the cow's lead, licking at the tears which trickle down his face.* SABELITA *takes a path through the cornfields which leads to the river bank, the red apple heart-shaped in her pale hands.*

Scene Four

The bank of the river. Two hags stoop down to do the wash, and a family of sparrows sings in the reeds that spread out like a woman's luxuriant tresses over a mirror. In the distance one can make out the contours of a Roman bridge which a mule-driver is crossing. SABELITA *walks along the riverbank against the current with a dazed and vacant expression. The two laundresses regard her with surprise. They are* JUANA CREEPY-FINGERS *and* CROSS-EYED ANDREA.

JUANA CREEPY-FINGERS
Hey, you recognize who that is?

CROSS-EYED ANDREA
No, who is it?

JUANA CREEPY-FINGERS
You won't believe it! It's Lady Sabelita. Even in that old apron, I can tell it's her. She sees us now.

CROSS-EYED ANDREA
What's she doing here all by herself? I heard a rumour, though I don't believe it, that she's no longer with Lord Don Juan Manuel.

JUANA CREEPY-FINGERS
I'm pretty sure she's in trouble. See how she's walking into the river?...

CROSS-EYED ANDREA
  Mother of God!

The two hags rise up in alarm. SABELITA *reaches the middle of the river when the current takes her. The women wave their arms and cry for help. Their shouting rouses* THE FERRYMAN *who had been dozing on the other bank of the river. He unties his boat and casts off, rowing rapidly downriver. He catches sight of her bobbing up and down like a lifeless sack.* THE FERRYMAN *sets down the oars and probes the water to gauge the current. He then stands and dives in, immediately swallowed up by the greenish water. Several seconds pass. The two hags grow pale and silent, watching the river with terror.* THE FERRYMAN *finally surfaces, swimming with one arm and with the other hauling the girl by the hair.* JUANA CREEPY-FINGERS *and* CROSS-EYED ANDREA *fall to their knees to give thanks.* THE FERRYMAN *squints and catches sight of them and swims back upriver in their direction. Finally, his feet touch bottom, and he emerges from the river bearing the unconscious body of* SABELITA. *The two sisters run to him.*

JUANA CREEPY-FINGERS
  We thought you were gone!
CROSS-EYED ANDREA
  We prayed to the Holy Virgin for your safety!
THE FERRYMAN
  I owe her a candle on the altarpiece!

THE FERRYMAN *stands on rock and shakes the water off just like a wet dog, calmly regarding his boat, which has drifted into a bed of reeds.* SABELITA *lies still on the riverbank, and the two sisters unbutton her jerkin and try to warm her body. Along a path by the river a pilgrim on the way to Santiago calls to them.*

THE PILGRIM
  You need to turn her over so she can spit out the water she's taken in.

Scene Five

The path by the river. DOÑA MARÍA *sits side-saddle on her mule, guided by a* MULETEER *who shoos the gadflies that pester the animal.*

THE MULETEER
  Something is happening down by the river, my lady. Do you see all those people gathered there?
DOÑA MARÍA
  I see nothing. The years have taken their toll on these eyes.
THE MULETEER
  All the peasants have gone to the riverbank. Would you like me to see what's

going on, my lady? I will only be a moment, and when I'm there, I can talk to someone and confirm that we're travelling in the right direction.

DOÑA MARÍA

They say the house is just past Gándara de Brandeso. You don't know the way?

THE MULETEER

When I was a boy I knew this area well. It was like the back of my hand!

THE PILGRIM

Our Lady's blessings upon you! If you wish to remain in good humour, I advise going around the riverbank here. Local folk have gathered to gape at an unfortunate woman who appears to have drowned.

DOÑA MARÍA *crosses herself and mutters a prayer for the drowned woman, and* THE MULETEER, *without waiting for his lady's permission, races off toward the riverbank.* DOÑA MARÍA *continues on down the road. An* OLD WOMAN *tending three goats sits down by the side of the road and questions her in a sing-song voice.*

THE OLD WOMAN

Kind soul, would you tell me if the sun has set?

DOÑA MARÍA

Yes, a while ago now, grandmother.

THE OLD WOMAN

I wasn't born blind, but five years I've lived in the darkness of night. I tend these goats that belong to another poor woman in exchange for a few crumbs of bread. The animals know me well, and I know all the good grazing spots. My name is Liberata the Magnificent, and long ago people knew me for my apples and pears I'd bring to market. Those were the days! Then my youngest girl got married and left our house with nary a thought of me again. I tend these goats that belong to another poor woman in exchange for a few crumbs of bread.

DOÑA MARÍA

You will find your reward in heaven! I wish the Lord would show me such an easy road to paradise!

Her mule resumes walking but, with no one leading it, begins munching grass. THE OLD WOMAN *with the three goats hobbles behind, her sibylline voice trailing off in the silence of the night.*

THE OLD WOMAN

How sorrowful this life is! These goats care more about me than that daughter of mine. I just heard that a young woman drowned in the river. My heart stopped: I thought it was that she-wolf. At that moment I wished for my sight back, just so I could see her corpse. But even the dead won't have her. It was someone else, a poor girl who'd lost her wits! She used to bring her cow here some afternoons, and one day she told me that she knew my daughter and the gentleman who keeps her in one of the mills. Women should all be barren as mules! Our offspring give us nothing but grief, and we are all cursed only to bring more sinners into the world. Youth's lust compels us to swell the ranks of Satan's armies, and even innocent babes suckling at their mothers' breasts grew up and helped crucify our dear Lord. Oh, may sweet death bring relief! Oh, may sweet death bring relief! Oh, may sweet death bring relief!

THE OLD WOMAN's voice fades away as she falls behind the mule's pace. Between the poplars which gird the river one can make out the faint light of some lamps. DOÑA MARÍA allows the mule to walk at its own pace, and occasionally it stops worriedly to look back for THE MULETEER. The lamp-bearers approach between the poplars. The peasants' footsteps and talking can be heard. Greyhounds draw near, sniffing at the roadside. Trailing them is DON GALÁN.

DON GALÁN
My lady, go no farther! That white dove is no longer with us!

DOÑA MARÍA
Our Lord in heaven, You show me no mercy! Lord Jesus, cast no more shadows over my life! Lord, my old age was already full of sorrow, why add such remorse? Lord, this cross is too much for me to bear!

A whimpering DOÑA MARÍA sits down at the edge of the road, and the greyhounds run and jump around her, barking happily. The mule pricks its ears at their racket. DON GALÁN scolds the hounds and cries.

DON GALÁN
Cursed beasts, cut it out! You irrational creatures can't understand the sufferings of the world, things that we Christian people know so well. Shut up, you rogues! Greymane, Liberal, don't scare the mule. And be still, for the love of God! Not long ago you jumped around just like this at that poor lamb. Ingrates, remember how you licked at those hands, which fed you and which have now grown cold.

The lamps among the poplars grow brighter as they approach. On a makeshift berth some peasants carry the woman covered in a white linen shroud. Only her hanging tresses can be seen.

THE PILGRIM
I encountered this poor woman on the road. It seemed to me that she had lost her wits.

CROSS-EYED ANDREA
She was clutching at the river bottom, that's how badly she wanted to die.

The ferryman has algae under his fingernails from trying to wrest her free.

JUANA CREEPY-FINGERS
Looks like she's dead!

CROSS-EYED ANDREA
She's not dead, her heart's still beating.

JUANA CREEPY-FINGERS
I laid my ear on her breast, and I couldn't hear anything.

CROSS-EYED ANDREA
It's beating faintly, very faintly…

THE PILGRIM
Where should we take her?

A SHEPHERD BOY
She was staying at the weaver's place. Just today she was tending the cow there…

JUANA CREEPY-FINGERS
I think it's best to take her into town.

THE PILGRIM
Does she have any family there?

CROSS-EYED ANDREA
She used to live the life of a queen, but now she doesn't even have a plot of hay to die on.

Some voices are heard behind the trees. Figures approach the assembled group. The night fog obscures the people and their lamps. With effort DOÑA MARÍA *stands and walks to meet the arrivals.*

Final Scene

A room in DON JUAN MANUEL MONTENEGRO's *home. It is night, and a tallow candle gives off a faint light. Two servants remove a tablecloth from the cupboard. In a peevish mood,* DON JUAN MANUEL *enters and sits in an ornate armchair at the head of the table.*

DON JUAN MANUEL
Summon your mistress to the table.

TAINTED JUANA
Lady María has gone.

DON JUAN MANUEL
Everyone has abandoned me!… Liberata! Liberata!

LIBERATA
At your service, my lord.

DON JUAN MANUEL
   Sit and dine with me.

Hunched despondently over the table, he clutches his head in his hands. LIBERATA *enters the room with a feverish expression in her eyes. Sensing her presence,* DON JUAN MANUEL *sits upright in the chair. The two servants begin serving, gliding around the table and to and from the kitchen.* DON JUAN MANUEL *drinks copiously and eats with a rustic, animal gusto, like a Homeric hero of old. His mistress takes a place at his side in order personally to keep his plate and goblet full.*

DON JUAN MANUEL
   Has that husband of yours stuck his horns through my door today?[13]
LIBERATA
   He was here at dusk…
DON JUAN MANUEL
   I thought I heard his voice.
LIBERATA
   He is a good man, and for that reason he will lose his shirt. Again, one of my lord's sons showed up at the mill.
DON JUAN MANUEL
   What did the blackguard want?
LIBERATA
   He left his horse there and took two cows. He mounted one and, facing backwards, crossed the river, using the tail for a brake.
DON JUAN MANUEL
   And why didn't your miller greet him with some buckshot?
LIBERATA
   I told you, he's a good man.
DON JUAN MANUEL
   Didn't I give him my shotgun and promise to keep him out of jail if he used it?
LIBERATA
   Yes, but it wasn't Don Pedrito this time.
DON JUAN MANUEL
   Who then?
LIBERATA
   Golden Boy, who's gone off to join the Carlists… He took the shotgun too.

DON JUAN MANUEL *knits his brow and scowls for a moment, then erupts into his violent, feudal laughter. The miller's wife takes her cue again to tend his goblet,*

---

[13] A reference to the common image of the cuckold.

which fills with the sanguine juice of the grapes that GOLDEN BOY's steed used to graze on. When the nobleman finishes his drink, MICAELA enters.

MICAELA
  Master, why do you break bread with this evil woman, when death stalks your hallways?

DON JUAN MANUEL
  What are you on about, madwoman?

MICAELA
  Hark! The voices of the good souls who have gathered down by the river!... Hark! The howling of the dogs!

DON JUAN MANUEL
  I hear nothing, thanks be to God. More wine, Liberata. Her hundred years have deranged her! I'm sure she nodded off in the kitchen during her prayers and then had a bad dream.

LIBERATA
  Oh dear! Her words struck home somehow.

From the kitchen comes the voice of a peasant woman who solemnly and piously describes to the servants how she caught sight of a young woman's hair and pale hands poking out of the river. Other beggar folk amend her narrative as they wait for handouts, bragging about their roles in saving the poor girl who lost her wits. Above the expectant jabbering rises the authoritative voice of DON JUAN MANUEL.

DON JUAN MANUEL
  What's going on in my house? This riff-raff is talking or praying? You say death has crossed my threshold?

MICAELA
  I do.

DON JUAN MANUEL
  Death for whom?

MICAELA
  For all the innocents.

DON JUAN MANUEL
  In that case we sinners have nothing to worry about.

DON JUAN MANUEL *drains his goblet again.* DOÑA MARÍA *approaches from the long hallway, a vague shadow still some distance away. The long-suffering lady walks slowly and stops at the doorway, a grave and severe expression on her face.* DON JUAN MANUEL *kicks over the chair of the miller's wife, who dares not rise from the floor.*

LIBERATA
  Sweet Lord, I hope she doesn't see me!

DON JUAN MANUEL
  Get under the table, bitch.
MICAELA
  Rabid bitch!
DON JUAN MANUEL
  (*to Micaela*) Silence! (*turning to Doña María*) I thought you had abandoned me, María Soledad.

With quiet dignity the long-suffering lady is met by the farce of her husband's attempting to hide his mistress under the table. A few moments pass before she finds her voice, which sounds pious and languid, like the whisperings of errant souls wandering the land.

DOÑA MARÍA
  You will leave this house, and you will not return while this poor creature remains here. Our Lord was not ready to receive her, and she was rescued from the river… I have forgiven her; she is daughter to me once again.
DON JUAN MANUEL
  Where is she?
DOÑA MARÍA
  Here!… But make no attempt to see her.
DON JUAN MANUEL
  Who'd dare to stop me?
DOÑA MARÍA
  I do… And when she is well enough I will take her away with me, and the first house to show us charity and offer us a corner to lay our heads, we will stay there.
DON JUAN MANUEL
  This is the house of my ancestors! For three hundred years it's been with us!
DOÑA MARÍA
  Do not worry, you will return to it soon.

DON JUAN MANUEL, *his hand trembling, passes a steaming plate of food under the table to his mistress, who still hides there.*

DON JUAN MANUEL
  Eat your fill.
DOÑA MARÍA
  Farewell forever!
DON JUAN MANUEL
  Wait. You've really forgiven her?
DOÑA MARÍA
  I forgave you, did I not?

DON JUAN MANUEL

María Soledad, your heart is big but volatile! María Soledad, you are a saint — Devil take me if I'm lying! Let's go, woman!

He kicks at the table, shifting the tablecloth, stained blood-red by the spilled wine, and knocking everything onto his cowering mistress. DOÑA MARÍA *leaves.*

LIBERATA

Please don't hurt me! Remember what I carry in my belly!

DON JUAN MANUEL

Stop yelping, you bitch! Come with me.

LIBERATA

I can't move!

DON JUAN MANUEL

Enough with the yelping, I said! We're leaving this house… Come!

Their footsteps echo throughout the halls as they descend the white stone staircase. They come to the deserted, silent square outside. Above the doorway, the coat-of-arms with its knight's spurs and triumphal eagles stares down at the weeping lord of the manor, and the moon shines upon his bare head. The fool also exits the house and approaches his master, who does not notice his presence.

DON GALÁN

With the weight of our sins on our shoulders, where can we go?

DON JUAN MANUEL

I have no idea…

LIBERATA

Sweet mother of God, the night is fierce!

DON GALÁN

No matter to us — we are three stars in the night sky.

DON JUAN MANUEL

Perhaps you are a star, for you are one of God's own… But this one here is a mongrel bitch, and I am a lecherous old wolf, a lecherous wolf, a lecherous wolf…

He moves away, fleeing his companions. His words and his footsteps resound in the empty square. His shattering pronouncement lingers in the air. Gusts of wind dishevel his hair and hoary beard. The fool and the mistress walk behind, finally losing all sight and sound of him in the darkness.

Wolves Rampant

Dramatis Personae

DON JUAN MANUEL MONTENEGRO aka the Mayorazgo, the Lord of the Manor, the Vinculero

His sons: DON PEDRITO, DON ROSENDO, DON MAURO, DON GONZALITO and DON FARRUQUIÑO

His servants: DON GALÁN, Ginger-MICAELA, THE CATTLE-HAND, ANDREIÑA, REBOLA and RECOGIDA

His CHAPLAIN: Don Manuelito

THE MARINER

Abelardo, the ship's CAPTAIN, THE SAILORS, and THE BOY

DOÑA MONCHA and BENITA THE SEAMSTRESS, various FRIENDS OF THE FAMILY

The band of beggars: THE MENDICANT OF SAN LÁZARO, DOMINGA DE GÓMEZ, THE ONE-ARMED MAN FROM LEON, THE ONE-ARMED MAN FROM GONDAR, THE CRIPPLE FROM CELTIGOS, PAULA 'THE QUEEN' and the BABY at her breast, ANDREIÑA THE DEAF, CIDRÁN 'THE BAT', CIDRÁN'S WOMAN, and ADEGA THE INNOCENT

ARTEMISA OF CASAL, the illegitimate daughter of DON JUAN MANUEL, with her young son, FLORIANO

THE BLIND MAN OF GONDAR with his GUIDE

FILTHY FUSO, a madman

The group of seven herdsmen: MANUEL TOVIO, MANUEL FONSECA, PEDRO ABUÍN, SEBASTIAN DE XOGAS and RAMIRO DE BEALO with his TWO SONS

DOÑA ISABEL aka SABELITA, the mistress of Don Juan Manuel

THE WIDOW with her FOUR ORPHANED SONS

PENITENT SOULS partaking in THE PROCESSION OF THE DAMNED

Act One

Scene One

A road. The air is thick with the pungent verdure of the village cemetery, which can be seen in the distance. It is night, and fresh moonbeams shine through the cypress trees. The Lord of the Manor, DON JUAN MANUEL MONTENEGRO, *returning home drunk from the fair, crosses the road on a colt that is clearly restive and unaccustomed to the saddle. The nobleman totters atop the beast, riding him in ungainly fashion, tugging at the reins and at the same time spurring him on. The rearing steed finally elicits both the consummate horsemanship and the fiercest execrations of its rider.*

DON JUAN MANUEL
   Damned beast!... Possessed by all the demons of Hell!... May the Lord smite me right here and now and get it over with!
A VOICE
   Sinner! Utter no profanity!
ANOTHER VOICE
   Your soul is black as coal dug from the depths of Hell!
A THIRD VOICE
   Think of the hour of your death, O sinner!
A FOURTH VOICE
   Seven demons prepare a cauldron of boiling oil, ready to receive your sinful mortal flesh!
DON JUAN MANUEL
   Who are you that speak to me? Voices from beyond the grave? Souls in pain, or simply miserable whoresons?

At the sound of thunder rending the air the colt rears and nearly throws its rider. In the cornfields shine the lights of the Procession of the Damned. Goosebumps and a sudden sobriety visit DON JUAN MANUEL *as he hears agonized groans and the clanking of chains being dragged through the dark night — tortured souls who have returned to earth in order to do penance. Like a cloud the white procession passes over the cornfields.*

A VOICE
   Sinner! Join us!
ANOTHER VOICE
   Take a candle and join our company, sinner!
A THIRD VOICE
   Join us on the road to the churchyard, sinner!

DON JUAN MANUEL *feels the cold chill of death as a candle's flame seems to flicker suddenly in his hand. The procession of souls surrounds him, and a gust of cold and graveborn wind pulls him to the centre of the pale phantoms who clank their chains and chant psalms in Latin.*

A VOICE
   Join the dead and pray for those about to die! Pray, sinner!
ANOTHER VOICE
   Walk among us until the black cock crows!
A THIRD VOICE
   You are a brother to us, and our sire is Satan himself!
A FOURTH VOICE
   Sin runs through our veins; it proves our kinship!
A FIFTH VOICE
   The hairy teats of the Demon Mother gave you suck as they did us! We are drunk off her unholy milk!
MANY VOICES
   Hear the pots breaking? It's the lame cross-eyed mother! That she-goat who ties corded belts onto whoring monk-brothers! Belts that string up the hanged man, fruit of thrice-accursed womb! Cross-eyed crow mother, delousing herself with an old hag's-tooth comb! Mangy bitch mother who squats to piss in the flames! Who keeps pins in a goat horn cinched to her waist! Who sews the girls' hymens shut, who's drunk on disgrace! Who mends cuckolded husbands' soiled underthings!

DON JUAN MANUEL *feels a jolt that knocks him from the saddle, and his steed bolts off with unholy speed. Still clutching at the candle, he looks to its wavering light and discovers to his horror that he holds only a bone from a human skeleton. He shuts his eyes and feels the ground give way beneath his feet, and then he is borne aloft through the air. When he finally dares open his eyes, he sees that the company has halted at the river bank where witches seat themselves in a ring formation. On the opposite bank passes a funeral procession. A cock crows.*

THE WITCHES
   The white cock has crowed! Sing now!

The phantoms disappear in a cloud, and the witches begin raising a bridge as bats flutter atop the river which seems as wide as the sea. On the opposite bank the funeral train has now stopped. Another cock crows.

THE WITCHES
   The brown cock crows, let him sing!

Through a dense mass of smoke the arches of the bridge begin to rise. The waters, black and sinister, spume below, roiled by the fires of Hell. With only one stone left to put in place, the witches make haste, for the dawn will break at any moment. The funeral train, now perfectly still, waits for the bridge to lower so that the company might cross. Another cock crows.

THE WITCHES
  The black cock crows, let him sing!

Having taken the form of a whirlwind, the witches drop into the bottom of the stream the stone they had been carrying. Then, transforming themselves into bats, they fly off. The funeral procession turns toward the village and disappears into the fog. DON JUAN MANUEL, *as if awakening from a dream, finds himself sprawled out in the middle of the path. The moon has passed behind the cypress trees, crowning them with a golden nimbus. The horse grazes over the fragant and dewy grass which grows by the wall.* DON JUAN MANUEL *mounts it and takes the road home.*[1]

Scene Two

DON JUAN MANUEL MONTENEGRO *bellows outside the entrance of his house. His dogs, chained in the orchard below, start barking wildly. In the tower, high above the nobleman's head, a window opens, and the gnarled face of an old woman, wearing only a nightgown and holding a candle, peers down.*

DON JUAN MANUEL
  Put out that light…
MICAELA
  I'll be right down to open the door.
DON JUAN MANUEL
  Put out that light…

He puts his hands over his eyes and, holding that position, waits for the old woman to step away from the window. The horse scrapes its hoof, and DON JUAN MANUEL *does not dismount until he hears the door being unlocked. The old servant appears with the candle in her hand.*

DON JUAN MANUEL
  Blow out that light, you evil hag!
MICAELA
  Mother of God! So ferocious! Like opening the door to a snarling wolf!

---

[1] The whole scene calls to mind Goya's Black Paintings. This play, as well as Valle's *Bohemian Lights*, sees the author developing the aesthetics of 'Esperpento' (see Introduction.)

DON JUAN MANUEL
I witnessed the Procession of the Damned![2]
MICAELA
Begone, foul witches! I deny thee, Satan!

The old woman blows out the candle and crosses herself in fear. She shuts the front door and hurriedly gropes toward her master, who is already ascending the steps.

DON JUAN MANUEL
Having seen the lamps of Death, I can endure no other lights... for the Reaper comes for me.
MICAELA
You act as if you'd seen the light.
DON JUAN MANUEL
And if more life be granted to me, I would remain blind until the light of the sun is reborn.
MICAELA
Amen!
DON JUAN MANUEL
My heart has tidings for me, but what they are I do not know... I feel as if a bat were circling over my head, and the echo of my footsteps on this dark stairway fill me with fear, Micaela.
MICAELA
Get thee behind me, Satan! Get thee behind me, Satan!

At the top of the stairs DON JUAN MANUEL *is halted by the neighing of a beast and a banging on the door.*

DON JUAN MANUEL
Did you hear that, Micaela?
MICAELA
I did, master.
DON JUAN MANUEL
What in the Hell?
MICAELA
Do not curse, master!
DON JUAN MANUEL
I forgot about the beast!
MICAELA
The goblin's steed!

---

[2] According to some traditions, witnessing the Procession of the Damned augurs death.

DON JUAN MANUEL

My steed! Wake Don Galán so he can stable him.

MICAELA

I tried to rouse him before to get him to open the door, but he's dead to the world. Begging my lord's pardon, I even kicked him with my wooden shoe on.

DON JUAN MANUEL takes a seat in the anteroom, and the old woman crouches by the bar to the door. They still hear the occasional whinny and hoof beating against the door.

DON JUAN MANUEL

Try waking him up again.

MICAELA

He's sleeping like a rock.

DON JUAN MANUEL

Give it to him again with your clog.

MICAELA

Even a swift kick to his backside won't get him up.

DON JUAN MANUEL

Then take your candle and set fire to the straw of his bed.

MICAELA

Holy Mother!

The old woman shuffles off to carry out the errand, groping her way in the darkness. A cock crows, and the nobleman, sunk into his chair in the antechamber, puts his hand over his eyes and waits. Suddenly he shudders. He believes he has heard a cry, one of those cries in the night which are incoherent and for that reason all the more dreadful. Sitting up alertly, he listens. The wind worries at the window sills, the rain beats at the panes, and the locked doors tremble in their frames. Clatter!... Clatter!... Those doors with their antique ironwork and embellished latches feel the pressure from unseen hands in the darkness. Clatter!... Clatter! A sudden rush of silence lends the house the atmosphere of a tomb. Eventually footsteps and murmuring voices sound in the hallway: the old woman and DON GALÁN appear, bickering as they enter.

MICAELA

We stabled the horse. What a night, Most Holy Mother of God!

DON GALÁN

The sky's booming and flashing — pretty scary.

MICAELA

And not to be able to light the wick of a single blessed candle!

DON GALÁN

What, you don't have one?

MICAELA
Oh, I have one, but there's no lighting it this fierce night. I have two half-candles left over from the vigil for my cousin Celana.
DON JUAN MANUEL
Did you hear that?
MICAELA
What, master?
DON JUAN MANUEL
A voice...
DON GALÁN
The wind goblin's cackling...

A pounding at the door resounds in the darkness of the manse. DON JUAN MANUEL *rises to his feet.*

DON JUAN MANUEL
My shotgun, Don Galán. I'll wing that wind goblin, just watch!
DON GALÁN
Hear how he cackles!
MICAELA
He'll only disappear in a puff of smoke, you'll see...

DON JUAN MANUEL *opens the window, and a wind rushes in with a tempestuous swirl, seizing and shaking everything in the room. Lightning illuminates the deserted courtyard where the cypresses sway desperately in the wind. Another flash reveals the face of a mariner in a sou'wester and raincoat. His hand is on the door knocker. The rain hits the face of* DON JUAN MANUEL MONTENEGRO.

DON JUAN MANUEL
Who's there?
THE MARINER
A sailor, one of Abelardo's crew.
DON JUAN MANUEL
Did something happen?
THE MARINER
A letter from the good chaplain. Lady María has fallen very ill.
DON JUAN MANUEL
Dead!... She's dead!... My poor Russian doll![3]

He steps away from the window, whose panes clatter in the pounding wind, which swirls from one side of the room to the other in the darkness. The old woman and the fool, now speaking only in whispers, descend the stairs to let in THE

---

[3] An affectionate nickname recalling the earlier, happier years of their marital relations. The Russian nesting doll is called a 'Matryoshka'.

MARINER. The saturnine wind writhes throughout the antechamber. Violently the windows swing shut; then with tragic inevitability they burst open again. Joining the servants is THE MARINER, *who stops at the threshold, not daring to step into the dark room. As* DON JUAN MANUEL *puts questions to him, a flash of lightning illuminates their livid faces.*

DON JUAN MANUEL
 You have a letter?
THE MARINER
 Yes, my lord.
DON JUAN MANUEL
 I can't read it at this moment. You tell me of the misfortunes it contains... Is she dead?
THE MARINER
 No, my lord.
DON JUAN MANUEL
 She has been ill for a long time?
THE MARINER
 No, it came on all of a sudden. But they say she's been very sick for a while now.
DON JUAN MANUEL
 She is dead! It was her funeral train I saw this night, and what seemed to be a river was actually the sea that divided us!

He falls silent in the shadows. No one dares respond to his words, and all that can be heard is the murmur of a prayer. DON JUAN MANUEL *senses in the darkness a shadow kneeling at his side. He shudders.*

DON JUAN MANUEL
 Is that you, Micaela?
MICAELA
 Yes, master.
DON JUAN MANUEL
 Give this man food and drink, so that he'll be able to travel again presently. Ah, black night!

Scene Three

Night on a storm-battered beach. Some poor women, wrapped in black cloaks, stand motionless on the rocks, awaiting the return of the fishing boats. The sea, howling and dark, breaks against the rocky beach, lapping at their bare callused feet. The seagulls swoop around the beach, and their incessant squawking mingles with the wailing of a baby whose mother has it wrapped tightly in her cloak, and joining this cacophony is the awesome voice of wind and sea. Among the shadows burns the light of a torch. DON JUAN MANUEL *and* THE MARINER *are heading down to the beach.*

THE MARINER
>My lord realizes that this is no weather to be setting sail in?

DON JUAN MANUEL
>Where is your boat moored?

THE MARINER
>Leeward of Castelo.

DON JUAN MANUEL
>We can sail the same course you took to get here.

THE MARINER
>We had clear daylight then, and no wind like this when we set out from Flavia-Longa. The sea still tore at us. Look to the south-east, how rough it is. How black the clouds are!

DON JUAN MANUEL
>How black indeed… like your cowardice!

THE MARINER
>The sea is a very different creature from the land, my lord Don Juan Manuel, and must be accorded her due respect!

DON JUAN MANUEL
>You're no mariners, just old women!

THE MARINER
>We are sailors who don't ignore the dangers that the crossing can set before us. And the sea, yes, the more we know her, the more we fear her. Those who don't fear her, they don't know her.

DON JUAN MANUEL
>I know her and I don't fear her.

THE MARINER
>My lord doesn't fear her because he fears nothing, unless perhaps he fears God.

DON JUAN MANUEL
>How many of your crew?

THE MARINER
>Five, plus a cabin boy who doesn't count. We tried to reef the mainsail but ended up having to bring it down in order to make it past La Bensa.

DON JUAN MANUEL
>Such a fierce night!

THE MARINER
>Not a star in the sky.

DON JUAN MANUEL
　Who needs stars? A real seaman would find his courage in these skies.
THE MARINER
　Only baleful storms there!
DON JUAN MANUEL
　Always preferable to a dead calm!

They arrive at the berth where the boat is moored. Dominating the place are huge rocks crowned by the ruins of a castle. THE MARINER *goes on ahead with his torch to check on the path down to the shore. The path over the slimy sea-spattered rocks is perilous, and they lose their footing again and again. Up ahead they can just make out the outline of the covered boat. A point of light from a lamp hung on the mast; all else is darkness.* THE MARINER *shouts.*

THE MARINER
　Abelardo!
DON JUAN MANUEL
　That's the captain?
THE MARINER
　Yes, sir.
DON JUAN MANUEL
　Abelardo, son of Peregrino el Rau?
THE MARINER
　The same, sir.
DON JUAN MANUEL
　That father of his was a real sea wolf.
THE MARINER
　The son is saltier still... Abelardo!
A VOICE IN THE SHADOWS
　Who's there?
THE MARINER
　Come out and give a hand to Lord Don Juan Manuel... It's too much for me when I'm holding the torch.
DON JUAN MANUEL
　Stay where you are, Abelardo! I can manage on my own.

They walk down to the shoreline. The flight of seagulls ushered in by the wind and the night can be heard. A shadow approaches, its footsteps glowing in the wet sand. Chimerical flashes of lightning over the mountainous sea outline the black boat, which pitches against its rocky moorings.

DON JUAN MANUEL
　Is that you, Abelardo?

THE CAPTAIN
   At your service, my lord Don Juan Manuel.
DON JUAN MANUEL
   I don't seem to know you… But your father I knew well. I recall a bet that he won, to swim all the way to the Island.
THE CAPTAIN
   Little good his swimming skills did the poor man!
DON JUAN MANUEL
   He drowned?
THE CAPTAIN
   He did, my lord.
DON JUAN MANUEL
   When do we cast off?
THE CAPTAIN
   When the weather permits.
DON JUAN MANUEL
   You won't die your father's death, that's for certain! You need the weather's permission in order to set sail. By the time we reach her, the saintly woman will be stone cold. Death doesn't share your patience, son of Peregrino el Rau!

The lightning shows the old nobleman standing tall, his beard blown back over his shoulder. His dolorous, disdainful voice is shattered by the winds. The son of Peregrino el Rau shouts into cupped hands.

THE CAPTAIN
   Boys, we're casting off.
A MARINER
   The wind's in our faces the whole way, it'll take all night and then some to get there. If we don't meet with an accident before, that is.
ANOTHER MARINER
   Better to wait.
A THIRD MARINER
   Maybe with daybreak will come a more favourable wind.
DON JUAN MANUEL
   Is that your mama's milk on your lips? I'll be damned if you all aren't milksops and cowards.
THE CAPTAIN
   All aboard, mates! Weigh anchor!

Following their CAPTAIN's *order, the four crewmen grumble in protest but hop on board one after the other.* THE CAPTAIN *gives the order to set sail and leans over the aft gunwale to take the tiller. He then crosses himself. The boat teeters atop a wave's foaming crest. The crossing has begun.*

Scene Four

A ransacked room on an estate at the edge of Flavia-Longa. Drifting through its walls are the lamentations of the servants who have just witnessed the passing of their mistress. Her sons have gathered in the dining room to bicker over the division of the spoils. They are DON PEDRITO, DON ROSENDO, DON GONZALITO, DON MAURO *and* DON FARRUQUIÑO. *The five brothers share a resemblance: tall, slim, good-looking, with penetrating eyes and an aquiline curve to the nose.* DON FARRUQUIÑO *stands out from the others by his tonsure and clerical garb.*

DON ROSENDO
Can you believe that they ate with wooden spoons in mother's house?
DON FARRUQUIÑO
Evidently they did.
DON ROSENDO
Doesn't seem right. Who's the thief who ran off with the silver we all know was here?
DON FARRUQUIÑO
Well, it's gone now. Just have to grin and bear it.
DON ROSENDO
But there definitely was some here.
DON PEDRITO
Whistle for it and maybe it'll come back!
DON FARRUQUIÑO
I seem to recall the chaplain taking it and having it melted down when he joined the Carlista forces.
DON ROSENDO
Lies! I've seen it since, even eaten with it. And not so long ago either!
DON MAURO
I've seen it too.
DON GONZALITO
All the silver disappeared just today, and it wasn't the chaplain who stole it.
DON ROSENDO
Who was first to arrive at the house?
DON PEDRITO
I was. So what?
DON ROSENDO
Then you are the thief.
DON PEDRITO
And you're a son of a whore!

DON PEDRITO *and* DON ROSENDO *go at each other and begin to grapple. With much commotion the other brothers intervene.* THE CHAPLAIN *looks on from the doorway. He is a dried-up old man with leathery skin and hairy hands, dressed in a raggedy green cassock which trips him up.*

THE CHAPLAIN
> Your mother's corpse is still warm and here you fight with each other, like a bunch of Cains. Respect the sleep of the dead, you blasphemers! Wait for your father; he will give to each his due inheritance. Do not act like crows who feast on the dead. Crows, Cains — that is what you are!

The five brothers, still massed together in the centre of the room, continue shouting at one another, their arms snaking menacingly above their hateful heads.

DON FARRUQUIÑO
> Don Manuelito, this affair will not be settled by sermons.

THE CHAPLAIN
> Even your hands — hands you placed at the service of our Lord — are stained with this impious looting! Just wait for your father to arrive. He will give to each his own. The wolves in the mountains know more of brotherhood than you do! You are sprung from one womb and yet you fight like beasts in the wild.

DON FARRUQUIÑO
> Who informed Don Juan Manuel?

THE CHAPLAIN
> I sent word. This afternoon Abelardo set sail carrying my letter.

DON PEDRITO
> Aha, a conspiracy!

DON MAURO
> Indeed, you presumed to bypass us and send word to our father!

DON GONZALITO
> Instead of respecting mother's wishes. She never called for him when she lay on her deathbed.

THE CHAPLAIN
> Because you all prevented her from doing so. But you know perfectly well that his name was on her dying breath. Carrion crows! Wolves!

DON PEDRITO
> Enough with the insults! I am fresh out of patience!

THE CHAPLAIN
> And you! You are chief crow, the most rapacious wolf in the pack!

DON FARRUQUIÑO
> And you are quite bold with a bit of wine in your belly!

DON MAURO
> God smite you down, Don Manuelito!

THE CHAPLAIN

Save your nasty talk for your women and children, it doesn't frighten me, you profaners! Don Juan Manuel will come and cast you out of this house which your concupiscence now desecrates.

DON PEDRITO

I'll be damned if later on today I'm not snacking on priest's tongue.

DON FARRUQUIÑO

Marinated in wine!

THE CHAPLAIN

Sacrilegious beasts! You could do it too; you are capable of laying hands upon a man of the cloth!

DON FARRUQUIÑO

Not I! I could never allow such a thing!

THE CHAPLAIN

And you, you are the worst of the lot!... But you will receive your punishment, if not in this life then in the next... I leave you now, leave you embroiled in this impious scavenging... Do you hear the tolling of the bell? It calls for me just as it calls for all of you... I go to say the first mass for the repose of your mother, my benefactress, my mother. You clan of Cains, you could not hear it anyway. It would be a travesty! You are like dogs who should not be admitted into the Lord's house.

THE CHAPLAIN *leaves, and the tolling of the bell resounds in the ransacked room, putting a halt momentarily to the looting in which the five rogues have been engaged since dusk.*

Scene Five

The bedroom where DOÑA MARÍA *passed her final days. It is dawn, one of those bleak winter sunrises during which the wind howls like a wolf and the sleet whirls 'round. In the bedroom, the new rays of the rising sun struggle with the candlelight surrounding the pillows of the deathbed and flutter on the walls like the shadow of a bird. Rain lashes at the window panes, and there is a cold stubborn cry of monotonous sorrow which seems to express all of winter's — and life's — indelible sadness. The window opens onto the sea, which is vast, green and frightening. It is one of those narrow apertures carved into the depths of the wall, almost like a confessional booth, and flanked by stone seats, one of which typically serves as a bed for the cat and the other a place for doing needlework. Two women tend to the corpse. One is tall and withered, with tufts of white hair and flaming black eyes: she is the departed lady's niece,* DOÑA MONCHA. *The other, small, timid, composed, and renowned for her skill in making funeral shrouds, is pale with* the stale pallor of aged ivory, a shade which stands out with a certain devout expression against the colour of her habit. She is BENITA THE SEAMSTRESS.

BENITA THE SEAMSTRESS
Shall we put the shroud over the mistress?
DOÑA MONCHA
Have you finished the robe?
BENITA THE SEAMSTRESS
Have a look here... I didn't finish threading the seams because, trust me, a shroud does not need the same care as a dress. No one's going out dancing, after all. My dear Doña Monchiña, look how pretty this gold braid is!

DOÑA MONCHA *gestures her approval.* BENITA THE SEAMSTRESS *folds the shroud and snuffs out the candles with the scissors she keeps cinched in her belt, tied there by a special blue ribbon.*

DOÑA MONCHA
Pour aunt, she looks like she's only asleep!
BENITA THE SEAMSTRESS
Her soul departed like a bird in flight... No suffering for her at the end.
DOÑA MONCHA
No, God preserve us from a suffering like hers... Thirty years her agony dragged on!
BENITA THE SEAMSTRESS
I can still picture her on her wedding day wearing her veil... The same year, same day as the queen visited... Such wonders in the world!... I sewed her wedding gown, and now it's up to me to stitch her funeral shroud.
DOÑA MONCHA
Twice you have sewn her a shroud. Everything you sew is a shroud.
BENITA THE SEAMSTRESS
Doña Moncha, my soul, don't say that! Holy Mother in Heaven, there are so many wicked folk about, someone might overhear and go repeating what you say!... Doña Moncha, my dear, please don't spread talk like that about me!
DOÑA MONCHA
I would not so much as try on a thing your hands had stitched together.
BENITA THE SEAMSTRESS
Oh... don't say that, Doña Monchiña!... Tell me, do you think we should wash and comb the body before putting on the robe?
DOÑA MONCHA
That custom seems sacrilegious to me.
BENITA THE SEAMSTRESS
How so? Will she not be coming before the presence of Our Lord? It is only natural that she should attend as if at a great feast, all washed and perfumed.

We should not have allowed the body to turn cold, Doña Monchiña. You will see how much harder it is now to make her ready... And the more time passes, the more difficult it will be... I'm stepping out for some warm water, Doña Monchiña.

THE SEAMSTRESS tiptoes off as if the corpse might awake at any sound. DOÑA MONCHA prays in a quiet voice during the time she is left alone in the darkened room filled with the mysterious, vague murmur of orisons and sputtering, wax-dripping candles. A cat pushes open the door and stalks silently up to the deathbed where it begins to meow mournfully from time to time. Following the cat in is BENITA THE SEAMSTRESS.

BENITA THE SEAMSTRESS

Doña Monchiña, there's no hot water! I had to set fire to some straw... it's as if rebel troops had commandeered the place. Just like five wolves, the five sons are dividing the spoils. And the servants too are taking all they can. God forgive me for even thinking it, but I'd say they actually wished for the death of our poor, saintly mistress.

DOÑA MONCHA

Her eyes had not even shut for the final time when they began raiding the closets and cupboards. They descended like carrion crows on a corpse.

BENITA THE SEAMSTRESS

Look what these godless ones did with Lady Sabelita! From the mistress's bedside, dragged by the hair and thrown out on the street. And the language they used! Mother of God! They wouldn't even let her fetch a black shawl for mourning among her own things! There was nothing of value to be looted from the house, so they assumed she, their father's god-daughter, had squirreled away both money and jewellery...

DOÑA MONCHA

They found nothing because they had already divided it all up before their mother even passed away.

BENITA THE SEAMSTRESS

And without even waiting for Lord Don Juan Manuel's arrival! They say that the sons even cursed at the chaplain because he sent word to him. It seems so unreal, does it not, Doña Monchiña?

DOÑA MONCHA

I would believe anything said of those beasts.

BENITA THE SEAMSTRESS

Sweet Jesus, what a lot of Cains they are!

Dipping a towel into the bowl of hot water she brought, BENITA THE SEAMSTRESS sets to washing the face of the deceased. Bloody spittle keeps gurgling stubbornly between bluish lips which needle-pricked, irreverent hands wipe, and the livid, lifeless head lolls about in the recess of the pillow.

BENITA THE SEAMSTRESS

The body's starting to swell... Doña Moncha, don't you have a kerchief or something to tie round her face, to keep the jaw in place? Good Lord, it seems like she's grimacing at us!

DOÑA MONCHA

Poor woman!

BENITA THE SEAMSTRESS

When the funeral robe is on, we can put a salt shaker on her belly.

DOÑA MONCHA

What will that do?

BENITA THE SEAMSTRESS

It will make the swelling less pronounced. See how it's affecting the legs, Doña Monchiña.

DOÑA MONCHA

Don't wash her anymore.

BENITA THE SEAMSTRESS

But she's soiled herself! You want her to appear like that before our Lord? And her body so pale! The whiteness of her bosom — a complexion that many a maiden would die for!

DOÑA MONCHA

Leave her be... I will put the robe on her myself.

With brusque and sombre movements, she takes the shroud and approaches the corpse, brushing aside BENITA THE SEAMSTRESS. *With one arm she moves to lift the body, whose cold hands, folded on the breast, fall and flop down senselessly at her side as the head rolls in place and falls forward toward the bosom which they have vacated.*

BENITA THE SEAMSTRESS

Let me help you, Doña Monchiña. Step aside.

DOÑA MONCHA

Cut the shroud in back. That's best.

BENITA THE SEAMSTRESS

Not necessary... Leave it to me. Step aside.

DOÑA MONCHA

Let's be done with it, I can't stand it anymore! Cut it!

BENITA THE SEAMSTRESS

But how sad, Doña Monchiña!

DOÑA MONCHA

Cut it, I tell you. Where have you put the scissors?

BENITA THE SEAMSTRESS

As you like. Such a waste of time and stitching!

BENITA THE SEAMSTRESS *gives in with a regretful gesture, and then the two women, grave and silent, enshroud the body of* DOÑA MARÍA.

Scene Six

A pine-covered beach. In this deserted expanse, the voices of the wind and the sea mingle in a dark and terrible dissonance. The boat, its masts broken and sails torn away, has struck the reef offshore. One of the crew hops out to find out where they have run aground. THE CAPTAIN *shouts from the deck.*

THE CAPTAIN
   From the sand it looks like this is the beach of Las Inas. Look around and see if you can make out Friar's Reef.
THE SAILOR
   Can't see two feet ahead. Looks like Del Rey Pines.
DON JUAN MANUEL
   So we must have landed between Campelos and Ricoy.
THE SAILOR
   The beach is very wide here.
THE CAPTAIN
   Until the sun comes up we won't know where we are.
THE SAILOR
   Nothing to do for it this night. We're lucky we didn't capsize.
DON JUAN MANUEL
   Lucky for us, not for the fishes who missed out on a meal.

A bell peals in the distance, one of those village bells which to the people sound as familiar as their grandmother's voice. The night fog lends it a haunting sound.

DON JUAN MANUEL
   We must be near San Lorenzo de Andras. I know that bell.
THE CAPTAIN
   We really have gone far off course then! There's no way we're casting off before sunrise... and even then, I don't know. We'd need to be bailing water the entire voyage.
DON JUAN MANUEL
   You can leave on your own. I'm out of time and patience.
THE CAPTAIN
   There's nothing we can do, Lord Don Juan Manuel.
DON JUAN MANUEL
   Nothing for you perhaps, but I intend to set out for Flavia-Longa on foot.
THE CAPTAIN
   Now? In this weather?

DON JUAN MANUEL
What do I care about the weather?
THE CAPTAIN
But it's three leagues, maybe four.
DON JUAN MANUEL
Three hours' walk.
THE CAPTAIN
Three hours in nice weather, but not in this complete darkness…
DON JUAN MANUEL
My night vision is like a wolf's, I just hope that the storm hasn't destroyed any of the bridges…

DON JUAN MANUEL disembarks and strides ashore. The wind carries the voice of the bell, soft and inchoate in the distance. The lord tries to find his bearings by following that sound through the pine forest in which the wind ululates plaintively.

DON JUAN MANUEL
God has commanded me to repent of my sins… A whole life's worth! A whole life's!… The bell peals so far away, I can hardly make it out! I've lived the life of a heretic. The Devil's true best friend!… Perhaps I'm mistaken and it's not the bell of Andras. That saintly woman has probably passed away by now… She will intercede for me in heaven… For me, her tormentor!… And yet I truly loved her, and if I survey my life's deeds, the only sin that I genuinely regret is causing that poor woman so much pain. I should have concealed my other women from her. But my problem is that I don't know how to lie, to be something that I'm not. So many sins! They've blackened my soul!… Religion is dry and bloodless as a bony old hag!… The face of a pious woman in prayer, the body of a starved greyhound… A man needs many women, but the Church allows him only one. He needs to find others on his own. With ten women perhaps I could have lived like a true patriarch… I would have loved them all, their children as well, and their children's children…. Stuck with only one wife… no wonder my life seems like a giant sin. My children are dispersed throughout the region, and I will never be able to recognize them. I can't even count them all. And those brigands, my legitimate sons, they fear that I'll confer their inheritance on my bastards… So they conspire to rob me, kill me even… But I have nine lives. That saintly woman sheds tears for all of us. Where am I? I can hear the bell no longer.

The wind whistling within the pines drowns out the other sounds of the night. It is muffled, fierce, hoarse, dark; the bolts of lightning seem born from it. DON JUAN MANUEL *halts from time to time, trying to find his bearings with the help of the sudden flashes which illuminate the pitch-black landscape. At one such moment he sees the huge rocks of a quarry which resemble the ruins of a castle. Thunder echoes between these stones. Approaching them, he hears a dog barking and makes out a band of beggars seeking shelter there. These barely visible figures seem like nothing more than nightmarish outlines. Immiserated patriarchs, emaciated women, crippled youths — all speaking in muffled tones, their voices distorted by the wind, dark and grotesque tones that resonate in what seem to be chimerical ruins guarded by a winged dragon.*

A VOICE
 Who're you barking at, Carmelo?
ANOTHER VOICE
 Someone's out there.
A THIRD VOICE
 Somebody must have lost his way.
A FOURTH VOICE
 Must be a stray dog.
DON JUAN MANUEL
 Is this Del Rey Pines?
A VOICE
 Yes, they call it that… But right now it belongs to us, who seek shelter on this terrible night.
DON JUAN MANUEL
 Is there any room for me?
A VOICE
 Certainly! Plenty of room!
DON JUAN MANUEL
 That bell that tolled a short while ago, was it the bell of Andras?
A VOICE
 The old bell of Andras, yes.

DON JUAN MANUEL *finds shelter among these beggars, who are in fact pilgrims on a holy journey. Like worms writhing about on the dusty roads, they ambulate slowly towards their destinations — country fairs, farmers' markets and the like, where they are quick to disperse and seek alms, only to cluster together again like a bunch of grapes on the vine. They are known in all the houses, all the towns, and they in turn know all the places where charity is to be found. Membership in the group is unchanging:* THE ONE-ARMED MAN FROM GONDAR, THE CRIPPLE FROM CELTIGOS, PAULA 'THE QUEEN', *who breastfeeds an infant,* ANDREIÑA THE DEAF, DOMINGA DE GÓMEZ, THE ONE-ARMED MAN FROM LEON, CIDRÁN 'THE BAT', *and* CIDRÁN'S WOMAN. *Another bell chimes in the distance.*

DON JUAN MANUEL
 Sounds like bell at the Nunnery of Belvis.
CIDRÁN 'THE BAT'
 How can you recognize it?

CIDRÁN'S WOMAN
   He's probably from the area. Please excuse the question. Are you from around Belvis?
DON JUAN MANUEL
   You don't recognize me? I am Don Juan Manuel Montenegro.
CIDRÁN 'THE BAT'
   Blessings upon you.
THE CRIPPLE FROM CELTIGOS
   I thought it was you.
DOMINGA DE GÓMEZ
   I recognized him immediately.
DON JUAN MANUEL
   How far are we from Flavia-Longa?
CIDRÁN 'THE BAT'
   Maybe a league or so.
CIDRÁN'S WOMAN
   I'd say three, Morcego.
DON JUAN MANUEL
   The night is so dark, I cannot find the way.
THE ONE-ARMED MAN FROM GONDAR
   I heard the cuckoo's song already, the sun will be up soon.
THE ONE-ARMED MAN FROM LEON
   Noble lord, here is a place where you will find safe haven and shelter from the storm.
CIDRÁN'S WOMAN
   Scoot over, Andreiña, and make room for Lord Don Juan Manuel.
ANDREIÑA THE DEAF
   Who's that you say?
CIDRÁN'S WOMAN
   The lord of the manor at Flavia-Longa.
ANDREIÑA THE DEAF
   Yesterday on the way to Bealo I heard that the lady of the manor was preparing to yield her soul up to God.
CIDRÁN'S WOMAN
   Mother of God! We're in the master's presence.
DON JUAN MANUEL
   I travel to her... With the hope of seeing her alive one last time, I recently came ashore on a nearby beach.
CIDRÁN'S WOMAN
   I believe you will find her alive still, my lord. I'm fairly certain that none of what Andreiña says is the truth!

CIDRÁN 'THE BAT'
She's deaf.... There's a lot she doesn't understand.
DOMINGA DE GÓMEZ
People make fun of her, telling her lies that they know she'll try to pass on to others!
ANDREIÑA THE DEAF
The Blind Man from Gondar told me that he was on his way to Flavia-Longa to pay his respects.
CIDRÁN 'THE BAT'
If the Blind Man from Gondar told you that, it must be a lie.
ANDREIÑA THE DEAF
They'll be giving alms at the manor house, and poor folk like us will get more there than we could at Santa Baya Church. I'm considering going there too, for they've always showed great charity.
DON JUAN MANUEL
And they will continue to do so. Alms for all who travel there.
ANDREIÑA THE DEAF
The late lady ordered alms to be distributed, to wash away her sins.
DON JUAN MANUEL
Her sins require no forgiveness! It is my sins which must be atoned for! All the corn in the granaries will be given out to you. It is my restitution to you, because so miserable are you that you dare not take back what is rightfully yours. Your souls are branded by the mark of the slave: a beggar's lot is what you deserve, it is your nature. But the day is coming when the poor will rise up and set fire to the fields, poison the wells — that will be the day that justice is delivered. And that day will come! A sun of fire and blood will rise, a sun that bears God's image. Houses will burn, and their burning will yield sweeter bread than the hearths therein. Women, children, the old and infirm — all will cry in the fires. You will be singing, and I will be as well, for I will lead you. You were born poor, and it is impossible for you to rebel against that fate. Your redemption will only come when we lords heed our conscience. For me that time has come. At this moment, here, I recognize myself as brother to you, one who could accompany you in your begging. But I was born a lord, and my nature would sooner permit me the life of a bandit than that of a beggar. You poor, miserable lot! You are resigned to this slave's existence. We noblemen will be your salvation, once we become true Christians!

The beggars heed his words, evidently moved by them, and begin to murmur among themselves with the same dramatic piety with which they season their prayers and interactions in the company of their benefactors. As their voices die down, a mendicant of enormous stature, with leprous eyes, speaks up. His murky, nasal tones express the millennium of dolorous servility imprinted upon his soul.

THE MENDICANT OF SAN LÁZARO
Our Lord God will grant us our heavenly reward for our sufferings in this life. It is His will that some folk are poor and some rich. Our Lord God demands that we show patience and beg for alms, and that the wealthy show charity to us. The rich man who shares his bread with the poor is more deserving of heaven than the poor who receive it ungratefully. Such is our Lord God's will!

DON JUAN MANUEL is shocked. The nasal voice is borne aloft by especially rancid breath from which he struggles not to recoil. The first rays of the rising sun illuminate the enormous figure of the leprous mendicant against the stones. DON JUAN MANUEL is filled with Christian feeling.

DON JUAN MANUEL
Are you the Mendicant of San Lázaro?
THE MENDICANT OF SAN LÁZARO
Yes, my lord.
DON JUAN MANUEL
And your sons, how are they?
THE MENDICANT OF SAN LÁZARO
All five are at the sanatorium.
DON JUAN MANUEL
They share your disease?
THE MENDICANT OF SAN LÁZARO
Yes, my lord… I was born a peasant, so I cannot abide the sanatorium. Not to see the open fields and roads — this is death to me. The sanatorium is like a prison, and I was rotting there… There the illness wouldn't do me in; rather, I'd die pining for the threshing floor. There, the grapevines and the chestnut trees.
DON JUAN MANUEL
Sunrise!… Job, if you can walk, accompany me…
THE MENDICANT OF SAN LÁZARO
Come, Carmelo! You've had your bone to chew for today.

Carmelo, an old and ugly dog who sleeps at the foot of the leper, rises and shakes himself. DON JUAN MANUEL sets off on the road, and the band of beggars shuffles after him with a mournful clamour.

THE BEGGARS
Oh, Doña María, mother to the poor! Yours was the most charitable house in all the world! Our Lord calls her to his side in Heaven, right next to the Holy Virgin! She was mother to the poor!
DON JUAN MANUEL
Why don't you walk in silence? She was mother to me too. She was all I had in this world, but you don't hear me weeping like a child!

The old nobleman's voice breaks from emotion and belies his harsh words. The band of beggars begins muttering the Our Father prayer, led by THE MENDICANT OF SAN LÁZARO.

Act Two

Scene One

The narthex of the Flavia-Longa chapel. All of the windows are closed and the dawn's rays shine through gaps in the shutters. Dust mites float among the beams of light. The aroma of candles and incense wafts within. After Doña María's funeral, the chapel sits dark and deserted and sealed off. Two of her sons enter furtively.

DON FARRUQUIÑO
   Shut the door.
DON PEDRITO
   What's going on?
DON FARRUQUIÑO
   You'll find out soon enough.
DON PEDRITO
   Why so secretive?
DON FARRUQUIÑO
   We can't have the others finding out!... They forgot about the jewellery that was here, and before they remember, we will grab it and share the spoils.
DON PEDRITO
   I've considered that too, but the chaplain has the keys.
DON FARRUQUIÑO
   We can let ourselves down from the balcony.
DON PEDRITO
   And the others won't suspect anything?... Don't think to cozen that damned lot... Remember that other business?... Honestly, I didn't even think of hiding it from them. I'm glad they know.
DON FARRUQUIÑO
   That silver we divvied up, that's nothing... What about all the wheat, the corn, the rye? The granaries are emptied out, yet they were full not even a week ago because mother had received the rent from András and Corón. Who stole all of it? They did, no one else!
DON PEDRITO
   All three of them?
DON FARRUQUIÑO
   Or maybe just one... What does it matter?
DON PEDRITO
   If it was one acting alone, we could make him cough it up.
DON FARRUQUIÑO
   I think it was all three!

DON PEDRITO
Thieves!... You think father has arrived yet?
DON FARRUQUIÑO
I don't know.
DON PEDRITO
I thought I heard some voices a little while ago...
DON FARRUQUIÑO
I didn't hear anything...
DON PEDRITO
I'm afraid of running into him.
DON FARRUQUIÑO
Me too.
DON PEDRITO
You think he's here?
DON FARRUQUIÑO
I doubt it, the house is too quiet... Don Juan Manuel's arrival would surely disrupt this sepulchral silence.
DON PEDRITO
Poor mother!... We her sons drove her to an early grave.
DON FARRUQUIÑO
Fine gravediggers we are, it's true... Look here, do you think I'll break my leg if I drop down from the gallery to the other side?
DON PEDRITO
Probably not.

DON FARRUQUIÑO *perches atop the balustrade, then hangs down on the other side where the chancel is, which still smells of candle wax and incense. He swings back and forth for a moment, then drops down below.*

DON PEDRITO
My turn now.
DON FARRUQUIÑO
Stay up there. You'll need to give me a hand when I'm ready to go. If you jump down, we'll be stuck here; all the doors are locked.

DON FARRUQUIÑO *ascends the chancel steps and, after a cursory genuflection at the altar, opens the sanctum from which he draws forth the pyx and the paten, which shine like golden treasure in his hands. Standing under the lamp light, he contemplates them with pious solemnity.*

DON FARRUQUIÑO
As luck would have it, there are no wafers on the paten. God has cast a shadow over our thieving brothers' memory, otherwise they surely would

have come here and desecrated this holy place in their quest for loot! Pedro, the solid silver lamp is all yours, and I will preserve these sacred vessels in order to put them to properly holy use. We must prevent sacrilege at all costs.

DON PEDRITO
We can make those arrangements later... The matter at hand is how to hide it all in old Andreiña's room.

DON FARRUQUIÑO
We can bury it in the wine cellar.

DON PEDRITO
If we bury it, I think it should go under the altar. It will be safe there... When the chaplain stowed away those contraband weapons for the Carlists, nobody ever found them.

DON FARRUQUIÑO
And how do we recover it? The moment Don Juan Manuel arrives, these doors shut us out forever.

DON PEDRITO
The trunk in the maid's room is the best option, no one will suspect...

As the eldest brother speaks, his tonsured sibling walks back up the chancel steps and blows out the lamp which was supposed to burn night and day. With an anxious chill running through his veins, he listens in the darkness to his brother's voice. DON PEDRITO's *body hangs over the gallery, his eyes shining feverishly, like one possessed.*

DON PEDRITO
Don't tread on mother's tomb... Grave robber!

DON FARRUQUIÑO
What's that you say?

DON PEDRITO
Don't tread on the tomb. She's buried before the altar. Don't step on her... She might rise up!...

DON FARRUQUIÑO
You're drunk. And you're the grave robber!

Leaning over the railing, the eldest brother steadies himself and wipes his brow with his hand, smiling and reeling.

DON PEDRITO
It's true, I'm drunk, yet I've had nothing to drink... I wish I really were drunk!... Don't forget the candle-snuffers, they're also silver.

DON FARRUQUIÑO
The only thing I'm going to leave is the church bell, you thief.

DON PEDRITO
That's the spirit!

DON FARRUQUIÑO *climbs onto the altarpiece and despoils the sculpted figure of his silver sword. The bloodshot eyes of Satan gleam maliciously under the foot of the Archangel.*

DON FARRUQUIÑO
   Glorious St Michael, sorry, but your work is clearly done!

DON PEDRITO
   Yes, you've crushed the Archfiend like a grape, so there's no need for the sword anymore, my little saintlet.

DON FARRUQUIÑO *affectionately pats the head of the evil one, who is depicted as a blackamoor, his forked tongue protruding in a pained grimace. The man of the cloth smiles in the knowledge that none of Satan's wiles are a match for the potency of his exorcisms. With the same smile he removes one of the Devil's horns.*

DON FARRUQUIÑO
   That should take you down a peg, Lucifer.

DON PEDRITO
   The horns are silver too?

DON FARRUQUIÑO
   Not sure, we'll take it just in case...

DON PEDRITO
   Well, then grab them both.

DON FARRUQUIÑO
   Not so loud, you thief! We'll leave him the other one to defend himself.

From the table before the altar DON FARRUQUIÑO *hops to the presbytery, which again upsets his brother who with madness and fire in his eyes leans over and shouts.*

DON PEDRITO
   Don't step on the grave slab!... She will rise!... She will rise!...

DON FARRUQUIÑO
   You're trying to scare me, you swine!

DON PEDRITO
   You've trodden on her breast. I saw her in the coffin, her hands crossed over her heart, from which protruded many swords, just like Our Lady of Sorrows. They were silver too, Farruquiño. Don't forget them! Don't forget them! Don't forget them!

DON FARRUQUIÑO
   Some thief you are! Shut up, you're giving me goosebumps! Shut up, why don't you!

DON PEDRITO
   What happened?... Why is it that even without the light of the lamp I see these bright spots?

DON FARRUQUIÑO
Shut your eyes and your mouth, that's the wine at work in you.
DON PEDRITO
I only took a sip!
DON FARRUQUIÑO
Then our hornless friend over there must be playing tricks on you.
DON PEDRITO
Give him his horn back, Farruquiño.
DON FARRUQUIÑO
Not a chance! You just need to recite the Credo.
DON PEDRITO
I saw mother's shadow and heard her voice. Don't tread on her grave, because she will rise, Farruquiño!
DON FARRUQUIÑO
You're mad!
DON PEDRITO
What would cause her more pain? The swords that pierce her heart, or our removing them? They are seven, that's the truth! Seven, like the swords of Our Lady of Sorrows! We've got the seven of swords, Farruquiño, and St Michael gave us the ace… Put them all together in the grave… It's a better hiding place than Andreiña's trunk.
DON FARRUQUIÑO
You can't scare me if I bash your head in, you lout!

He spins around to look for something to throw at his brother and force him to move. He settles on a statuette of Saint Roch's dog. The object smacks DON PEDRITO *in the middle of the forehead. Blood trickles from the point of impact. He leans back, his face pale and calm.*

DON PEDRITO
Brother of mine, I don't want any of that silver! Come here and I'll hoist you up. Light the lamp again and put everything back the way it was. St Michael's sword and Satan's horn too.
DON FARRUQUIÑO
How about you go to Hell instead?
DON PEDRITO
Dear brother, come away from that darkness. Here, take my arm. But please, don't step on her resting place. She will rise!… She will rise!… She will rise!…

DON PEDRITO *backs away slowly. Terrified, he makes for the stable where his horse is tied. He saddles up and rides out on the main country road, which is green and overgrown with untended trees.*

Scene Two

Farther along the same verdant roadway there is a place marked by poplars and ponds. There the eldest brother runs into his father, who walks among the band of beggars. DON PEDRITO *reins in his horse and moves aside to allow them passage.* DON JUAN MANUEL *does not recognize him until he walks by. The father then regards his son with an air of superiority — without anger, but disdainful, scornful, sad.*

DON JUAN MANUEL
 Ah… It's you, you rogue.
DON PEDRITO
 Verily I am a rogue!
DON JUAN MANUEL
 Our paths finally cross. Did you hear word of my curse upon you?
DON PEDRITO
 Yes, sir.
DON JUAN MANUEL
 And you don't care?
DON PEDRITO
 No, sir.
DON JUAN MANUEL
 Then it's true that 'a curse brings no worse'.

DON JUAN MANUEL *strokes his beard and laughs heartily, the weird laugh of an old madman, disdainful and mocking.* DON PEDRITO *gathers the reins.*

DON PEDRITO
 Let me pass, father!
DON JUAN MANUEL
 Before I do, you will tell me why you do not fear my curse. It makes you laugh?
DON PEDRITO
 It doesn't make me laugh…
DON JUAN MANUEL
 It makes me laugh to hear myself issuing excommunications like the Pope.
DON PEDRITO
 Allow me to pass, sir!
DON JUAN MANUEL
 A bandit son like you deserves more than a curse; I should bash in your skull.
DON PEDRITO
 I am not your son, Don Juan Manuel.

With one hand DON JUAN MANUEL *seizes hold of the reins, and with the other brandishes his walking stick. The eldest son ducks down and spurs his mount. The father, still grasping the reins of the rearing steed, brings the stick down repeatedly on his son.*

DON JUAN MANUEL
    More than a curse! I'll break your head open. Kill you! Bury you!
DON PEDRITO
    Don't provoke me. Don't bring out the wolf in me, because I will devour you!
DON JUAN MANUEL
    Dismount, and we will see who has the sharper fangs here.
DON PEDRITO
    Don't push me, sir!
DON JUAN MANUEL
    Dismount, and we will see who the real wolf is!

Quivering, with eyes afire, the firstborn leaps to the ground to face his father who, still brandishing his walking stick, awaits him in the middle of the road. Spread out behind him is the beggar band, some of whom, shivering with fear and cold in their ragged clothing, make tremulous attempts to stand between the two enraged figures.

THE MENDICANT OF SAN LÁZARO
    Lord Don Pedrito, this is your father — he gave you life, and he can take it away. A father's authority should be like that of Our Lord in Heaven!
THE ONE-ARMED MAN FROM LEON
    Young squire, your noble blood should tell you what is right: turn back now.
DOMINGA DE GÓMEZ
    No need to puff up our feathers before our fathers.
THE MENDICANT OF SAN LÁZARO
    A father may lay hands on us to correct our behaviour. Even if he draws blood, we must kiss those hands.
DOMINGA DE GÓMEZ
    Oh, how I wish I could see my father come back from the dead to tug my hair again, even though I don't have much to pull anymore.

DON PEDRITO *stands motionless in the road for a moment, trying to regain his composure as he watches his mount gallop away through the fields, hooves tangled in the loose reins.*

DON JUAN MANUEL
    What's stopping you, you ingrate?
DON PEDRITO
    I'm waiting to see if any of your missionary friends will go fetch my horse.

DON JUAN MANUEL
   And you call yourself a wolf!
DON PEDRITO
   Rest assured, the wolf will come out if my father again dares to swing his stick at my head.

DON JUAN MANUEL *takes note of the threat and moves closer to his firstborn.* DON PEDRITO *cautiously turns away and with a sudden movement grabs at one of the leper's staves. Armed with this new weapon he begins twirling it around to make a menacing whooshing sound. Just as father and son are about to clash, the huge and tragic figure of* THE MENDICANT OF SAN LÁZARO *moves between them.*

THE MENDICANT OF SAN LÁZARO
   This staff that has served me on so many journeys shall not be raised by son against father. Our Lord gave it unto me, just as the cross was given unto Our Lord Jesus Christ.
DON PEDRITO
   Out of the way, leper.
THE MENDICANT OF SAN LÁZARO
   Before I move, you must return to me my staff with which I travel the world. For if you fail to give it to me, I will take it.
DON PEDRITO
   You'll be sorry if those rotting hands of yours touch me!

Walking slowly, with a potent and solemn humility, THE MENDICANT OF SAN LÁZARO *walks forward. He wears a soldier's cloak which highlights the tragic, hulking figure of the formidable beggar.* DON PEDRITO, *clearly intimidated, backs away and casts the staff aside. The shadow of* DOÑA MARÍA *seems to spread out behind him.*

DON PEDRITO
   Here's a cross for you, brother!
THE MENDICANT OF SAN LÁZARO
   My thanks, noble sir.
DON PEDRITO
   Tell me then, where might I find my own?
THE MENDICANT OF SAN LÁZARO
   I cannot say... That, no one can know until the time of night when, as we repose in a manger or walk along the roads, an angel from heaven appears to us in the name of Our Lord.
DON JUAN MANUEL
   Enough of your babble, Job!... We can exchange crosses whenever you're ready...

The old nobleman offers his walking stick to the leper and moves to retrieve the latter's. His eldest son walks away, muttering to himself, trudging through the fields to fetch his horse which now grazes there, its reins still dragging along the ground. He mounts and gallops away. DON JUAN MANUEL *knits his brow and rejoins the beggar band which resumes its plaintive moaning and chanting when they catch sight of the towers at Flavia-Longa.*

THE BEGGARS
    She was mother to the poor! Her door was always open to us! Our Lord God will take her up to heaven to sit by the side of the Holy Virgin! She was mother to the poor!

Scene Three

The kitchen at the Flavia-Longa estate. DON ROSENDO, DON MAURO *and* DON GONZALITO *sit by the hearth, comfortably enjoying their breakfast of fried bread and fine wine.* ANDREIÑA, *the old serving woman and the brothers' accomplice, informs them of* DON JUAN MANUEL'S *arrival.*

ANDREIÑA
    I can make him out over by the Three Crosses.
DON GONZALITO
    Then we have time to finish our breakfast.
DON ROSENDO
    The hounds can lick my plate clean.
DON GONZALITO
    My horse is saddled, the saddlebags full.
DON MAURO
    Mine too, all I need to do is put on my spurs.
DON ROSENDO
    Where are my spurs, Andreiña?
ANDREIÑA
    Look, they're hanging on that nail over there.
DON MAURO
    Where are our brothers Don Pedro and Don Francisco?
ANDREIÑA
    They left some time ago!
DON ROSENDO
    You saw them actually leaving?
ANDREIÑA
    Lord strike me dead if I lie.

DON GONZALITO
   Maybe they're hiding out somewhere?
ANDREIÑA
   Where could they be hiding, my lord?
DON GONZALITO
   As if there are no places to hide here! The stable, the tower, the chapel... Damn it! We forgot about the jewels in the chapel.
DON ROSENDO
   Curse the luck!
DON MAURO
   Is there time enough to search?
ANDREIÑA
   The master is well on his way, he'll be here any minute.

DON MAURO drains his glass, then casts it hard onto the floor. He turns. With one hand he grasps the old servant by the throat and with the other draws his knife. ANDREIÑA cries in fear.

DON MAURO
   I'll cut out your tongue if you breathe a word to our brothers. If those jewels are gone, you'd better confess the truth. Otherwise I'll skin you alive and nail your witch's hide to my front door.
ANDREIÑA
   In all my life I have never betrayed another's trust!
DON MAURO
   You let them take the silver, no use in denying it.

The clamour of the beggar band can now be heard outside the door, as can the commanding, stirring voice of the old nobleman who climbs the stairway.

DON JUAN MANUEL
   Oh, the earth has received you already! María-Matryoshka, my Russian doll, why have you left me all alone? Oh, how I wish to buried next to you!... My Russian doll! My Russian doll!
THE BEGGARS
   She was mother to the poor! Sweetest fruit of a special tree grown from holy soil!

The three ruffians scramble out of the kitchen, grumbling curses and threats, and escape through the door to the garden, where they mount their horses and gallop away. The old servant pulls her hood over her face, huddles up by the fire, and mumbles a lament in unison with that of the beggars. Another serving woman enters, black and dwarfish but with an enormous bosom. As hideous and stunted as a pagan sculpture, she lurches forward awkwardly. She is referred to pejoratively as REBOLA.[4]

REBOLA
What a fright I've had!... I heard a voice coming from under the chapel when I was walking through.

ANDREIÑA
Quiet, damn you!... Cover your head and weep with me, quickly!

REBOLA
My lady, my mistress! My lady, my mistress!

ANDREIÑA
You're not very convincing! Watch and learn how to lament properly. Rose of Jericho! Rose with no thorns! My queen, whose white hands knitted garments for the poor!...

REBOLA
Sweet gentle dove! Dove from heaven!

ANDREIÑA
Tree that gave us all shade!

REBOLA
Pear tree bursting with sweetest fruit!

Down the long hallway resound the voices and footsteps of the beggars who follow DON JUAN MANUEL. *His imposing figure appears at the kitchen doorway. The two women, kneeling by the fireplace with covered faces, increase the volume of their laments.*

DON JUAN MANUEL
You two, stand and serve my guests. Give food and drink to all. Come, warm yourselves by the fire.

ANDREIÑA
There's not enough food here for so many hungry mouths.

DON JUAN MANUEL
Silence, you old serpent!

DOMINGA DE GÓMEZ
Allow me to sit by the fire, I am so cold.

THE ONE-ARMED MAN FROM LEON
God preserve you, noble sir!

CIDRÁN 'THE BAT'
What a grand kitchen!

CIDRÁN'S WOMAN
Fit for a convent, Morcego.

---

[4] Carries a connotation of 'bouncy', i.e. fat.

THE ONE ARMED-MAN FROM GONDAR
   Fit for such a fine house!
THE MENDICANT OF SAN LÁZARO
   Twenty servants could sit around the fireplace here, and in the old days they did! I sat with them in such a place, before the sickness took me.
DON JUAN MANUEL
   Now you will sit beside me so that one day I can take my place beside my departed wife. Old witch, go to the stove and pull out the bread to distribute to my friends here.
ANDREIÑA
   Ah, my lord and master, there's nothing baking in the stove!
DON JUAN MANUEL
   Light it, then knead some dough from the finest flour you have.
ANDREIÑA
   Oh, my lord, there is no flour left, nor is there even grain for the mill!
DON JUAN MANUEL
   What about all the wheat and rye in my granaries?
ANDREIÑA
   Oh, my lord, it was devoured by rats, all of it!
DON JUAN MANUEL
   Light the stove… If there's no bread to bake, we'll burn you for the witch you are.
ANDREIÑA
   So sad that my lady passed away! If she were here, she'd never allow me to be treated this way! Witch? No one on this earth has called me such a name. My parents were good Christian folk, no one can say they've seen me spitting on the doorway of the church or making devilish signs during mass. Oh, dark spectre of death, you always take the best of us!

DON JUAN MANUEL sits alone on a bench near the fireplace, stooped and sombre, his eyes gazing at the smouldering grape vines. The golden-tongued flames lick against the black fireplace in which the wind laughs cruelly. At the other end of the kitchen, the beggars mutter to one another.

DON JUAN MANUEL
   Come, warm yourselves. All I can offer is a fire and a roof over your heads. Don Juan Manuel Montenegro is as poor today as you are.
DOMINGA DE GÓMEZ
   You are rich in soul.
THE MENDICANT OF SAN LÁZARO
   Where the hearth is, the Lord is there too. The home fire means more than bread, water or salt. All things on this earth require a spark from the fire.

Wine, blood, the eyes which need light, the soil which yields fruit. This affliction of mine is due to a coldness which runs through my body, so when the fire touches me, I cannot feel its warmth against my dead flesh. Nothing can be seen in the dark of night, only the fire, and from the sky only water and fire fall, for they are brothers...

From the kitchen issues the crying of a baby who suckles at the breast of PAULA 'THE QUEEN'. The beggar woman tries to shush him by humming a lullaby as she heeds the leper's words and switches the hungry baby to her other breast.

PAULA 'THE QUEEN'
(*singing*)
My child
By St Thomas...
Who is your mother?
Who is your father?
My child...

DON JUAN MANUEL
Why not wring the creature's neck, Paula? You don't hear him shrieking?

PAULA 'THE QUEEN'
Murder the flesh of my flesh?

DON JUAN MANUEL
What gives you the right to pass your misery onto him? Cover your breasts and grant him death. You do not see that it is hunger that fuels his cries? Cries that he will make his whole life? Have you no pity, woman? Break his neck and put an end to his suffering; free his angelic soul... May all of our necks be wrung at birth! I wish I had given that gift to all of my sons! Have those gravediggers been here, Andreiña?

ANDREIÑA
When my lord was arriving, they slunk away furtively.

DON JUAN MANUEL
Did they dig a suitably deep grave for their mother?

ANDREIÑA
They didn't do anything.

DON JUAN MANUEL
Deep enough, deep enough, so that I may join her in the ground?

ANDREIÑA
Good Lord, what fever makes you utter such things!...

DOMINGA DE GÓMEZ
The sadness clouding his heart makes him speak so.

DON JUAN MANUEL keeps silent. The group gathers around the fire, hugging themselves and bundling up in their rags, trembling with the happiness of beggars who know how to appreciate the warmth and shelter of the hearth. THE CHAPLAIN *enters.*

THE CHAPLAIN
> Back from the dead!... The man before me does not resemble Don Juan Manuel! I've come from the seaside, where I awaited the vessel of the unfortunate Abelardo!

DON JUAN MANUEL
> It still hasn't arrived?

THE CHAPLAIN
> No!... It was wrecked...

DON JUAN MANUEL
> Everyone on board perished?

THE CHAPLAIN
> Everyone!... The skipper's body washed up on Rajoy Beach... I thought you were with them, Lord Don Juan Manuel. It must be Providence!

DON JUAN MANUEL
> God saw fit to grant me more time to repent of my sins!

THE CHAPLAIN
> Then heed His wishes, Lord Don Juan Manuel!

DON JUAN MANUEL
> I forced them to cast off, and I was with them all through the night!... Death lay in wait the whole time, and I could feel him right by my side. The Reaper was on that vessel, and he is in this house of mine... Wherever I go, I see his footsteps. I have seen his lights!

THE CHAPLAIN
> Death walks at our side from the moment we are born.

DON JUAN MANUEL
> I can hear his steps in this vacant house... This house which also looks dead, covered in silence, cold, darkness, orphaned by the loss of that poor soul... I was not there to close her eyes when she died, nor could I kiss her waxen hands! Why not wait for me to give her body unto the earth?

THE CHAPLAIN
> Her body was beginning to decompose, my lord.

DON JUAN MANUEL
> Curse of the flesh!

THE CHAPLAIN
> The worms were feeding on her. Clusters on the head and under the arms.

DON JUAN MANUEL
> Cursed life of ours!

THE CHAPLAIN
> They say the worms were quick to appear, the way it happened with one of the Spanish kings.

DON JUAN MANUEL
Where did she die? I want to see her bedchamber. Her shadow will be there waiting for me... These corporeal arms cannot touch her... But our souls, like shadows, might yet embrace, and the living might still commune with the dead.

The old nobleman departs the kitchen, followed by the chaplain. A few moments later, around the fire, under the canopy of the chimney in which the wind's laughter echoes, the beggars, heretofore silent and solemn, grow animated.

DOMINGA DE GÓMEZ
How is it that in a mansion such as this, there is no bread to be had!... It's unheard of!

ANDREIÑA
The bread was for them who had teeth.

CIDRÁN 'THE BAT'
That rules you out.

ANDREIÑA
Eaten by someone who was at least grateful.

CIDRÁN'S WOMAN
Don't get all riled up, sweetie.

DOMINGA DE GÓMEZ
No flour or grain in such a rich house!

THE ONE-ARMED MAN FROM LEON
Not only death but a hurricane seems to have swept through the place.

THE MENDICANT OF SAN LÁZARO
Like candles, these grand houses die out, as sons turn on fathers and quarrel over their inheritance.

CIDRÁN 'THE BAT'
And I was hoping for a nice cut of meat to chew on!

CIDRÁN'S WOMAN
You can forget about that, Morcego.

DOMINGA DE GÓMEZ
The glorious St Baya visits this punishment upon us because we missed her pilgrimage.

THE ONE-ARMED MAN FROM LEON
Lord Don Juan Manuel won't forget the promise he made to us.

THE ONE-ARMED MAN FROM GONDAR
He has always been a generous lord.

CIDRÁN 'THE BAT'
You don't think there's anything in the cupboards or larder, Andreiña? Surely the clergy who performed the funeral rites must have left behind something?

ANDREIÑA

Rats must've gotten to it.

Arriving at the kitchen doorway are THE BLIND MAN OF GONDAR *and the boy who leads him. The blind man has a clerical look about him, wearing a tobacco-coloured cape which reaches down to his wooden shoes. The pan-flute he carries in his rucksack under the cape makes him look like a hunchback. His guide carries their belongings in bags. He is a village boy in woollen clothing, whose bowl haircut lends him a medieval appearance.*

THE BLIND MAN OF GONDAR

May I come in?

ANDREIÑA

You don't need our permission.

THE BLIND MAN OF GONDAR

There's a place next to the fire for me?

ANDREIÑA

That's not much to ask for. Come in!

THE BLIND MAN OF GONDAR

I ask also to speak with you, Andreiña.

ANDREIÑA

To speak with me?

THE BLIND MAN OF GONDAR

And we must keep it between ourselves.

CIDRÁN 'THE BAT'

Strike me dead if he doesn't want to ask her to marry him. You'll put out a nice feast for us?

ANDREIÑA

I'll put out some nice goat horns for you, roasted black.

The old serving woman with her withered witch's hand pushes the boy aside toward the fire where the beggars are gathered. She and THE BLIND MAN OF GONDAR *begin conversing in loud tones which gradually diminish in volume as secrets pass between them.*

THE BLIND MAN OF GONDAR

My sweetheart, come here if you like. If you don't like, there're plenty of other fish in the sea.

ANDREIÑA

You're all talk!

THE BLIND MAN OF GONDAR

My little dove, bring your beak close to mine, for I am no hawk.

ANDREIÑA

Say what you have to say, the fire needs tending.

THE BLIND MAN OF GONDAR
So blow on it, my sweet one. We can work the mortar and pestle with only a few ingredients, knead the dough, put it in and out of the oven. Don't laugh, people, I'm quite serious.

The beggars enjoy these old jokes, and as they have a good laugh over them, the old woman and the blind man begin speaking in hushed tones.

ANDREIÑA
What's going on?
THE BLIND MAN OF GONDAR
I'll tell you now. I was sitting outside the chapel taking shelter when I heard some strange knocking from within. I knocked in response, and that's when I heard the voice of Don Farruquiño.
ANDREIÑA
You're sure?
THE BLIND MAN OF GONDAR
He's locked inside, and asked for me to help you find a way, in secret, to go and talk with him from the balcony.
ANDREIÑA
You're giving me goosebumps. The other brothers could kill me.
THE BLIND MAN OF GONDAR
I'm just the messenger.
ANDREIÑA
Alright, I will leave right away…

ANDREIÑA *departs the kitchen, and the blind man, feeling his way with his cane, approaches the fireplace, guided by the beggars' voices which now discuss the sinking of* CAPTAIN ABELARDO's *boat.*

THE BLIND MAN OF GONDAR
Are you talking about those five young men who drowned?
PAULA 'THE QUEEN'
The poor souls!
DOMINGA DE GÓMEZ
We still don't know if all five are in fact dead.
THE BLIND MAN OF GONDAR
On the shoreline all you can hear are the laments of the women and the little ones.
PAULA 'THE QUEEN'
Poor little creatures, such a sad fate awaits them!
DOMINGA DE GÓMEZ
The same as ours: asking for coins door-to-door.

THE BLIND MAN OF GONDAR
   So far the sea has returned only the bodies of the skipper and a boy.
CIDRÁN'S WOMAN
   Whose son was the boy?
THE BLIND MAN OF GONDAR
   Not sure.
REBOLA
   He was the youngest son of Garula.
CIDRÁN 'THE BAT'
   That Garula, she doesn't need another excuse to guzzle the wine!
THE ONE-ARMED MAN FROM LEON
   That's fine. *In vino veritas* — the jug of wine is our best friend in the end.
THE BLIND MAN OF GONDAR
   Everything bad comes from water. Look at Garula's son! All the water that she never touched in her life, he drank up in one night.
PAULA 'THE QUEEN'
   Oh, death hath no mercy!
THE MENDICANT OF SAN LÁZARO
   He's in a better place now!
DOMINGA DE GÓMEZ
   In this world only the rich can get by.
THE MENDICANT OF SAN LÁZARO
   No one can get by in this world. What can a rich man do if he's fettered by illness? The world is a dark prison through which our souls wander until at last they can glimpse the light. Moments ago when the lord Mayorazgo encouraged you to throttle your baby's neck, he was certainly thinking about his life's trials and tribulations.
DOMINGA DE GÓMEZ
   He sure was blessed to have washed ashore from that wreck!
CIDRÁN'S WOMAN
   Everybody else went down with the ship!
THE BLIND MAN OF GONDAR
   Even the sharks and the demons from below spat him back up.
THE MENDICANT OF SAN LÁZARO
   Our Lord God awaits him now.

Footsteps in the hallway can be heard, and the beggars grow silent. REBOLA *adds dried grape vines to the fire which crackle and smoke before bursting into flames. The troupe of beggars huddle 'round, timorous and fearful.* BENITA THE SEAMSTRESS *appears at the doorway, mumbling unenthusiastic salutations.*

BENITA THE SEAMSTRESS
   God be with you!

THE BEGGARS
Blessings also unto you!
BENITA THE SEAMSTRESS
Andreiña's not here?
REBOLA
She's on her way back.
BENITA THE SEAMSTRESS
Where was she?
REBOLA
Running an errand.
BENITA THE SEAMSTRESS
Alright, then you can take care of this. Hurry into town, to the Curuja's bakery... Don Juan Manuel's orders! Go there and tell her to give you all the bread to serve to the poor... Later on we'll gather wine from the cellars, we'll roast twelve pigeons.

Benita wipes the film from her eyes with a rag that reeks of a tree-sap salve, then she departs. The beggar troupe mutters their thanks from lips which express both sadness and conviviality. The collective noise seems to issue from the ulcerous mouth of a single leper.

Scene Four

The chapel. DON FARRUQUIÑO *is seated before the altar on a chair covered in velvet and studded with huge bronze nails. Framing him is the arch of the gallery which opens to reveal the dark figure of the old crone,* ANDREIÑA.

ANDREIÑA
This gives me the willies, my lord!
DON FARRUQUIÑO
The blind man told you what to do?
ANDREIÑA
He mentioned something... But the others swore to slit my throat!
DON FARRUQUIÑO
Find the key and toss it down to me...
ANDREIÑA
I don't see how I can; the chaplain has it on him.
DON FARRUQUIÑO
Lift it off him.
ANDREIÑA
But how do I trick him?

DON FARRUQUIÑO
>   When he's asleep. Does he sleep with you or Rebola?

ANDREIÑA
>   Good Lord! Such talk from you!... He'd have to be blind to lie with Rebola! And as for me, I'm too old for all of that fleshly temptation... My lord, keep trying to sting me with your words and a wasp will land on your tongue... I'm willing to serve you as best I can. I'll bring you all of the keys from the house just in case one or the other will let you out.

DON FARRUQUIÑO
>   Without a key I'll have to set fire to the door.

ANDREIÑA
>   I will do what I can for you... But don't forget your promise to me, that one day you'll take in one of my daughters as your housekeeper.

DON FARRUQUIÑO
>   As I said, if I'm assigned a parish, I'll take in both of your daughters.

ANDREIÑA
>   I don't ask for so much. Christ in Heaven!

The old woman and guardian of the brothers' secrets crosses herself, and the tonsured junior son rises to his feet and peers at the door leading into the main house, a small door in a dank corner framed by a wet stone wall. A rusty key turns the lock. DON FARRUQUIÑO *hides in the darkest corner and waits. The door opens and a shadow moves aside to make way for* DON JUAN MANUEL. *Another shadow, black and witch-like, scurries away from the gallery.*

DON JUAN MANUEL
>   Father, why is the lamp not lit?

THE CHAPLAIN
>   Perhaps an owl has drunk up the oil.

DON JUAN MANUEL
>   I sense wings rustling in this darkness.

THE CHAPLAIN
>   That windowpane is broken. An owl could have followed the wind inside.

DON JUAN MANUEL
>   The wings I sense beat not on the outside, but from within.

The two shadows advance toward the altar. Their hollow footsteps echo in the solitude of the chapel, and their words hang in the air, umbrous and full of mystery.

DON JUAN MANUEL
>   Where is she buried?

THE CHAPLAIN
That slab there covers her, my lord.
DON JUAN MANUEL
We must remove it, Don Manuelito. I wish to see her!
THE CHAPLAIN
We lack the necessary strength, my lord.
DON JUAN MANUEL
Stone, stone, rise now!

DON JUAN MANUEL *kneels before the tomb and, his tenebrous figure breathing heavily, begins to pray in a low voice. Meanwhile,* THE CHAPLAIN *senses that something is amiss and he scrutinizes the shadowy interior. Suddenly, in a loud and stentorian voice, he shouts.*

THE CHAPLAIN
The lamp is missing!
DON JUAN MANUEL
What deviltry is this!?
THE CHAPLAIN
It wasn't owls who got in, it was wolves!
DON JUAN MANUEL
Not even a lamp to light your resting place, my poor Russian doll! They've left nothing! My dear, pray for me and for those thieves who suckled at your breast! For they are our sons, María Soledad!
THE CHAPLAIN
They fear not the Lord's wrath!
DON JUAN MANUEL
Or mine, Don Manuelito!
THE CHAPLAIN
The Lord might have struck them all down with thunderbolts!
DON JUAN MANUEL
Or bullets from my gun might have done the same work.
THE CHAPLAIN
They are like wild beasts!
DON JUAN MANUEL
They are cubs, sired by a wolf.
THE CHAPLAIN
Lord Don Juan Manuel has never been such as they.
DON JUAN MANUEL
I have ever been the worst sort of man! And now that it is time for me to depart this world, I wish to repent. The light that they extinguished now burns in the shadows which darken my soul, and so that my line, which

numbers among its members both saints and great warriors, may not be remembered for my sons hanged as thieves on the gibbet, I will apportion to them my property and live out my days as a pauper... Now let us together move this gravestone... I wish to see my departed bride!... She may have a message for me!

THE CHAPLAIN

You are delirious, Lord Don Juan Manuel.

DON JUAN MANUEL

Rise, Oh stone!

THE CHAPLAIN

Don Juan Manuel, we are old men! We are old, and old age has no strength. Years ago we might have managed it, but there is no lifting it up now...

DON JUAN MANUEL

There is.

THE CHAPLAIN

We are too old.

DON JUAN MANUEL

A heavier burden than that slab now rests on my shoulders.

THE CHAPLAIN

You, who bend for nothing and no man, are stooping now.

DON JUAN MANUEL

Yes, I am stooped, and my one desire is to leave this life behind, Don Manuelito.

THE CHAPLAIN

You have had the consolation of praying over her grave... Let us leave now... But, what was that noise?...

DON JUAN MANUEL

I shifted the slab a bit.

THE CHAPLAIN

You have muscles of iron!

DON JUAN MANUEL

My hands are bleeding!

THE CHAPLAIN

Let me help you, my lord. Where can we find something we might use to pry it open?

DON JUAN MANUEL

It's almost impossible to see in this darkness.

THE CHAPLAIN searches around the altar and then the entirety of the chapel. In its dark recesses his keen eyes suddenly espy a still form, shapeless and featureless, which takes on the appearance of an ancient carving of a saint. The chaplain approaches. His hand gropes in the shadows, but before he touches anything solid, he intuits the presence of DON FARRUQUIÑO.

THE CHAPLAIN
  Ah!... I knew a heretic was desecrating this holy place!
DON FARRUQUIÑO
  Hush your mouth.
THE CHAPLAIN
  Not content to rob only the house!
DON FARRUQUIÑO
  Hush now... Let us talk out of earshot from father.
THE CHAPLAIN
  How could you sink to such impious thievery? Why break into this sacred place? Speak!
DON FARRUQUIÑO
  I desired to make peace with my conscience.
THE CHAPLAIN
  By blatant profanation!
DON FARRUQUIÑO
  No, to prevent profanation by others. I realize what my brothers are capable of, so I came here that I might forestall their foul deeds.
THE CHAPLAIN
  Where are the treasures of the chapel?
DON FARRUQUIÑO
  Stolen already...
THE CHAPLAIN
  Don't lie, vile apostate!

DON JUAN MANUEL *descends the steps of the altar and advances a few paces in the darkness of the chapel. His dignified figure, at first vague and ghostly, grows more substantial as he enters the nave, and his voice, imbued with lugubrious gravity, resounds with a martial and patriarchal grief. The two clerics are silent.*

DON JUAN MANUEL
  Why do you hide, wayward son of mine?
DON FARRUQUIÑO
  I am not hiding, sir.
DON JUAN MANUEL
  You fear my wrath?
DON FARRUQUIÑO
  The innocent have naught to fear.
DON JUAN MANUEL
  You have extinguished the only lamp that lit your mother's tomb!
DON FARRUQUIÑO
  If my father says so, it must be true.

DON JUAN MANUEL
You are as crafty in words as you are in your deeds. What do you have to say for yourself?
DON FARRUQUIÑO
Our Lord God in Heaven has selected my innocent head for the sins of others to fall on.
DON JUAN MANUEL
Don't try to pull the wool over *my* eyes… Come here and help me lift the gravestone… I am not long for this world, but if I do tarry in this life, you all would lack the patience to wait me out… So that you do not all end up on the gallows, I have had the notion of dividing my property among you. You will receive your inheritance while I still live… Come here and lend me a hand… If you have sons, they will avenge me… The vows you've taken will not stop you from procreating. Come here so that we can raise the slab.
THE CHAPLAIN
Come on. For once in your life, act like a Christian.
DON FARRUQUIÑO
Hard to believe it's really Don Juan Manuel.
THE CHAPLAIN
And he speaks the truth: he will die soon.

They reach the altar and slowly move about the tomb, trying to determine how to carry out the task at hand. Eventually, bending down, each on one knee, in tacit agreement they begin to hoist the slab. They gasp for breath. The gap below opens up, pestilential and moist, to which the patriarch adds his bitter tears, sobbing and choking like an old lion. The son, his eyes clouded with fear, withdraws.

DON FARRUQUIÑO
No more! I cannot!
THE CHAPLAIN
I fear the strain is driving your father into apoplexy.
DON JUAN MANUEL
María Soledad, I am here! Speak to me!
THE CHAPLAIN
Enough, my lord…
DON JUAN MANUEL
I want to see her face one last time!

DON JUAN MANUEL *raises the lid of the coffin. In the cavernous dark the funeral shroud gleams white, and the crucifix laid over her breast shines between her rigid hands.* DON JUAN MANUEL *bends down, and the dank pestilent reek, which instils in him death's utter horror, chills him to the marrow.*

DON JUAN MANUEL
María Soledad, wait for me!... Your eyes are open and I feel their gaze upon me... I take my leave now, but I will return to lie forever by your side... God!... God!... My God, why hast Thou stolen my Russian doll from me?...

THE CHAPLAIN draws near and raises the now unconscious body of DON JUAN MANUEL. The son approaches more circumspectly, either from fear or from lack of any filial devotion, and helps out. They carry his limp form out of the chapel. DON JUAN MANUEL makes them pause at the doorway so that he can kneel down.

DON JUAN MANUEL
My grave is dug! My curse upon any who try to put back the slab before I have been laid to rest next to her. Wait for me, María Soledad!

Scene Five

The bedroom where DOÑA MARÍA passed away. In the background, under the curtains of crimson damask which have a liturgical look to them, the antique bed of polished carved walnut lies neglected and cold. In the shadow of the doorway DON JUAN MANUEL barely stands, supported by his son and THE CHAPLAIN. His pallid face and silver beard are sunk into his breast.

DON JUAN MANUEL
This is where I wish to die, in the same bed where that saint of a woman breathed her last... Until now I have lived a heretical life, never thinking of the hereafter; but now I feel a light within me.
THE CHAPLAIN
It is the light of Divine Grace.
DON JUAN MANUEL
Good Father, I need absolution from my sins so that I can be reunited with my spouse in heaven.
THE CHAPLAIN
You must confess to all of them.
DON JUAN MANUEL
I have only one sin to confess... Only one, which has haunted me my whole life!... I will confess it publicly... Summon the servants... gather them all... Servants of my house... My spiritual brethren who accompanied me here!... Where are you? Don Juan Manuel would take confession before you! Where are you? Come one and all!

Son and CHAPLAIN exchange curious glances. The eyes of each reflect the same thought: are not these words born aloft on wings of madness? With sedate murmuring the servants and beggars begin to gather around from the kitchen, their eyes frightened, their gestures confused, and they halt at the doorway.

SEVERAL VOICES
Holy Mother of God!

DON JUAN MANUEL
My grave is dug!... Death has crossed my path, and my days — my hours — are numbered... After you put me in the ground, replace that stone which my own two hands have moved — but not before! A curse upon him who tries! As for you, scoundrel of a son, do not pretend to grieve... Spread the news of my benefaction, and rejoice in your thieves' den, your wolves' den, where no one can see you. Tomorrow you inherit everything that was mine. The maggots that await me in the grave are greater reward than what is coming to you... My servants, my brothers — do not weep. These doors will always remain open to you, and even though my hand be cold in death, it shall still reach out to you in welcome. This I command as expiation of my crimes, and if my order is not obeyed, I shall rise from the grave. Weep not and be silent. I wish now to confess my sins to my chaplain. I have only one sin to confess... only one, which has haunted me my entire life... I was my good wife's torturer. I tortured her with all the pitiless cruelty of one of Nero's Roman centurions... A fresh sin for every day, for every hour and every moment... This is my sole sin to confess. Lust for gambling, women and wine — this is man's nature... It is a grave sin to have been the tormentor of a human soul, to have dug into it hooks forged in the fires of Hell — the sort of hooks that Satan drives into the flesh of the damned... And now I kneel in order to receive absolution... Father, I pray that you will absolve me... and that you will too, vile son of mine, for the Lord still works through your impure hands. Grant me absolution, then nail shut the window and door. Leave me as you would someone tossed down a well — leave me to die alone.

THE CHAPLAIN makes the sign of the cross over the nobleman's head, and the murmur of the villagers and peasants, elevated by their religious zeal, rises up in a sonorous wave.

Scene Six

The countryside, at a crossroads. A field sparsely covered in grass and chamomile flowers, and between four cypress trees, a roadside shrine. It is a place where travellers can rest and the old women can pray in the evening. DON ROSENDO, DON MAURO *and* DON GONZALITO *repose in the shade of the trees, their horses tied up by the reins. Farther off, a young villager lets his cows graze, and along the road, which leads off into green and rustling fields of corn, groups of mounted herdsmen head to market, rigid and ceremonious, dressed in old woollen clothing. Their fat, copper-coloured oxen, glistening and grand as pagan idols, have green oak branches entwined between their horns.*

DON MAURO
What happened to the cleric?
DON ROSENDO
I'd bet he's attending to some girl's spiritual needs.
DON MAURO
I keep hearing that Pedro's up and left by himself. Why'd they part ways?
DON GONZALITO
Probably got to fighting over what they stole from us.
DON ROSENDO
Too bad they didn't kill each other!
DON MAURO
We need to go back there…
DON GONZALITO
If they haven't beaten our hand already.
DON MAURO
I can't believe we forgot the chapel!
DON ROSENDO
Hard to remember everything when the grief is still so near…
DON GONZALITO
Poor mother! She helped everyone in need, and we always had someone to go to… What will become of us now?… We ruined her final moments with our bickering. We are like wild beasts!
DON MAURO
We only did what we had to. If we hadn't, those thieving brothers of ours would have left us without a stitch.
DON GONZALITO
Still, it's sad.
DON MAURO
Yes, it is.

For a moment the three brothers remain silent. Meanwhile, a group of herdsmen arrives in order to rest in the shade of cypress trees. They let their mounts roam free in the green and fragrant field over which the country roads criss-cross and fade away in the distance. Clusters of peasant women, young and old, take their rye and corn to the mill. There are seven herdsmen: MANUEL TOVÍO, MANUEL FONSECA, PEDRO ABUÍN, SEBASTIÁN DE XOGAS *and* RAMIRO DE BEALO *with his two sons. The elder of these,* OLIVEROS, *has the noble and masculine air of a Suebian nobleman of the highlands. His coppery beard, emerald eyes and aquiline nose evoke dim memories of the sybaritic youth of* DON JUAN MANUEL MONTENEGRO. *Back home in the village, both mother and son pride themselves on his resemblance to the Mayorazgo. And* RAMIRO DE BEALO *has managed, thanks to this affinity, to secure from the old nobleman four yokes of oxen and some land in Lantañón in fief.*

THE HERDSMEN
A good morning to you!
THE BROTHERS
And to you!
RAMIRO DE BEALO
Is Lord Don Mauro on his way to his house at Bealo?
DON MAURO
Yes, I'm on my way there.
RAMIRO DE BEALO
Are you returning from the funeral of my lady, who now basks in God's glory?... May He continue to watch over her!... And may God comfort you in this dark hour!... I suppose you saw Sabelita there? When we left for the fair, she told us that she'd decided to go to the funeral. You must have seen her there? We would have gone too, but one of the oxen went lame and there was no yoke to plough the earth... If God continues to bless us with life and health, we will head to town Sunday to hear mass and pay our respects to Don Juan Manuel.
DON MAURO
I'm telling you, dogs are more welcome in church than you are in my father's house. I'm telling you.
DON GONZALITO
You've milked that udder for all it's worth, so don't think that just because mother's dead...
OLIVEROS
We'll go there anyway, don't need your permission.
RAMIRO DE BEALO
Quiet, boy! Don't make trouble.
OLIVEROS
I'll say what I see fit, father.
DON ROSENDO
How fit will you find it to have your tongue ripped out of your mouth?
OLIVEROS
It has teeth to defend it.
RAMIRO DE BEALO
Watch your mouth, boy.
DON ROSENDO
Indeed. The mouth is a woman's weapon.

OLIVEROS
A wolf's also.
DON MAURO
Don't make me yank out your little fangs and plant them in the ground!
OLIVEROS
Big talk!
DON GONZALITO
If you value those teeth of yours, keep them in your mouth.
OLIVEROS
Look at them!

OLIVEROS furiously bares his healthy young white teeth, drawing back his lips which quiver with a primitive and bloodthirsty ferocity.

DON MAURO
Teeth of a peasant, not a predator!
OLIVEROS
They can still bite!
DON GONZALITO
A crust of stale bread maybe.
DON ROSENDO
Mangy little mutt!
OLIVEROS
My mange comes from the same bloodline as yours.
RAMIRO DE BEALO
Watch out now, boy, they outnumber you.
OLIVEROS
It is your turn now to be silent, father.
RAMIRO DE BEALO
They are nobility.
OLIVEROS
Whatever nobility they claim is also mine.
DON ROSENDO
Whoresons don't qualify as nobility. Or didn't they teach you that?
DON MAURO
You'll always be the son of the cuckold Ramiro de Bealo.
OLIVEROS
My mother's no whore, my father's no cuckold. No one's ever said as much to me twice.

The young herdsman advances toward the brothers and brandishes the long prod he uses to guide his cattle along the fields and paths. The other herdsmen band with him, and together they surround the brothers.

DON MAURO
  Three for me!
SEBASTIÁN DE XOGAS
  Here's one who'll be quite enough for you!
DON ROSENDO
  Don't go easy on them, Gonzalo!
OLIVEROS
  Look at these teeth!...
RAMIRO DE BEALO
  My boy, they're killing me!... Come here!...
DON MAURO
  Three for me!

In the middle of the field DON MAURO *shouts the triumphal battle-cry of an epic hero of old. At his feet,* SEBASTIÁN DE XOGAS *and* PEDRO ABUÍN *wallow in the dirt, blood gushing from their heads. However, the other brothers are nearly succumbing to the combined attack of the other herdsmen.*

DON GONZALITO
  Seven on three!... Despicable!
DON ROSENDO
  They could be seventy and pose no more of a threat!
OLIVEROS
  Leave just one for me!

The boy, all the time waving his prod, stalks toward DON MAURO. DON JUAN MANUEL'*s legitimate and bastard sons exchange savage glares.* OLIVEROS, *pale with battle lust, trembles in his desire for victory. And* DON MAURO *stands strong and proud, with bared head and bloody hands, like a hero in ritual combat from an old Castilian ballad.*

OLIVEROS
  Now you'll see what a bastard is good for!
DON MAURO
  I'll serve that tongue of yours to my greyhounds!

They clash: the herdsman brandishes his cattle prod, and DON MAURO, *with a robust arrogance, keeps his eyes fixed on him, raising his blood-stained hands to guard his exposed head. The goad swooshes through the air before* DON MAURO *intercepts it, tears it out of its owner's hands, breaks it in two, and casts the pieces aside. Their fight continues, a dance marked all the while by ferocity, boldness and beauty. The spooked horses run off, trailing their reins behind them, halting only in the distance to whinny in middle of the road.* MANUEL TOVÍO, MANUEL FONSECA, RAMIRO DE BEALO *and his youngest son are harrying* DON GONZALITO and DON ROSENDO. *Suddenly, among the sounds of staves cracking against skulls and fists beating on chests,* DON MAURO's *war cry rises like a game-cock's clarion call.*

DON MAURO
 Three for me!
DON ROSENDO
 Come on, my brothers!
DON GONZALITO
 Come on!

The young squires' victory slams the group of herdsmen with the force of a storm. In tacit agreement the latter begin to yield, unashamed of being overcome by these three high-born warriors. For what other outcome is possible with noblemen, lords of the land? OLIVEROS, *on the ground, face down, growls, but his fury is smothered by the hands of the gigantic* DON MAURO. *Like a bright bugle call* DON MAURO's *war cry resounds through the fields.*

DON MAURO
 Three for me!

Act Three

Scene One

A corner of the Flavia-Longa church. The voice of the abbot, an uncloistered monk who leads the prayers in the church's Chapel of Jesus the Nazarene, buzzes nasally, dissonantly, for he is deaf. A peasant woman, her cloak pulled over her head, sighs in completion of her prayers and kisses the ground with her tongue. She is stooped and wizened, her skin the dark hue of centuries-old chestnut. She walks slowly through the nave, the clack of her wooden shoes revealing her age. This is the woman who since childhood has served the house of DON JUAN MANUEL MONTENEGRO: *Ginger-*MICAELA, *who entered the service of the Mayorazgo's parents when she was only a girl, tending the cows in exchange for clothing and food. Now, cane in hand, she limps from one shrine to another. She opens one sanctuary's sad and rusted iron door and walks up to a woman absorbed in prayer. It is* SABELITA, *who at one time was the mistress of* DON JUAN MANUEL. *In hushed tones they converse, their heads bowed together in the damp, prayer-infused shadows. Two lights burn low at the altar, two ornamental candles whose excessive volutions and colouring call to mind a pair of aging demi-mondaines.*

MICAELA
I had a feeling I'd find you here!

SABELITA
You were not mistaken.

MICAELA
When you've finished your prayers, you must come with me.

SABELITA
Where?

MICAELA
To the manor.

SABELITA
Micaela, I have no wish to see anyone there, neither the father or his sons…

MICAELA
You're right to avoid those boys… But you must see the master. My lamb, that's why I've been out searching for you. The poor soul has been suffering so ever since he first witnessed the Procession of the Damned and its blinding lights.

SABELITA
He saw the Procession?

MICAELA
Yes, he did… A long procession of souls in torment, dressed all in white.

They appeared one night at the Temple Green.
SABELITA
Yonder, in Viana?
MICAELA
And at the same time as Doña María was departing this world!... The sailor arrived later with the news... Don Galán came downstairs with me to open the door.
SABELITA
You came here with Don Juan Manuel?
MICAELA
No, we came by land. Dear me, I thought we'd never make it! And the master, he came on his own on a boat which capsized on the way.
SABELITA
How terrible! Let us pray for the eternal rest of those poor departed sailors.
MICAELA
The Lord willed that they perish and that the master survive.

The two women pray in hushed tones, their voices pious and muddled, mingling with the flickering of the candles in the shadows of the chapel. Their heads are bowed, their eyes rolled back in ecstatic union with the image of Our Lady of Sorrows above the altar, whom the candlelight lends a lifelike impression: the violet, crying eyes, the sorrowful mouth, the tear-stained cheeks. SABELITA *and the old woman cross themselves and complete their prayers.*

MICAELA
They'll be closing the church soon. Let's be off!
SABELITA
I'm not going...
MICAELA
Show some charity and offer him this consolation.
SABELITA
You know that's not possible...
MICAELA
He's finally repenting of his sins.
SABELITA
What is he saying?
MICAELA
He won't speak with or even see anyone. He's locked up in the room where his saint of a wife passed away, you can hear him pacing around. And when anyone comes near, he picks up his shotgun and threatens to shoot.
SABELITA
Have you seen him?

MICAELA
No, my dove. He has a notion of starving himself to death.
SABELITA
What can I do?
MICAELA
Go to him. Beg him to stop acting this way.
SABELITA
He will not listen to me.
MICAELA
No, you're the only one he will listen to… You can't allow him to die alone like a dog!
SABELITA
I don't know what to do!
MICAELA
What does your heart tell you?
SABELITA
It tells me many different things!
MICAELA
And is any one voice louder than the rest?
SABELITA
Oh, yes!
MICAELA
Then heed that one.
SABELITA
I'm afraid of falling back into sin!

SABELITA makes the sign of the cross, her withered rose of a mouth murmuring yet another prayer. Her eyes fix upon the altar, and then upon the two weeping candles whose flames conjure in her mind the image of two nude women writhing either in ecstasy or in the fires of Hell. A white-haired old man walks through the church jangling a ring of keys.

MICAELA
Let's go, my dove. St Peter already holds the keys.
SABELITA
Yes, let us go…
MICAELA
The Holy Virgin pointed the way to you?
SABELITA
No.
MICAELA
You still suffer in doubt?

SABELITA
   Yes, by God!

They exit the church. In the chancel the widows of the shipwrecked sailors await the abbot so that they can discuss funeral arrangements. These women smell of the sea. Their eyes are red from weeping, their hair dishevelled, their clothes wet and dark and briny with the grief of many bereavements.

MICAELA
   Lord Don Juan Manuel ordered that a load of corn go to each widow. For days those have been his only words!
SABELITA
   Let's go to him!
MICAELA
   God will reward you, my daughter!

Scene Two

An anteroom in the manor. ANDREIÑA *is weaving and the other servants husk corn around a basket. They speak in soft voices, heeding the footsteps coming from the bedroom where* DOÑA MARÍA *passed away. The door is closed, and occasionally one of the servants presses an ear against it. The others fall silent and look to their friend for details. When the eavesdropper rejoins the group, the hum of conversation begins again. The resounding footsteps determine the rhythm of the movements and gestures of these servants husking corn in the dimly lit anteroom.*

ANDREIÑA
   He's been going on like this day and night!
THE CATTLE-HAND
   At night you can hear him moaning!
RECOGIDA
   A voice of despair filling the whole house!
ANDREIÑA
   The voice of the Archfiend possessing him, burning to come out!...
REBOLA
   Holy Mother!
DON GALÁN
   Here he is, repenting like a friar for all the suffering he heaped upon Doña María!
REBOLA
   You really think he'll starve himself to death?

DON GALÁN
 Even a rabid dog remembers to eat.
REBOLA
 He is not a dog!
THE CATTLE-HAND
 My hands ache! Is that one easier to husk, Rebola?
REBOLA
 It practically husks itself.
THE CATTLE-HAND
 I never pick up any of those.
REBOLA
 Put that one in the oven for a minute to dry it out.
DON GALÁN
 If you give me yours, I promise to marry you.
ANDREIÑA
 Does it have to be her cob? What about mine?
THE CATTLE-HAND
 A woman giving the cob? That's a first!
DON GALÁN
 So we'll have two. The more the merrier, right?
ANDREIÑA
 Too bad you lack one of your own!

DOÑA MONCHA *enters the anteroom, after which the servants immediately fall silent, assuming in that dim chamber the grave air of phantoms. With their faces obscured, their movements slow and reserved, their shapes seem shrouded in mist.*

DOÑA MONCHA
 Can you hear his footsteps?
ANDREIÑA
 Yes, my lady.
DOÑA MONCHA
 He never stops!
DON GALÁN
 Some worm gnaws away at him from the inside!
ANDREIÑA
 As if he were already dead!

DOÑA MONCHA *approaches the door to listen. The footsteps fade. She waits. The pacing resumes. She knocks timidly at the door. An expectant hush falls on all.*

DOÑA MONCHA
 Uncle!... Uncle!... You're killing yourself! Uncle!... Uncle!... This is a grave sin! Uncle!... Uncle!...

ANDREIÑA
He won't answer!
THE CATTLE-HAND
His mind's made up, he's going to starve himself!
DON GALÁN
He suffers great pain! His soul is somewhere else!...

Silently, slowly, DOÑA MONCHA *moves away from the door and sits among the servants to help husk the corn cobs. Breaking the silence from time to time is a faint voice, the roar of the wind and the pacing footsteps. Having filled one basket with shucked corn, they bring in another. In the anteroom now drifts a dark shadow, cast by* THE CHAPLAIN.

THE CHAPLAIN
Day in and day out, the footsteps never cease.
DOÑA MONCHA
Day and night!
THE CHAPLAIN
He's driving himself mad!
DOÑA MONCHA
He's already mad!
THE CHAPLAIN
He should not be left alone!
DOÑA MONCHA
What are we poor folk to do? Just standing near that door gives me the shivers.
DON GALÁN
Some worm gnaws away at him!
ANDREIÑA
It eats and eats away at him as if he were already dead!...

THE CHAPLAIN *walks up to the door and raps on it with his knuckles. He waits a moment and, hearing no reply, knocks again. The pacing inside continues.*

THE CHAPLAIN
Don Juan Manuel!... Don Juan Manuel!... The Lord would have us take courage! We must tend to this mortal life of ours as if it were a tender rose, despite its thorns.
ANDREIÑA
He won't answer!
RECOGIDA
He is like a king; he listens to no one!

The priest's shadow again drifts about the anteroom. The servants resume their talk in hushed tones. With solemn, deliberate movements they resume their work around the basket of corn, and in the darkness their superstitious chatter shifts from one mysterious topic to another. The pacing in the bedroom continues.

ANDREIÑA
  Just like that, day and night!
RECOGIDA
  He never rests!
DON GALÁN
  He'll have a long rest soon!
RECOGIDA
  Eternal rest!
THE CATTLE-HAND
  He won't listen to anyone!
ANDREIÑA
  He will hear the voice of Our Lord!
RECOGIDA
  All of creation hears that voice.
ANDREIÑA
  Stronger than a hurricane is that voice!
THE CATTLE-HAND
  And louder than thunder!
DON GALÁN
  Its crashing more powerful than stormy waves on the seashore.
RECOGIDA
  All last night you could hear the surf pounding off Corrubedo.
REBOLA
  They say it could be heard fifteen leagues off!
ANDREIÑA
  But the voice of Our Lord rings all over the world!

The servants continue to husk their corn, but their disquisitions come to a sudden end. ARTEMISA OF CASAL *appears at the doorway. She's a pale, blonde young woman, vivacious and attractive, wearing a hooded sailor's coat. People believe her to be* DON JUAN MANUEL's *illegitimate daughter. She holds by the hand a young boy with mischievous eyes who totters atop his white wooden clogs, worn for the first time outside his home. Hanging across his chest like a military band is a yellow sash which holds up his shorts. One of his little hands briskly doffs his Phrygian cap, and the other squeezes the life out of a frog.*

ARTEMISA
  Good evening to you all! Say hello, Floriano.

THE CHILD
Blessed and praised be the most holy Sacrament of the Altar!...
ARTEMISA
Kiss the reverend Chaplain's hand. Kiss Doña Moncha's hand as well.
DOÑA MONCHA
What brings you here?
ARTEMISA
I was wondering if there's been any change with the master.
THE CHAPLAIN
He seems set on seeing this fatal fasting through to the end.
ARTEMISA
The Holy Virgin of Gundarín won't allow it!
ANDREIÑA
And what if the Holy Virgin wants him to?
DON GALÁN
Then they'll have to settle the matter in the court of Heaven!
ARTEMISA
All day I've been so worried. This little one, how he comforted me when he noticed me fretting and sighing. And no change in the master?
DOÑA MONCHA
No change.
ARTEMISA
Why is he being left like that? All of his blood is going to rush to his head.
DOÑA MONCHA
Talk to him yourself and see what kind of answer you get. As for me, there's no way I'm going near that door again!

ARTEMISA OF CASAL walks up to the door, holding her child by the hand. In the bedroom, the pacing back and forth continues persistently, strangely, like the thought process of a madman. ARTEMISA pauses to listen.

ARTEMISA
He's pacing around in the dark!
THE CHAPLAIN
As soon as he entered the bedroom, he ordered the windows boarded over.
ARTEMISA
My lord!... My lord!... You don't remember me? It's Artemisa!... My lord, open the door! For the sake of the saintly departed lady. My lord, it's Artemisa here!

The pacing ceases, and the door flies open with a crash. In the doorway, against the bedroom's dark interior, towers the figure of DON JUAN MANUEL MONTENEGRO. His eyes glare with rage, and his aged-ivory coloured hands brandish a shotgun.

His quivering hoary beard cascades over his chest.

DON JUAN MANUEL

   Must I kill one of you so that you will let me die in peace? Damn you all to Hell, hovering around this door with no thought of my pain! And you damn me as well, for you will not allow me to die repentant! My hours are numbered!... My grave is open; it beckons me! Leave me! All night the hounds have been howling!... I close my eyes to die, and your voices disturb my rest! You are like hyenas who feast on buried corpses!... I'll have to kill you! Leave me alone, you hyenas, you wolves, you scorpions! Leave me, and let the gravedigger's shovel spread earth over me, covering my eyes forever!...

The old nobleman crosses the anteroom, his footsteps echoing down the long corridor. Those assembled stare wide-eyed at one another and approach, one by one, the doorway of the bedroom, from which the stench of death emanates. Huddled together, none is so bold as to enter, for it is as if they can still hear the obsessive steps, can still see in the darkened space the shadow of the pacing figure.

ARTEMISA

   The way he's talking, it chills me to the bone!

DOÑA MONCHA

   It's enough to give anyone the chills!

RECOGIDA

   He's set on dying!

ANDREIÑA

   He's seeking out death!

ARTEMISA

   Condemning his very soul!

RECOGIDA

   Where will he go?

DON GALÁN

   If he didn't scare me so, I would go after him!

THE CHAPLAIN

   No point in goading a lion!... If our eyes have lost sight of him, let us keep him in our prayers.

THE CHAPLAIN *walks across the room, muttering a prayer, and the servants, once again gathered around the basket of corn, converse in hushed tones. Suddenly, the hoof beats of a horse being reined in outside the gate can be heard.*

DOÑA MONCHA

   Who can that be at this hour?

THE CHAPLAIN

   The wolves descend from their hilltop dens. Who else could it be but the sons?...

DON GALÁN
They come to divvy up the inheritance.
ARTEMISA
Didn't take them long to find out!...
DON GALÁN
Some witch must've told them!...
ANDREIÑA
From this day on, it is they who are our masters!

Scene Three

DON JUAN MANUEL MONTENEGRO *wends his way through the streets, narrow alleys enclosed and shaded by high walls, above which cypress and fig trees loom. Ancient alleyways in a feudal town full of churches, huge old houses and convent gardens! Rain drips from the blackened drain pipes, and in the narrow windows which open below them occasionally appears the silhouette of a cat.*

DON JUAN MANUEL
Where can I wait for death without their voices pestering me?... In what dark den of wolf or lion might I hide away?... Life brings me no peace!... I raised a pack of wolves, and now these cubs would tear me apart. I begat monsters. I am accursed! How could the womb of that saintly woman have produced vile demons, and not winged angels? How? Because he who sowed the seeds was one accursed! Accursed was the seed he sowed! Death, do not tarry! Pull me out of this snake pit and deliver me to your worms instead!... Better for your children to devour me than mine! Tarry not, Oh Death! If, dear God, my sins render me unworthy of your company, at least do not deprive me of Satan's as well!

DON JUAN MANUEL *passes by two women who are clearly startled by the encounter. He continues on without seeing them, stopping only when they plaintively cry out to him. He then recognizes his old servant as well as* SABELITA.

MICAELA
Master, where are you off to at this hour?
SABELITA
Holy Mother of God! Don Juan Manuel!
MICAELA
Master, where are you off to in this rain, with nothing on your head?
DON JUAN MANUEL
From what hell do you come? Why do you delay me? Why do you talk to me when I try to flee from your voices?... Isabel, what do you want of me? One

day you desert me, and now you return in the company of a witch! From what sort of hell have you come, Isabel? Or is that still what you call yourself?

SABELITA

I am Isabel, my lord!...

DON JUAN MANUEL

The Archfiend does not call you Isabel. The Archfiend calls you the mother of lies, the raven of ingratitude, the serpent of hypocrisy, the ember of lust! Only the saintly woman whom we both drove to the grave called you Isabel! With a mother's kindness she spoke to us all!... But from Satan's mouth there issues none of that love which passed from those lips, now and forever mute! Isabel, to me your true name is Remorse, and you, old woman, are nothing but a witch. A witch!

DON JUAN MANUEL disappears into the darkness. The two terrified women do not dare to follow. For some time hollow footsteps echo in the solitude of the street. DON JUAN MANUEL walks down to the shore, where the wind pounds against the sea.

DON JUAN MANUEL

Great sea, your waves would not drag me down to your depths!... You took those sailors' lives yet you rejected mine! If you, O sea, you would only swallow me up forever, never spitting my body back up on any beach! Entomb me, preserve me in your depths!... You showed no love for me that night, yet I am reduced to flotsam, much more so than the naked bodies your waves have taken in their rough caresses. As poor and bare and cold as a castaway am I! I know not where to go!... If death still will not have me, I will take to the roads and beg!... The sea that night could have covered me forever, like the dirt over a grave; but it would not have me!... Now I am truly wretched! I have passed on everything to those beasts! In that other life, that life from which I flee, my soul was also a sea, a sea with its own storms, its pitch-black nights, its monsters whom I begat! And now I am nothing but a miserable old beggar! Among my sons I divided up all my possessions, and while they warm themselves by the fire which I kindled and tended, I wander the earth aimlessly. And one day, O sea, if you will not have me, I will die shivering at the foot of a tree as old as I am! The oaks planted by my hand will not deny me their shade the way my monstrous progeny deny me their affection!...

Three black figures walk along the beach. They carry over their shoulders long poles, the tips of which seem to rise toward the moon like horns or like the fangs of an old crone. The three figures come before DON JUAN MANUEL. From time to time they pause to stretch out their poles over the spindrift, and the witches' teeth at the ends plunge and disappear into the sea. DON JUAN MANUEL moves among these three figures who, to their astonishment, recognize him. In the wake of a storm these three beggars often come to the beach hoping to salvage pieces of wreckage. Their shadowy figures also jar the old nobleman's memory. They are CIDRÁN 'THE BAT', *his woman and a madman known as* FILTHY FUSO.

DON JUAN MANUEL
What goblin or witch has brought the likes of you here?
FILTHY FUSO
The moon...
CIDRÁN'S WOMAN
We hope to salvage the wreck of a large ship coming from... we're not sure where...
CIDRÁN 'THE BAT'
A large brig that went down somewhere off Corrubedo.
CIDRÁN'S WOMAN
Perhaps the waves will show more charity than human hearts and throw us something tonight to relieve our poverty.
DON JUAN MANUEL
The waves show no charity!
CIDRÁN'S WOMAN
They've shown it to many...
CIDRÁN 'THE BAT'
And there's no other beach like this one, where so much timber washes up from the ships.
CIDRÁN'S WOMAN
And sometimes quite valuable things...
FILTHY FUSO
Fine silverware, fine jewellery...
DON JUAN MANUEL
And also sometimes a bloated corpse, gnawed at by the fishes!
FILTHY FUSO
Years ago the body of a king washed up, he had a crown of gold and precious stones... The crown was stuck on so tight, there was no removing it... the head had to be cut off...
DON JUAN MANUEL
How many castaways has your greed brought to a similar fate!
FILTHY FUSO
Oh, but that was a king of the Moors. The blood that poured out of his neck was black as night.
DON JUAN MANUEL
If a storm had tossed me into the sea that night, your kind would have lopped off my head as well, crown or no crown. You would have sold it to my sons, and they would have paid you well for your work.

CIDRÁN'S WOMAN
Don't say such things, my lord!
FILTHY FUSO
We'd have served it up on a silver platter as they were seated at the table.
DON JUAN MANUEL
And they would waste no time devouring it as a fine delicacy.
FILTHY FUSO
Don Pedrito would say, 'I want the tongue!' Don Gonzalito would say, 'I'll have the eyes!' And how they would all dig in with their teeth!
DON JUAN MANUEL
They'd murder one another fighting over the portions!
FILTHY FUSO
The bones would go to the dogs.
DON JUAN MANUEL
Dogs do not eat their masters.
CIDRÁN'S WOMAN
But can sons really devour their fathers, my lord?
DON JUAN MANUEL
Mine tore the heart from my chest, that much is certain.
FILTHY FUSO
Even though they tore it from your breast with their fangs, don't worry, another heart will come and grow in its place... Sprouting up like bay laurel... Nothing to fear!
CIDRÁN'S WOMAN
The only thing that devours its own source is the worm of death. Life is like a fountain: as long as it endures, it is like a fountain to which all come to drink and which none can exhaust.
CIDRÁN 'THE BAT'
A fountain has enough water to slake everyone's thirst.
DON JUAN MANUEL
And have you ever seen a well gone dry?
CIDRÁN 'THE BAT'
Only when the weather is very hot.
CIDRÁN'S WOMAN
But it was the sun that exhausted those wells, not thirsty men's mouths.
FILTHY FUSO
The wolves who try to drink a well dry end up bursting like bloated wineskins.
DON JUAN MANUEL
Why do you compare the human heart to a fountain? The waters of a fountain can be poisoned, bringing death to those who would drink from them.

CIDRÁN 'THE BAT'
The human heart also comes with its own poison!
DON JUAN MANUEL
The poison issues not from the heart, but from those who gnaw at it.
FILTHY FUSO
The heart is like the pupil of the eye. It holds within itself that which it sees on the outside. Sometimes a fountain, sometimes a stone... Sometimes the snarling fangs of a wolf, other times the resplendent sun's rays.
DON JUAN MANUEL
Why do they say you are crazy, Filthy Fuso?
CIDRÁN'S WOMAN
He started the rumour himself, to get out of working.
FILTHY FUSO
The kids say it, so they can pelt me with rocks. Every village needs its idiot and its mayorazgo.
CIDRÁN 'THE BAT'
The tide is low again. The waves chose not to make our fortunes on this day.
CIDRÁN'S WOMAN
But perhaps my lord Mayorazgo can spare a little something!...
DON JUAN MANUEL
I am now as poor as you are. If an open grave did not await me, I would join your paupers' caravan on the open road, begging for crusts of bread. Death has already numbered my hours, and I have turned my back on all my relations, all my possessions, so that I might die in peace.
CIDRÁN'S WOMAN
And where are you off to this dark night?
DON JUAN MANUEL
As I said before, I am setting off in search of my death.
CIDRÁN'S WOMAN
Death comes in his own time; he needs not be sought out. Do not commit a grave sin, my lord!
DON JUAN MANUEL
I seek nothing... I await death, who has given me his calling card!... A great candle, illuminating everything, has been lit within me, it guides and enlightens me. I have gazed into the abyss known only to those whose graves are already dug. I have learned, at the end of my days, that what awaits us all is a dunghill for a deathbed, and it is there that I go now. The earth will provide me with that long before the sea yields up any of that shipwrecked treasure for which you yearn...

DON JUAN MANUEL *walks away slowly. The three beggars stare after him until he disappears among the rocks on the beach. The moon seems to enhance the figure of the old nobleman and place a halo around his bare white head.*

Scene Four

A rocky beach leading out to green and daunting waters. Sandy dunes strewn with tattered pines and brackish tidal pools. A cow's pale bones. Under the dawn's grey skies, carrion crows circle about, picking at the corpse. Deep within a sea-formed cave, the hoary nobleman waits for death like an old lion. In his clouded vision he espies the shadow of FILTHY FUSO *approaching.*

FILTHY FUSO
    Too-too-too!... Just the two two two of us.

DON JUAN MANUEL
    Even here I cannot die in peace!...

FILTHY FUSO
    The honourable Mayorazgo has his palace and his canopied bed... Why choose the aches and pains of this place?... Filthy Fuso's bed is too rough and hard for my lord's noble body.

DON JUAN MANUEL
    You sleep in this cave?

FILTHY FUSO
    Sometimes I sleep, sometimes I lie awake.

DON JUAN MANUEL
    I ask only that you allow me to die here!

FILTHY FUSO
    So the nobleman, my lord Mayorazgo, becomes a hermit? Then maybe the madman can reign in the palace? With a dirty white linen mantle and a paper crown? A table stacked with fresh bread and wineskins full to bursting. One with Rivero another with Ramallosa, yet another with white Alvariño, and still another with the really good stuff, like what the abbots drink when they're performing mass. And if my serving girl's busy having a baby, she can stay in bed. The madman can run my lord's estate!

DON JUAN MANUEL
    I have no palace. Everything I had I divided among my sons to keep their thieving, dishonourable necks from the gallows. It's all gone!

FILTHY FUSO
    Too-too-too!... Then we are brothers!

DON JUAN MANUEL
    My final bed is being prepared. By candlelight an angel and a demon dig my grave. The angel digs at the head of the bed, the demon at the foot... The demon wields his reaper's scythe, the angel his golden shell. Can't you see

them, Filthy Fuso my brother? The angel digs, the demon digs... One at the head, the other at the foot...
FILTHY FUSO
The angel digs, the demon digs... Yes, I see them clear as day! The demon's lighting up a cigar with the embers from his tail.
DON JUAN MANUEL
That's what you see, Filthy Fuso?
FILTHY FUSO
Yes, clear as day!
DON JUAN MANUEL
You are sure?
FILTHY FUSO
Yes, I see it all now!
DON JUAN MANUEL
I thought perhaps I was delirious... I can barely make out your shadow in this cave. I came here to die... I lived the life of a rabid wolf, and like a rabid wolf I will starve to death in this cave... Filthy Fuso my brother, you must cut the head off my corpse and deliver it to my sons. You do that, and you will see how these monsters born of my flesh reward you with silken finery.
FILTHY FUSO
How many sons?
DON JUAN MANUEL
Five.
FILTHY FUSO
Five candles burn for five demon-kind, five tails trail five demon behinds!
DON JUAN MANUEL
Demons they are!
FILTHY FUSO
Spawn of the Demon-in-chief who five times bedded her who is recently departed from this earth.
DON JUAN MANUEL
Keep her name out of your miserable mouth! Scorpion's mouth! Serpent's mouth!
FILTHY FUSO
So we are no longer brothers?... All because I pointed out the Demon-in-chief's trickery! All five sons are the issue of his dark lore — Lord preserve us from it!... From his right hand the Demon gave each son a taloned finger to claw at my brother the Mayorazgo's heart with. Brothers forever, brothers on the road, begging door to door, and in death here in this cave... Brothers forever... Too-too! We've lived as strangers all this time, but now we recognize one another as brothers... We've travelled the same path — only

now we find one another. We travelled the same path. Too-too-too!

DON JUAN MANUEL

We are brothers and sisters, all of us, we are all the spawn of Satan! And we just never realized it before!...

FILTHY FUSO

But there are also children of Our Lord God...

DON JUAN MANUEL

On the Earth's side we are all siblings, for she is our mother. You say the Devil doled out his fingers to my sons especially? But we were all made for robbing, killing, for sticking our middle fingers at our fellows...

FILTHY FUSO

Your five sons are the product of the Demon-in-chief. He made each of them on a Saturday, around midnight, which is the time when the witches start to kindle his lust, so all horny and barking like a dog, he cavorts on the rooftops, breaking the shingles, before he jumps down the chimney and mounts his chosen women whom he knocks up thanks to a special trick all his own... Without this trick of his, which this fool of a devil knows so well, he couldn't have any children... And the women realize that they're being taken by the Archfiend because the seed he plants in them runs ice cold. The Big Demon frequents the fairs, markets, the harvests and the sacred processions in the guise of a seductive young woman, to tempt the menfolk. Monks and aristocrats are the most easily tempted. Oh, brother of mine, how many times have we lain with a young woman under the grape vines, not realizing that it was actually the Chief Demon of Hell? The dirty thief leaves us sleeping while he makes off with the seed of our lust. He takes the form of a husband so he can have his way with the wife. See how the trick works? With the warm sperm that he stole, he can knock up women and make children.[5] You've always loved the ladies, my lord Mayorazgo, so the Devil made use of your form and got with Doña María, making a cuckold out of you.

DON JUAN MANUEL

I am no cuckold.

FILTHY FUSO

The Devil made you one.

DON JUAN MANUEL

If Don Juan Manuel Montenegro is a cuckold, then all men are cuckolds.

FILTHY FUSO

They are indeed, that's why so many of Satan's children walk the earth!

---

[5] The idea that the Devil, in the form of a succubus, could steal semen from a man, and then use it (taking the form of an incubus) to impregnate a woman, is very old. It is common in early modern writing on witchcraft and demonology, and goes back at least to the medieval period, possibly having come from older folklore beliefs. The incubus or succubus was often said to take the form of a person known to the victim.

Here FILTHY FUSO *pulls out from under his shirt a crust of stale bread, which he starts to gnaw on with a sullen and determined expression.* DON JUAN MANUEL *shuts his eyes and lies down on a bed of seaweed made by* FILTHY FUSO. *The wind and waves pound against the shore outside.* DON JUAN MANUEL *sighs without opening his eyes.*

DON JUAN MANUEL
Are you hungry, Filthy Fuso?

FILTHY FUSO
Noblemen and monks sit 'round a table covered in seven tablecloths, and they fill their bellies with fresh bread and fried pork rinds. And stuffed, they nod off, not waking until the morning. Roasted horse mackerel!... Pans without handles!... An old hag with blood-red eyes!... The madman here is always hungry!...

DON JUAN MANUEL
Your furious chomping allows me no rest!

FILTHY FUSO
This crust is hard as a rock!

DON JUAN MANUEL
I haven't eaten in two days, and now my dormant hunger is awakened by your munching!...

FILTHY FUSO
I must look like a dog!

DON JUAN MANUEL
What makes that noise? The pounding surf or your jaws?

FILTHY FUSO
Like the roaring waves!

DON JUAN MANUEL
I don't know if it's the sea or your teeth that is making this racket that has bored its way into me!

FILTHY FUSO
It's the voice of the cave!

DON JUAN MANUEL *continues to lie on* FILTHY FUSO's *bed of seaweed. At the back of the cave some invisible creature beats its wings rhythmically in time with the sound of the wind and the waves. The ashen grey curtain of rain swirls in the shaft of light that outlines the opening of the cave. Some shadows approach, preceding their owners who seek shelter from the rain, huddled together and out of breath. There are four barefoot children with curly, matted hair, and a woman in mourning clothes.*

THE WIDOW
Time of deluge!... Time of storms!... Cursed time!... Misery for the poor!...

For the hungry and the bereaved!... The sun nowhere in sight!... Sit on the ground and rest, my sons!... We still have a long way to go down this sandy beach!... Your feet will start aching if you don't rest now!... Share this bit of bread between you!... Time of storms, time of sorrows!....

FILTHY FUSO

If only we had some kindling, we could make a fire.

THE WIDOW

Hard to see in this darkness... Is that you, Filthy Fuso? Have you come from that sandy, wolf-ridden wasteland? You must've seen the body of a drowned man washed up on shore. In the middle of the night they came to my house. They banged at the window. I didn't know who it could be.

FILTHY FUSO

The sea hasn't given up Venturoso's body yet?

THE WIDOW

The voice at the window told me it was at the beach at Campelos. I'm going there now to identify the body... The four children awoke crying when they heard the knocks at the window... They thought it was the ghost of their father! This morning at first light I went to the manor to ask for some food before we set off on this long journey. They loosed their dogs on me!... Damn all the rich folk!

FILTHY FUSO

It's a long walk for the little ones. Why not sit them on a log, tie a rope to it, and tow them from shore? Much easier!

THE WIDOW

...And they say that they help widows and orphans. Ha! The Mayorazgo up and left because he couldn't keep his word! Five young wolves he left circling his empty seat. Oh, you black-hearted tyrant, Montenegro! On your orders those poor sailors set out to sea on that stormy night! When you grow up, my sons, you confront him, you tell him that it was he and he alone who left you fatherless! May a rabid dog tear out your heart and drag it all up and down this beach! May a carrion crow peck out your eyes! May sharp prickly nettles take root in your innards! May a wasps' nest grow on your tongue!

DON JUAN MANUEL

Silence, woman! Your curses are already coming to pass!

DON JUAN MANUEL sits up on the bed of kelp. THE WIDOW *and her four children tremble when they see who it is. In the blackness of the cave the outline of the old nobleman is barely perceptible, and his voice echoes darkly, seemingly issuing from the depths of the cavern itself.*

THE WIDOW

Ah! My soul is in such torment that I am talking nonsense!... For the sake of

these four wee ones, do not harm me, my lord Mayorazgo!
DON JUAN MANUEL
So you went to my house and found the door closed to you!
THE WIDOW
They sicced the dogs on me!... All I wanted was to beg for some money to bury my husband!...
FILTHY FUSO
Five candles, five tails, five demons crowned!
DON JUAN MANUEL
I will dig your husband's grave myself! And if there is no shovel to do it with, I will use my bare hands. And for the shroud, I will go to my own house and beg. If they lock the doors on me, I will beat them down so that you and your children may enter...
FILTHY FUSO
Don't forget to bring your crazy brother!
DON JUAN MANUEL
They will bend to my will! The dead shall be buried, and the living cared for. All of my commands shall be obeyed. Come with me, witness me begging for alms at the threshold of my own house. After that, let your curses fall and come true. I will rip out my own despairing heart and give it to the dogs to drag down this desolate shore.

DON JUAN MANUEL strides out of the cave. The rain falls on his hoary head, and the wind blows his patriarchal beard from one shoulder to the other. THE WIDOW, the madman and the children follow him like shadowy vestiges of his delirium. The children clutch at their mother's skirt, sobbing with fear. The entire group seems lost in that vast wasteland.

DON JUAN MANUEL
I am fainting with hunger!... I cannot see!... I can barely stand!... Let the children share a small crust of their bread.
THE WIDOW
There is nothing left, my lord!
DON JUAN MANUEL
God grant that I do not drop dead in the middle of the road! Let us go!

Scene Five

The band of beggars rests in the open air before the door of the manor house, reclining in the sun along the side of the road. Atop the raised stone barn the weathercock shines, its golden majesty itself a kind of clarion call.

DOMINGA DE GÓMEZ
>   In all my life, it never changed! When the noonday bells rang they'd give out bread and cabbage to the poor folk who gathered at this door. A tradition of charity passed on from the first generations of lords.

THE ONE-ARMED MAN FROM GONDAR
>   And this door, which had always been open to those in need, is now shut!

THE ONE-ARMED MAN FROM LEON
>   The sons inherited none of their fathers' honourable customs!

CIDRÁN'S WOMAN
>   Some masters they are! The mother dies, and the father ditches everything and wanders out into the world. We came across him at the seashore. The rain was lashing at his bare head.

CIDRÁN 'THE BAT'
>   He's begging for death to take him!

THE MENDICANT OF SAN LÁZARO
>   He cast aside everything to be like us and to have his golden throne in Heaven.

THE ONE-ARMED MAN FROM LEON
>   His heirs will rest on seats of thorns in Hell.

DOMINGA DE GÓMEZ
>   They bar their doors to the poor, who are Our Lord God's children.

ADEGA THE INNOCENT
>   Holy Jesus also walked the earth begging, carrying nothing but a small embroidered saddle-bag the Holy Virgin made for him.

THE ONE-ARMED MAN FROM LEON
>   And where can the noble lord have gone?

CIDRÁN'S WOMAN
>   Who knows!

DOMINGA DE GÓMEZ
>   He must've retired to the hills to do penance. He has a big house there.

THE MENDICANT OF SAN LÁZARO
>   He keeps five young mistresses at that place, so he wouldn't be heading there if he were truly repentant.

CIDRÁN'S WOMAN
>   Listen! You can hear the sons shouting inside!

DOMINGA DE GÓMEZ
>   At each other's throats, they are!

CIDRÁN 'THE BAT'
>   They're fighting over their shares!

THE MENDICANT OF SAN LÁZARO
>   In the great city of Jerusalem, centuries ago, the same shouting could be

heard from the Jews dividing up the tunic of Our Lord Jesus Christ!
DOMINGA DE GÓMEZ
The sons are just like that!
THE MENDICANT OF SAN LÁZARO
Just like Jews they slam their doors on the poor and cast them out in the street! They give the crumbs from their table to their dogs!
DOMINGA DE GÓMEZ
Dogs have it better than we poor folk!
THE MENDICANT OF SAN LÁZARO
For the poor man accepts his fate, while a dog barks and howls!

*A small door opens on the great gate of the manor, and one by one the servants file out: Ginger-*MICAELA, DON GALÁN, RECOGIDA. *The doorway slams shut behind them.*

MICAELA
Nothing good comes with old age!
DON GALÁN
It's a bone no one wants to chew, except maybe Death!
RECOGIDA
Where do we go, Micaela ma'am?
MICAELA
You are still young, you will land on your feet soon... But me, poor me, nearly a hundred years old now, where am I going to go? Cast out of the house I've lived and worked in my whole life!... There's no way anyone's going to hire me now!... A mouth to feed, even if it's got no teeth, is a big burden to take on!... A big loaf shared by many people makes for small portions! And if the whole kingdom breaks apart, imagine the fate of a single house!... This house used to be great, but now, divided, it will fall!... How I wish death would come and spare me from seeing it happen!
RECOGIDA
Andreiña alone lucked out. They're keeping her on.
DON GALÁN
That's because three of her nanny goats bed down with the wolves.
MICAELA
I'll die somewhere on the roadside under a hedge.
RECOGIDA
We're both caught in this storm, Micaela ma'am!
DON GALÁN
The three of us, we'll wander far and wide begging for alms. I'll sit in a cart, you two can push.
MICAELA
I'd work if I was as able-bodied as you!

DON GALÁN
Can't say I really want to.
MICAELA
My heart breaks to leave this hearth!... To lose my masters, to lose them forever. I who saw them born!...
DON GALÁN
We are but lambs at whom these wolves bare their fangs!
MICAELA
They are noble lions!

DON JUAN MANUEL *approaches down the country road that wends its way through the verdure. He is accompanied by the madman,* THE WIDOW *and her children. He walks among them like a venerable patriarch with his family: an allegory of Pain, Sorrow and Madness.*

DON GALÁN
Look! The master returns!
DOMINGA DE GÓMEZ
The king comes home! To claim his throne!
THE ONE-ARMED MAN FROM LEON
The poor once again have their benefactor!
MICAELA
He seems to be in great pain!
RECOGIDA
We were like lost lambs. And now look, our shepherd is here!
DON GALÁN
No shepherd is he, but a fierce sheep-dog! We will see how he shows his teeth to the wolves inside!

DON JUAN MANUEL *plods forward weakly, leans on the gate and pounds on it. He rests against the door frame and waits. The beggars and the servants huddle together behind him, maintaining an expectant silence.* DON JUAN MANUEL *again beats against the door with his fist, bellowing in a deep voice.*

DON JUAN MANUEL
Open up, you Satan's spawn! Open these doors that your greed keeps shut! Open them wide, the way your foul deeds have opened the gates of Hell to you! Open this home to the homeless! I, who have given you everything, come to ask you for alms on their behalf! I, who am now as poor and miserable as they, knock at this closed door! Open up, you Satan's spawn! Do not stir my wrath and force me to enter this house as Don Juan Manuel Montenegro! Open, Satan's spawn!

DON JUAN MANUEL's *knocking echoes inside the wide hallway. Behind him the rancorous, obstinate voices of the beggars and dismissed servants swell like a wave.*

THE SERVANTS AND BEGGARS
  Open up for your father! Open up for your father!
DON JUAN MANUEL
  Break down the door! For you are my true children!
THE SERVANTS AND BEGGARS
  Show some charity to your father! Charity and respect! Charity and respect!
DON JUAN MANUEL
  These things come only with love!

Two tears run down the old nobleman's cheeks and lose themselves in his snowy white beard. The beggars and servants try to ram down the door.

THE SERVANTS AND BEGGARS
  Do the Christian thing here!
DON JUAN MANUEL
  Bring me an axe!
THE SERVANTS AND BEGGARS
  Do the Christian thing here!
DON JUAN MANUEL
  Set a fire at each corner of the house! Let these hellspawn burn!
THE SERVANTS AND BEGGARS
  Such a godless place! Godless!

Suddenly all is silent. Frightened now by the sound of their own voices, the beggars and servants listen as the door is unlocked. It creaks open, and in the doorway appears ANDREIÑA *like a shadow conjured up by some black art. At the same time, the four sons stride out onto the balcony, barbarism and violence following their every step. They take their places beneath the coat of arms, with its eagles and wolves, and speak in unison.*

DON MAURO
  The door is open!
DON ROSENDO
  Come on in, if you dare!
DON MAURO
  The one who comes in is not going to come out!
DON GONZALITO
  Come on, just try it!
DON FARRUQUIÑO
  You're quiet now, you misbegotten lot!
DON JUAN MANUEL
  Enter with me, all of you! You are my true children! Succour me so that I

might assuage your hunger for bread and your thirst for justice! Succour me as if you were my true children! Succour me as if you were hungry animals, archangels or demons! Even lambs can feel rage!

They all cower by the door, quiet and still. DON JUAN MANUEL *enters alone, and his booming voice fades as he strides down the vaulted hallway. The four sons take their belligerence and fury back inside with them.* ANDREIÑA *tries to close the front door, but finds it blocked by the towering figure of* THE MENDICANT OF SAN LÁZARO, *who pushes it back against the old crone and enters the house with a shout. The others echo his voice and his movements.*

THE MENDICANT OF SAN LÁZARO
    He is our father! He is our father!
THE SERVANTS AND BEGGARS
    He is our father!

Final Scene

The manor kitchen. In the hearth burns a large fire whose tongues lend a blood red hue to the faces of those assembled. The four sons appear through the dark back doorway at the very moment the kitchen is invaded by the noisy band led by DON JUAN MANUEL.

DON JUAN MANUEL
    I am returned from the grave to curse you all!
DON FARRUQUIÑO
    Enough, father!
DON ROSENDO
    Out of here, all of you riff-raff!
DON JUAN MANUEL
    They are my true children! I asked you for alms on their behalf, and you slammed the door on them!
DON MAURO
    It is open now!
DON JUAN MANUEL
    I am here to impart justice, because you are no children of mine!... You are the sons of Satan!
DON FARRUQUIÑO
    Precisely! Our father is Don Juan Manuel Montenegro.
DON JUAN MANUEL
    Ah, I have ever been a great sinner, and my life a pitch-black night full of lightning and thunder!... That is why I am punished now in my old age!... To

humble me, God willed it that I would engender you monsters of Hell in that saintly woman's womb!... I sense that my time has run out, but I still have a chance to redeem myself. I am here to disown you, you thieves, to disinherit you, to redistribute all this property of mine! God has prolonged my life so that I can strip these things from your despicable hands and pass it to my true children here! Leave this house, you hellspawn!

The sons respond to the nobleman's words with derisive laughter, and his companions assume an air of anxious piety. DON JUAN MANUEL *advances a few steps. His four offspring circle him, hurling crude insults and cruel mockery.*

DON MAURO
Maybe you should sleep it off, Lord Don Juan Manuel!
DON ROSENDO
Did you save any wine for us, father?
DON GONZALITO
Nice sermon. Perfect for Lent!
DON FARRUQUIÑO
Come now! Profanity has no place here!
DON ROSENDO
Find father a bed!
DON MAURO
You 'true children', you get out, unless you want me to sic the hounds on you! Now! Away! Take your begging on the road! You can rob the neighbours, but not us! De-louse yourself somewhere outside!

DON MAURO *walks into the miserable company and herds them toward the door with a violent shove, roaring like a giant. The group cowers in fear, groaning humbly at their mistreatment. At the threshold they turn and disperse, pious invocations on their lips. The noble and resplendent figure of* DON JUAN MANUEL *then moves between his gigantic son and the group: his eyes burn with madness and fury, and his face shows both regal pride and Christ-like pallor. His hand slaps the face of* DON MAURO. *The fire from the stove lends a sanguine colouring to the scene.* DON MAURO *howls and with his fist pounds the forehead of the old nobleman, who collapses to the floor. The servants recoil and gasp in horror, then kneel to his aid. At the same time, the sons go pale in the face and look on in dark, wide-eyed stupefaction. Suddenly, the shadow of the leper rises, and his hands move to grasp* DON MAURO *by the neck. The two giants grapple, each spraying the spittle of his fury. The huge young nobleman bares his white lupine teeth, and the leper the open sores in his mouth. Locked in combat, they fall together into the fire pit. Transfigured and engulfed in the primal beauty of the flames,* THE MENDICANT OF SAN LÁZARO *arises.*

THE MENDICANT OF SAN LÁZARO
   He was our father!
THE SERVANTS AND BEGGARS
   He was our father! He was our father!
THE SONS
   We are damned! Damned to at least twenty years of legal woes!

www.ingramcontent.com/pod-product-compliance
Lightning Source LLC
Chambersburg PA
CBHW071423150426
43191CB00008B/1017